"*Safe Passage* is essential reading for anyone
transition."
– Mary Russman
Director, International School of Latvia
Counselor Training Center, London
Recipient: National Distinguished Principals Award

"My synthesis of 1000+ meta-analysis relating to enhancing achievement
has systematically shown that mobility is the most disruptive influence. Ota
accepts this evidence, truly cares about this issue, and wants to make mobility
a positive not negative influence.

His book has a bit of everything – personal stories, attachment theory, brain
science, psychological cliffs, safe harbors, rafts – and messages in a bottle
for every person who influences mobility. This is the book you read when
thinking about moving, when someone moves to and from you, and when
you want a moving story."
– John Hattie
Professor, University of Melbourne
Author, *Visible Learning,* the largest study in educational research history

"Schools can neglect the importance of supporting families in coming to
a new school, new country, new city, new culture, and supporting those
repeatedly left behind.

This is a pragmatic and invaluable guide for those in schools with
mobile populations and those working with such schools: parents, students,
teachers and administrators, school Board members and school accreditation
agencies. *Safe Passage* is full of practical advice but also acknowledges that
each international school is different in its cultural context, aims and values.
This is also an intensely personal book, based on the author's personal and
professional lives, and is all the richer for it.

This will be a handbook for counselors, school leaders, teachers, and
families living and working in contexts of international mobility."
– Graham Ranger
Director of School Support and Evaluation
Council of International Schools (CIS)

"Children of highly mobile parents face unique social and emotional challenges. The better we understand those challenges, the better equipped we'll be to meet them. With *Safe Passage* Ota culls insights from the social and affective neurosciences to construct sound, concrete recommendations, with implications for both parenting and policy. His coverage of this work is lucid and accessible – after reading *Safe Passage* I understand my own work better than I did before. Certainly, I have a new appreciation for the implications of the work I do."

– James Coan, Ph.D, Associate Professor
Department of Psychology & Virginia Affective Neuroscience Laboratory
University of Virginia

"*Safe Passage* is a brilliant amalgam of inspiration, memoir, theory, and practical advice.

If you are a newcomer to the idea of a school Transitions Program, you will instantly know you are in good hands with Ota's step-by-step instructions for the initial stages of this approach. If you've been involved in these ideas for a while, you'll appreciate Ota's depth of expertise in and practical advice for how to sustain, nurture, and continually revise programs as they grow.

An inspirational and motivational read for anyone concerned with the needs of globally mobile adults and children who meet in an international school."

– Anne Copeland, Ph.D.
Executive Director, The Interchange Institute

"Every international educator and every expatriate parent should get this book. Ota's style will pull you in and his ideas will transform what you think is possible. Your response to his call to action can be one of those differences that makes a difference."

– Barbara F. Schaetti, Ph.D
Founder, Personal Leadership Seminars (www.plseminars.com)
Author, *Personal Leadership: Making a World of Difference*

"Reflection on identity is a critical first step for international educators who encounter change on a daily basis as they pursue careers in new countries and new cultures. *Safe Passage* took me on an emotional journey – one that helped me to understand the experiences that have shaped me. I believe it will help others too."
– Jane Larsson, Executive Director
Council of International Schools

"Only when you have experienced a great Transitions Program do you realize the importance it can make in a person's life. A good Transitions Program can make the difference between a great experience abroad and a rough one. Ota's book makes it possible for one person to start the wheels turning anywhere in the world. Working on Ota's team in the Netherlands allowed me the opportunity to learn a tremendous amount, and I was able to bring his ideas to Santiago, Chile. We invited Ota to come and share his energy with us in October, 2013. We were left wanting more information, anecdotes, and strategies from this very experienced and learned source. His book provides just that."
– Chica Strauszer, Parent, Founder of Transitions Program
International School Nido de Aguilas, Santiago, Chile

"Ota's book is indispensable for every therapist or teacher who works with Third Culture Kids (TCKs). He brings understanding as to why repeated moves impact TCKs so strongly and goes the extra mile to give specific guidelines on how to help them walk through the grief process. I love how he connects it all with attachment theory, sound psychological principles, and his own experiential wisdom. I can't put it down and highly recommend it as it is sure to be a classic in the TCK literature."
– Lois J Bushong, M.S.
Author, *Belonging Everywhere & Nowhere:*
Insights into Counseling the Globally Mobile

"Students, faculty, families. Arriving, staying leaving. This engaging text succeeds in identifying the challenges, obligations and opportunities international school communities face as constituents come and go. A compelling, systematic model for developing a multi-faceted transitions program is presented and supported by the literature. Practical examples from the successful 'Safe Harbour' transitions program at the American School of The Hague are incorporated, as are suggestions for revising accreditation standards. This volume is also relevant to any school that has a steady turnover of students who come from multiple cultures.

As the first parent member of the ASH Transitions Team, I attest that the Transition Program positively impacted the lives of my family and many friends. It continues to be regarded as a model program internationally."

 – Merry Lynne Hamilton, DPT, Ph.D.
   Associate Professor, Regis University, Colorado

"*Safe Passage* is one of these rare seminal books which compels us to become more human as we recognize ourselves and others with new understanding.

Clarity and rigor of analysis, evocative metaphors, strong supporting authors and recent research all complement Ota's elegant language, succeeding in profoundly touching the reader. Rooted in solid professional experience, practice, and reflection, Ota's call for understanding offers a plan of action one step at a time, structured and addressed to every international school.

The power of Ota's book resides in its confidence that challenges can lead to growth, that understanding will elicit genuine care, and that the quest to find safe passage is part of our common humanity."

 – Beatrice Caston
   Director of Development, International School of Dusseldorf

"An invaluable gift to the field of international education, this book makes a compelling case for a comprehensive approach to building Transitions Programming in international schools. Drawing from neuroscience and attachment research, as well as personal stories from his own life and work, Ota reviews how high mobility can affect our ability to learn and to form healthy identities and relationships. Compassionately and intelligently Ota practically outlines how schools can implement transitions support. If you work in an international school, support or parent an international student, this needs to be on your must-read list."

– Ellen Mahoney
  Founder and CEO, Sea Change Mentoring

DOUGLAS W. OTA

SAFE PASSAGE

How mobility affects people &
what international schools
should do about it

Summertime Publishing
by your side from inspiration to publication

First Published in Great Britain 2014 by Summertime Publishing

ISBN 978-1-909193-40-6

Grateful acknowledgment is made to the Council of International Schools (CIS) and the New England Association of Schools and Colleges (NEASC) for permission to use the Guide to School Evaluation and Accreditation - 8th Edition (Version 8.2).

Design: Tom Hubbard – www.tomhub.com
Cover Image: Tom Hubbard

To Astra
For joining me in building a harbor
And to Niels, Elsa, and Loek
That you may receive safe passage

"I am a swallow,

I am a swallow...

Hail, O ye gods whose odour is sweet...

I have advanced with a message...

Open to me.

How shall I tell that which I have seen?

Let me pass on and deliver my message...

I have completed my journey."

Chapter 86, Papyrus of Ani, 240BC
Commonly known as the Egyptian Book of the Dead
Translated by Sir Ernest Alfred Thompson Wallis Budge

ACKNOWLEDGEMENTS

Until writing a book of my own, the 'Acknowledgements' section in every book I've ever purchased seemed like an indulgence on the part of the author that innocent readers had to endure. You buy the book and listening to the author thank everyone – from grandmothers to goldfish – is part of the deal.

Now that I've written a book – and this book in particular – my thinking has changed.

It is no exaggeration to state up front that this book represents the culmination of millions of work hours invested by thousands of dedicated individuals, ranging from those managing screeching school hallways to those crunching statistics in secluded research labs. Many of them I have been fortunate to know. Some of them I have been fortunate to know well. Most I'll never know personally. The majority of the people I need to thank remain unnamed in the pages that follow, for the simple reason that the most significant acts of helping occur in the privacy of the relationship – however fleeting – between helper and recipient.

Let me honor and recognize right now those who have helped people in transition. Let me honor and recognize those who continue to help. Let me honor and recognize those who decide to help in the future, perhaps as a result of reading this book. The value of an act resides not in the applause from the perimeter, but in the heart of the recipient. Those who you've helped know it. Those you will help will feel it. And that's all that matters.

In my seventeen years at the American School of The Hague (ASH) in the Netherlands, many of them as High School Counselor, and in my years in private practice as a psychologist since, thousands of people have let me into the inner sanctum of their experience. To all who have told me their stories, I thank you. Many of you have distilled in me the truths I describe.

My dear soccer[1] coach, Sam Caycedo, once said, "The way you play on the field is the way you'll play in real life." Acknowledgements like these matter because, like effective soccer teams, comprehensive Transitions Programs demand effective teamwork. Mine might be the sole name on this book's cover, but that is simply because I found myself compelled to kick this project to completion. I've been fortunate enough to work on transitions-related programs closely with many brilliant people. Their ideas, inspiration, and energy infuse the pages of this book, just as it infused the Safe Harbour they helped build.

I obviously cannot thank every individual who made a contribution to ASH's 'A Safe Harbour' program, originally known as the 'Transitions Program Team.' I must thank clusters of people. In a very real sense, this book is a reflection of their contributions.

To begin with, I want to thank the founding members of the Transitions Program Team, or 'TPT': Carol Mecklenburg, Peter Loy, Dianne Banasco, Jessie Rodell, Merry Lynne Hamilton, Cheryl de Vries, Victor Ferreira, Drew Cardy, Sarah Nagata, and Chris Lewin.

Many played key leadership roles throughout the growth and development of the program and its team. In addition to the founders, the leaders I worked closely with that I would like to thank include:

Students:
Abhinav Kaul, Alan Nichol, Aleri Zama, Alette Bansema, Alice Dula, Andrea Koris, Anicka Slachta, Annie Love, Audrey Bernasconi, Ben Mahaffie, D'Ann Barker, Daniel Arvidsson, Daniel Goh, DJ Moreau, Emily Ackermann, Emily Wolff, Emma Harper, Floortje Beemsterboer, Fred van der Krogt, Gillian Wong, Giulia Donzelli, Grant Stephens, Guido Galligani, Gustaaf van Oosterom, Harri Narhi, Heather Worling, Ian Rider, Isabella Benestad, Jessica Batt, Jessica Si, Johan Lönn, Jules Kortenhorst, Kaity Allen, Kevin Guckian, Larske Soepnel, Laura van der Krogt, Leanne Hamilton, Luis Blanc, Margot van der Krogt, Mark Stephens, Michaela Botts, Mike Steenvoorden, Mimie Laurant, Molly Brass, Robert Limkeman, Saar Ziv, Sarah Bellotti, Sarah Tisel, Scott Love, Supriya Balachander, Tae-Hoon Lee, Tenley Wood, Timur Sumer, Victoria Sigurthorsson.

---

1   *I hereby betray my roots in the USA by not calling it 'football' like the rest of the world.*

Parents:

Alessandra Matussi, Andy Kirker, Ann-Kathryn Lippert-Larsen, Annamarie Fourie, Barbara Stoebe, Beatriz Negrin, Anneke Beeuwkes, Bev Coit, Carol Chew, Carolyn Matula, Geraldine Hilton, Carol Jeter, Charlotte Hubbell, Chica Strauszer, Corinne Portheine, Deppy Karavassilis, Ellen Barth, Elsa Figueroa, Geraldine Hilton, Geri Foster, Holly Bratsman, Ingrid Lenotte, Jane Love, Janice Koris, Janne Lunde, Jeanette Hansen, Laura Ackerman, Jo Hannson, Julia Sigurthorsson, June Goh, Karen Ispahani, Katrina Hele, Kaylynne Matheson, Jane Keilty, Kim Gundle, Lambrini Skulikaris, Lisa Chesson, Lora Lyn Frederick, Lotta Therme-Lindell, Marta Kapusta, Mary Beth Guckian, Mary Brass, Mercedes Bodega, Michiko Haru, Molly Boed, Pam Gartner, Pam Hall, Pat Sümer, Patricia Bazzoni-Maresi, Pippa Hill-Strathy, Rita Sunden, Rosemary Calnan, Rosemary Taylor, Sarah Fisher, Sarah Saul, Signe Hernes, Terry Potts, Venetta Morger, Viola Barbagallo.

Staff:

Annette Huizinga, Arlene van Staden, Arlette Stuip, Arnoud Hirs, Bob Johnson, Bobby Hendricks, Carla Abrams, Connie van de Broek, Corey Fries, Eileen Hagerty, Fabienne Gouverneur, Gera Klijnsma, Jessie Coyle, Jim Tisel, John Mugno, Jolette Moeliker, Karen Dobbie, Lani Gibbs, Laura Romains, Laurie Mackaill, Louise Dube, Maire Ni Shlatara, Margo Arango, Marja Pellerin, Michele Velthuizen, Mike Flaim, Nick Radvany, Nicole Whelan, Petra Drijkoningen, Rosemary Horn, Sara McMickle, Sheri Fischer, Stacey Ulery, Sue Nelsen, Tamara Palash, Tanya Peters.

Administrators:

Bill Gerritz, Brian Weinrich, Ellen Stern, Mary Russman, Paul Mackaill, Rick Spradling.

On two previous occasions, I attempted to lead the writing of a book about ASH's Transitions Program. I am grateful to Alessandra Matussi, Barbara Schaetti, Carol Mecklenburg, Jessie Rodell, and Merry Lynne Hamilton for joining me as editors in the first attempt at the writing of that book. I am particularly grateful to Alessandra Matussi for being the first of us to articulate the reality that the important changes called for in a book like this could only be widely achieved via changes in the standards for school accreditation. I am also grateful to the other chapter editors who gave of their time and energy to that first attempt: Daniel Goh, Jim Tisel, Lambrini Kiosse, Lani Gibbs, Margot van der Krogt, Peter Loy, Rick Spradling, Rosemary Taylor,

Ruth van Reken, Venetta Morger, and Victor Ferreira.

With the wisdom of hindsight, it is not surprising to me that this first attempt failed. Writing a book is profoundly difficult. Coordinating an entire team in writing a book is dizzyingly difficult. I asked the aforementioned five editors to join me in a second, more streamlined attempt to write the book. Again, they pooled their energy and brilliance, for which I was thankful. Again, the endeavor failed, for which I felt ashamed for years.

In *Chapter 2: Finding the Ship's Log*, you'll read about Dan McAdams' work on 'Redemptive Sequences.' Writing this book was my redemption. Life had forced a certain expertise down my throat. On two occasions, I had failed to distill that expertise into written form – a written form that those eager to address transitions in schools had requested for years. I needed to keep trying, not only for the people I felt I had let down, not only for the readers who might benefit, but also for myself. On some level, I knew 'transitions' as a theme would not relinquish its grip until I had.

This book simply had to be.

Looking back over the past two years of hard work, *Safe Passage* is not the book I first endeavored to write. I set out to write about ASH's Transitions Program, but ended up writing about Life. I thought ASH's Safe Harbour needed to be the origin of this opus – the Greenwich to which we all must adjust our clocks – but Safe Harbour has ended up seeming a solitary safe haven in a sea yearning for more. This is a book about how we cope with Life, in its unrelenting appeal to us to fly from one safe haven to another, from one set of stabilities to the next. Harbors provide the masts and shelters for swallows to alight, rest, and mingle, before the journey begins anew.

As I think about my gratitude to so many, my heart gets lodged in my throat. I am thankful to Barbara Schaetti for being a lighthouse that flashed at reliable intervals and crucial junctures in my journey with transitions. Ruth Van Reken has been a North Star whose presence provided orientation when skies were clear, and comfort when they clouded. Lani Gibbs has provided excellent GPS service; if you ever tackle a project of your own, may you too be blessed by a brilliant retired colleague looking for a project into which she can sink her intellect. Thank you, Barbara, Ruth, and Lani, for poring over earlier versions of this manuscript and reassuring me I was not sailing off the edge of a flat earth.

I am thankful to my publisher, Jo Parfitt of Summertime Publishing, for the patience, guidance, and professionalism she has provided in various iterations of this project for nearly a decade. Marnie Schaetti offered outstanding early editorial suggestions; I am even more grateful for her selfless satellite perspective, which allowed me to discern the best path forward. Jane Dean has been tireless in her devotion as an editor, helping this sailor hone his craft and keeping us on course, even when I fell asleep at the bridge. With Jane at my side, Jo helicoptering above, and Shelley Antscherl trolling behind for proof reading, what started as a solitary writing project felt at the end like a unified fleet. Thank you all for being such an outstanding and professional team.

As my designer, Tom Hubbard did what Tom does best. He listened straight through words and vague notions and identified the faint flutter of a migratory bird. And he taught me at the deepest of levels to let the process lead the project. A swallow alighted on our mast. We followed it wherever it led. I am profoundly grateful to Tom for his dedication to this journey.

I am thankful to Rick Spradling for his support throughout this project, and for introducing me to Graham Ranger, whose infectious enthusiasm for *Safe Passage* merged seamlessly with professional growth and camaraderie for us both. I am thankful for the emboldening and heartening words of the reviewers I haven't already recognized above: Anne Copeland, Beatrice Larose, Chica Strauszer, Ellen Mahoney, Jane Larsson, Jim Coan, John Hattie, Lois Bushong, Mary Russman, and Merry Lynne Hamilton.

The encouragement of my colleagues at 'Van Boetzelaerlaan 136' has been worth its weight in gold. Nick Radvany ran with this project on the beach, and Alp Soycengiz cheered from the sidelines. Anja Hammega has transmitted her friendship from GPS locations across the globe.

Sean O'Murchu saw these words inside me long before I dared notice them. When I forgot them, he sang them back to me. Throughout this ride, Sean has taught me the awesome experience of being known in friendship.

Graham Ranger recognized this book as a 'life work.' He was right. My mother's love and support infuse each page. My father's painful life story forms the backdrop. The scent of my stepfather Gene's memory wafts through the words, like his flowers. And Bill rides the prow of this vessel, like the sun god's sparrow. As a kid, I awed at my big brother's generosity as he paid for our sodas. I am in awe now at his lessons in grief, lessons that infuse these pages, lessons that Bill paid for with his life. I am eternally grateful to all in my family of origin.

I thank my in-laws, Edith and Simon, for being an endless source of support to me and my family. On more than a dozen occasions, my family heard me announce, "I've finished the book!" (Each time it was true. But that's a different issue.) Thank you, Astra, Niels, Elsa, and Loek, for putting up with this journey. You are the finest and safest harbor any husband and father could wish for, and I thank you for giving this book safe passage.

TABLE OF CONTENTS

THE LISTING OF GRAPHICS & TABLES

FOREWORD

*"Your pain is the breaking of the shell that encloses your understanding.
Even as the stone of the fruit must break, that its heart may stand in
the sun, so must you know pain. And could you keep your heart in wonder
at the daily miracles of your life, your pain would not seem less wondrous
than your joy; And you would accept the seasons of your heart, even as you
have always accepted the seasons that pass over your fields. And you
would watch with serenity through the winters of your grief."*
  – Kahlil Gibran, *The Prophet*

I will never forget the first moment I walked into the American School of The Hague (ASH). Despite having visited many international schools, this was an experience unlike any I'd had before.

A young man, about ten years old, came up to greet me. "Good evening, Mrs. Van Reken. My name is Michael. We're glad you're here tonight. Would you like to get some food and join me at this table?" and he pointed to a group of his peers who displayed equally welcoming smiles as they waved their hands in greeting.

Good grief, I thought, *Where are the adults?*
They were there, with more broad smiles as they watched Michael take me under his wing and shepherd me through the food line and back to the table where his friends were sitting. Obviously, the adults were aware and approved what was going on.

The conversation with these young people only brought me more astonishment. They asked me thoughtful questions about where I'd been, what I did, how I liked it here, and responded articulately when I asked questions in return. Who *were* these young phenomena?

And then I met Doug Ota.

"Hi, Ruth. I'm glad to see Michael and his friends have taken such good care of you. They're all part of our transitions team for the lower grades." Doug asked a few logistical questions and off we headed to the auditorium for an hour and a half seminar on the topic of third culture kids – children who grow up, for at least some time, outside the country their passport names as 'home.'

To be honest, I was more than a little nervous. I didn't want to complain, but Doug had initially handed me a daunting task – providing me with perhaps the most diverse audience I had ever faced. The attendees included students ranging from these ten year-olds through High School seniors, proud parents, teachers and staff. How could I begin to keep everyone's attention over such an extended time? The only thing I could think of was to use some students as panelists so at least their friends and family might pay attention to them. And so, before I arrived, I emailed Doug and asked if he could get a representative group of students to interview.

I expected about four students. When I entered the auditorium, I saw ten chairs lined up. Oops! Internally I questioned his wisdom.

"Are all these chairs for students?" I asked.

"Yes. The youngest is ten and the oldest is eighteen. I thought we should have a broad range. Some kids are leaving, some are staying, but they're all on various transition teams we have here. They'll be great."

I gulped and hoped Doug was right. The audience entered the room, the panelists came up on stage, and we began one of the most memorable nights of my life.

Doug had placed the students in age order and he was right: youngest to oldest, each was articulate, gave thoughtful answers and there was definitely an age related progression as to how the students answered questions such as, "If people ask you, where do you say you're from?" The younger children dutifully noted their passport country, the place where parents told them they were from. The older the children, the more abstract the answers came. "The moon." "Everywhere." But one girl replied "ASH." How could anyone name their school as the place they were from? And so I asked her.

"My parents are teachers here so I've been in The Hague my whole school career. But this is the one place all my friends who have come and gone, or who are here now, share in common with me."

The panel was indeed great. But there was one moment no one attending could possibly forget. I said something about how, when they returned to their passport countries, they might discover that not even their cousins really understood what life had been like for them here in The Hague. Michael had seated himself right in front of me in the audience and began to wave his hand madly. At first I ignored it. Time was already short. But Michael was so insistent, I finally stopped and asked if he wanted to stay something.

He stood up, barely tall enough for those in the back rows to see him. "You talked about our cousins. Last year I went back to Portugal and my cousins were laughing at me, telling me I wasn't Portuguese anymore. I felt so bad and I was crying. But I just realized something. I AM Portuguese, but I'm a TCK too."

We all clapped... and cried. I looked at him, at the panelists, at the audience who all understood what he had said. Here was a ten-year-old who, because of his role as an Ambassador in the Transitions Program, already had language and understanding for his story. He did not have to listen to the scornful judgments of others who didn't know why he was 'different.' Here were panelists who had already begun to think through how they would name themselves, and deal with the inevitable losses that happen in any international school as friends move in and out according to the dictates of their parents' careers. And here were parents and staff who had come and listened to the stories being told that night – who knew how important these stories were, not only for the students but also for themselves. Yes, they might be older, but they too knew the confusion of defining place and identity – at least to some degree – after their years away from what had always been home to them before.

That night I saw for myself the magic of what happens when an all-school transitions program is put in place and is working well. Bottom line, lives are changed. Instead of being defeated by the challenges of so many cycles of separation and loss, everyone involved in this community had learned how to process them well in order to walk through to the other side and use the many gifts involved.

And that is the journey Doug Ota invites you to share as you read this incredible book. Yes, it is about developing a transitions program for your school in terms of the logistics – Doug is a master teacher for giving you the 'how to's' of this important topic. But much more, he describes the human process we go through when transition stops the flow of our story and we lose those who once listened to us.

As one who has lived this globally transient lifestyle since the moment of my birth, and worked with countless others who have made a similar journey, I cannot recommend this book highly enough for what it says about who we are and why we need each other. A school Transitions Program is one way those needs can be met, but the principles here will apply in countless others arenas of life as well.

Enjoy reading this as much as I did!

Ruth E. Van Reken
Co-author, *Third Culture Kids: The Experience of Growing Up Among Worlds,*
Author, *Letters Never Sent,*
Co-founder, Families in Global Transition

PREFACE
My Reasons For Writing This Book

"That which is most personal is most universal."
  – Carl Rogers

What you have before you is an intensely personal book. This is the case not because I want to talk about me, but because I have found that when I have the courage to share my most human feelings, moments, and vulnerabilities, the people I'm speaking to feel safe to do the same. You cannot rush this process. When you give people a chance to go with you at their own pace, and when you make it safe for them by not putting any emotional pressure on anybody, people often want to share their own stories too.

We have an innate desire to connect with others. Our stories help us do so. But we have to feel safe in order to share them.

This book originates with three stories of my own.

THE FIRST STORY

The first story began when I entered kindergarten in 1975. Something felt wrong. It was so close to me I couldn't see it – like the color of my eyes. Only, as I looked around the room, it wasn't eye color I noticed. It was skin.

The other children had white skin. Mine was brown. A nascent self-awareness whispered to me that, if I had already noticed this difference in skin color in the first few days of school, the other kids would probably notice it too. Soon.

What would they ask me? More importantly, what would I say?
Forty years later, I can explain how my father was Japanese, and how his marriage to my mother, with her Anglo-Saxon roots, produced two children

whose ethnic roots were impossible for strangers to peg. In the white, Anglo-Saxon, Protestant and relatively affluent area of Southern California in which I was raised, my brother and I stood out like milk chocolate chips in angel food cake. That's at least how it felt to a five-year-old.

But what made that difference more poignant and pressing was that it remained unnamed.

My parents separated when I was three. My father's departure took in its wake any associations with my half-Japanese roots. He left, his Japanese furniture and paintings left with him, and my brother and I grappled with the resulting vacuum for the next decades, two chocolate chips with a caucasian mother who baked angel food cakes. I never questioned my mother's love, but that love provided no answers to the existential questions that dawned on the preschool playground.

Why do I look so different?

Where do I come from?

While I continued to have contact with my father throughout my early years – and up to this day – my father himself had needed to detach from his Japanese roots. His life depended on it. Born in Hawaii as the eldest in a family descended from Japanese immigrants, he was seven years old when the country of his roots bombed the country he called home. The blasts of Pearl Harbor blew his Japanese identity to bits. From one day to the next the family ceased speaking Japanese forever. Massive amounts of energy had to be channeled into a hypervigilant need to detach from their cultural roots, lest they join the ranks of thousands of other Japanese Americans deposed of their possessions and routed off to internment camps. My father underwent a trauma due to his own cultural identity that I have since described as "the trauma of his own reflection."

One could argue the unease I felt in that 1975 preschool classroom was a faint aftershock of a bombardment that had occurred on December 7th, 1941. I was brown. All the other boys and girls were white. Nobody stepped forward to help me with the questions I was wrestling with. Nobody – including me – even knew I was wrestling with those questions.

I didn't have a vocabulary to grasp or describe what was happening to me. Worse still, I didn't even know it.

THE SECOND STORY

The second story involves my graduation from college and moving to the Netherlands. The high-stakes pressure I had felt throughout secondary school in Southern California had successfully brainwashed me into believing – like far too many USAmerican[2] youth still today – that getting into a good college was the only reliable ticket to a successful future. The conviction brought with it a much less apparent and far more insidious additional conviction, namely that *once you got into and graduated from a good college, you had it made in life.* Nobody explicitly said, "They'll roll out the red carpet for you," but 'red carpet' was certainly an implicit part of the deal.

Now the 'red carpet' phenomenon may actually exist. The fact is I do not know. All I do know is that when I graduated from Princeton and moved to the Netherlands to be with my fiancée (now my wife of twenty years), I had unwittingly allowed my faith in the 'red carpet' to take on international and cross-cultural proportions. I assumed it would be self-evident that 'Princeton' would open doors for me across the Atlantic. Society had fed me this conviction. I had eaten what Society had served, and even asked for seconds.

Imagine my confusion when I arrived in Holland and nobody had heard of Princeton. Imagine how you would feel if you had steadily set aside a considerable portion of your wages, steadily saving for something grand, month by month and year by year, only to be told a decade later that the currency in which you saved had been discontinued. The Euro, the US Dollar, the Yen – sorry, they don't exist anymore![3] Dutch people I would speak to would tell me they'd "heard of Harvard," and then they would often go on to share their conviction that "American education is famous for being quite bad." When I wanted to begin graduate work in psychology at the University

---

2   Throughout this text, I will use the term 'USAmerican' to refer to citizens of the United States of America. This is a text that espouses sensitivity towards, and respect of, our cultural differences. That respect begins at the level of examining our own cultural programming, and the things we may take for granted. In other words, out of respect for other nations and cultures in North, Central, and South America, this text opts for the term 'USAmerican' as a micro-means of inviting the reader to question his or her assumptions in using the term 'American' for U.S. citizens.

3   For those of us in the Euro zone between 2011 and 2012, the period when I began writing this book, this was not merely an imaginary exercise!

of Leiden, I was told the university would not transfer a single credit from my degree at Princeton. With a feeling of helplessness that is difficult to describe, I watched the promissory notes issued to me by Society go up in smoke.

Back then, I was interning at the American School of The Hague, so my degree bore at least some residual value in that one setting. But leaving work every day and 'returning' to Dutch society, where I attempted to acculturate to Dutch norms and values and in-laws, remained an exercise in alienation. Dutch and American cultures do not appear so very different on the outside, but they could not be more different at their core. Confidence is a virtue in the States, whereas the Dutch embrace modesty. Americans tout success, while the Dutch downplay it. Many Americans – and certainly those from Southern California – put a premium on being outgoing and close to the "life of the party"; the reticent Dutch rap people on the fingers for being boisterous.[4] In moving to the Netherlands, the surface culture (the visible part of the ice, in the analogy that compares culture to an iceberg) seemed similar enough to what I knew, but the hidden culture (the part of the iceberg under the waterline) was fundamentally alien, with a mass and inertia I could neither fathom nor budge.

Again, nobody stepped forward to help me with the questions I was wrestling with. But more painfully, I didn't have the vocabulary to grasp or ask about what was happening to me. More clinically depressed than I realized, I spent my first long winter in Holland carpooling to work with a similarly displaced American colleague. She did the driving, while I stared into oncoming headlights, trying to get enough light to my Southern Californian soul in order to survive that dark Dutch winter.

THE THIRD STORY

The third story is about saying goodbyes.

When I would fly back to college as a young adult, my mother would always leave me at the airport. In the era prior to September 11th, when bags could be checked in at the curb, she would shower me with forehead kisses, get back into her car, and wave out the window as she sped to the airport exit.

----

4   A famous Dutch snub is, "Try to be normal. Then you'll be weird enough."

Is it harder to be the one leaving from the airport or the one being left behind?

So 'normal' was this ritual it never occurred to me to question how my family of origin dealt with goodbyes until I met my wife. She would wave goodbye as long as she possibly could. When departures involved an airplane (as was the case in our early long-distance relationship), I could see her waving from the observation deck at Schiphol airport until the view became obstructed. And nowadays, when departures usually involve catching a tram, I can see her waving from the front door until the moment I turn the corner.

Little did I know I would one day be an expert on grief and the process of saying goodbye. I'm sometimes asked how I ever became an expert on mobility across cultures when I only worked at one international school. In my earlier years, I'd be inclined to invoke my exchange student periods in France or Japan, or the year I spent trekking across Asia during college, steeping myself in enough cultural alienation to make me shun travel for a decade. Such explanations sound defensive to me now. More importantly, they miss the point.

Staying in one place and working at the American School of The Hague for seventeen years provided me with a very particular perspective. That perspective is not better or worse than the perspective of the international school veteran – the student or parent or teacher who has attended or taught in, say, five different international schools. The perspective is what it is, namely *the perspective of the stayer*. From this camera angle, *life seems to be passing through*. New people constantly arrive, and people we may be extremely fond of constantly leave. My perspective as a long-term stayer forced me to participate in the recursive cycle of attachment – what I will refer to in this text as 'the tightening and loosening of affectional bonds'– at a level that can only be described as wrenching. The late David Pollock was fond of saying that "many kids at international schools experience more grief in their developmental years than most adults in a lifetime." Such overdoses of grief pertain no less to the adults who work with, or parent, these kids.

When presenting on the topic of mobility, I often ask my audiences a question that was born on the curbside of San Diego's Lindberg Field Airport. *Do they think it's harder to be the one leaving from the airport or the one being left behind?*

Without fail, people recognize it's harder to be left behind. As you will read in *Chapter 1: Attachment*, this pain can probably be traced to our evolutionary ancestors, as we have a biological drive to keep our attachment figures in range. Being left behind by those we held dear was an invitation to danger – and predators. It could be argued that we carry this vestigial fear into the modern era, right into 'Terminal D, Gate 17.'

My mother never consciously examined or discussed the reasons why she converted my departures into an act of my saying goodbye to her. (My becoming a psychologist would take care of that.) But it is fair to say her Anglo-Saxon upbringing gave her neither the vocabulary nor the skill set to cope well with goodbyes. She learned to manage difficult topics with avoidance. She learned to morph difficult experiences, like saying goodbye to her departing son, into variations that were slightly less painful, such as having her son wave goodbye to her as she departed.

So as I left for college, my bag of vocabulary for understanding and articulating the feelings involved in loss was close to empty. The fact I probably shared this lack of vocabulary with billions of people on the face of the earth would provide little consolation later, when I started struggling with my first losses. (They say "misery loves company," but you have to know who your 'company' is and how to find each other. I certainly didn't.) The only tool I had for dealing with loss in my early twenties was avoidance.

For the first seven years of my time at the American School of The Hague, I avoided the annual goodbye party at the end of the year with excuses coated in Teflon. *I have too much to do. They're leaving anyway, so what's the point? That sob party's not going to help me get Orientation ready to go, and the new kids are going to be here in a few more workdays.* It wasn't until my counselor colleague Dianne Banasco left that I finally knew I couldn't come up with an excuse that would be good enough.

The old minister of my church had the cryptic saying that "grief is cumulative." I never had any idea what he was talking about. But when I said goodbye to Dianne, his words flooded me like an emotional tidal wave. Waiting in line to give Dianne a hug, I remember a surge of terror as sadness welled up out of my gut. I put my arms around her, and began bawling. I had enjoyed working with Dianne, and I would definitely miss her, but the depth and the intensity of that grief utterly overwhelmed me, leaving me spinning, drenched, and confused. Horrified, I fled for the safety of my bike and attempted to pedal in the direction of home, my vision blurred like a mask filled with salt water. Nearly crash-landing at the nearest park bench, I had no choice but to let the waves roll me over, like the Pacific breakers when I would tumble off my surfboard. Only months and years later would I come to appreciate I was shedding tears that were as old as my soul, as old as my parents' divorce, as old as my dear step-father's early death, as old as the loss of my country in exchange for the new life I hadn't yet built in the Netherlands.

At a visceral level, I learned that you shouldn't argue with a minister. Grief *is* cumulative. You can run, but Grief eventually catches up with you to settle the bill. Years of experience from the perspective of the stayer have branded me with an indelible appreciation for the pain of the grieving process – but also for its importance. David Pollock famously emphasized "you have to say a clear 'goodbye' in order to say a clear 'hello'." He was so right that this book labels his words 'The First Law of Transitions.'

My own clinical experience, including counseling at an international school and running the 'Safe Harbour' program at the American School of The Hague, have taught me the transformative power of saying effective goodbyes. Teaching our students the skills for how to say effective goodbyes converts an experience which can be crippling if avoided, into one that can foster immense personal growth if embraced. It takes time and energy to acquire this skill set – but that's no different from learning to drive. Or to type. Or to sail.

I'm going with the nautical metaphor. So get in, rig yourself to the lifeline, and get ready to learn how to navigate mobile lives through the hearts of international schools.

Doug Ota
www.SafePassage.nl

HOW TO USE THIS BOOK
A 'Quick Start Guide'

Modern gadgets get packaged with 'Quick Start Guides.' Spend one minute reading the overview on the next page, and you'll get the most out of *Safe Passage*.

A WORD ON THIS BOOK'S SCOPE

This book focuses upon transitions as they occur at international schools worldwide. But the issues discussed in this book pertain to other settings and contexts just as well: the transition to university, the transition to parenthood, the transition of grown children leaving the home, the transition to retirement, and the ultimate transition facing us all, the end of life.

While the focus throughout this text is upon transitions issues as they operate at international schools with a transient population, I wish to make it emphatically clear at the outset that the scope of this book can easily be extended to the contexts and situations mentioned above. I do not make these extensions explicitly throughout the text, but the reader is free – and encouraged – to make them in his or her own imagination.

IF YOU WANT TO…	THEN READ…	ON PAGE…
SEE IF IT'S **WORTHWHILE** TO WORK ON ISSUES RELATED TO MOBILITY AT YOUR SCHOOL	*THE INTRODUCTION*	XXXIX
READ A **LETTER** I WROTE TO YOU, TO CUSTOMIZE THIS BOOK TO YOUR NEEDS AND INTERESTS	THE APPROPRIATE 'MESSAGE IN A BOTTLE' ADDRESSED TO YOU IN *APPENDIX A*	221
UNDERSTAND THE **THEORY** ON WHY ANY SCHOOL WITH A TRANSIENT POPULATION SHOULD ADDRESS MOBILITY ISSUES	*PART I ON THE HIGH SEAS: WHY MOVING ACROSS CULTURES IS CHALLENGING*	LVIII
GET **PRACTICAL IDEAS** ABOUT ABOUT HOW YOUR SCHOOL COULD START TO ADDRESS ISSUES OF MOBILITY	*PART II FINDING A SAFE HARBOR: BUILDING PROGRAMS TO MATCH THE CHALLENGE*	72
SEE **'BEST PRACTICE'** EXAMPLES OF HOW ONE SCHOOL WENT ABOUT ADDRESSING MOBILITY	*CHAPTER 6: AN EXEMPLAR HARBOR*	143
EVALUATE THE QUALITY OF YOUR SCHOOL'S MOBILITY-RELATED SERVICES, OR THOSE OF A PROSPECTIVE SCHOOL	*PART III ENSURING SAFE PASSAGE: NAVIGATING MOBILE LIVES THROUGH THE HEARTS OF SCHOOLS*	170
UNDERSTAND WHY **NO SINGLE SCHOOL** CAN ADEQUATELY ADDRESS THESE CHALLENGES ON ITS OWN	*CHAPTER 10: ASSESSING NETWORKS OF SCHOOLS*	201
UNDERSTAND HOW **ACCREDITATION** AND QUALITY ASSURANCE AGENCIES ARE IN THE BEST POSITION TO EFFECT NECESSARY CHANGES	*CHAPTER 10: ASSESSING NETWORKS OF SCHOOLS*, AND *APPENDIX B* AND *APPENDIX C*	201
FORM A SUCCESSFUL TEAM TO ADDRESS THE ISSUES IN THIS BOOK AND UNDERSTAND YOUR TEAM MEMBERS BETTER	READ ALL OF THE 'MESSAGES IN BOTTLES' IN *APPENDIX A*	221

THE SIX LAWS OF TRANSITIONS

"A man is but what he knoweth."
  – Inscription above library, Columbia University, New York

You have to say a clear 'goodbye' in order to say a clear 'hello' *or* You have to grieve well to leave well. (In memory of David C. Pollock)

For every connection, there is an equal and opposite connection *or* For a person to connect to somebody else, that other person must be willing and able to make the connection.

The Transitions Team is the Transitions Team for the Transitions Team.

A person's role at a school with a high degree of turnover is subject to drift. Arrivers become stayers, and stayers become leavers. People are not consciously aware of this drift. Arrivers need to be helped to consider accepting the roles and responsibilities of the stayers when the time comes.

Humans need safe attachments to community. People in transition are looking for a community to attach to.

The international school should conceive of itself as a transitional attachment object for its clientele.

INTRODUCTION
All Hands on Deck!

"Humanity remakes the world in an accelerating cycle of change that strips away our stories as well as the topsoil."

> – Paul Salopek, National Geographic Explorer,
> as he walks around the world,
> *National Geographic,* December, 2013

A STUNNING DISCOVERY

In 2009, Professor John Hattie of the University of Melbourne published *Visible Learning,* the "largest ever collection of evidence-based research into what actually works in schools to improve learning." His book gathered every study ever published on what works in education. A study that pools data from separate studies into a larger overview is called a 'meta-study.' Professor Hattie's fifteen year investment produced the largest-ever 'meta-meta study.' It combined more than eight hundred meta-studies in education, involving a total of 52,637 different published studies that surveyed millions and millions of students worldwide.[5]

Hattie's was the largest educational study in history. His question was simple. *What actually works to improve student learning?*

Many factors improve learning. Hattie's book concludes with a ranking of 138 factors that impact how well students learn, from the most positive factors to the most negative. The point here is not to review *Visible Learning* and examine the factors that clearly do help students learn – things like having students self-report their estimated grades, the quality of the student-teacher relationship, and providing students with regular feedback. The point here is

---

5   *As this book goes to press, Hattie's database now includes over 1000 meta-studies.*

to examine what Hattie found at the *bottom* of the list, namely those things that hurt learning.

What emerges in 138th place – at the absolute bottom of Hattie's list – is mobility.

In other words, in the largest study ever performed in the history of educational research, the factor that has the single greatest negative impact on how much students learn is whether they have to move.

This book will explain why. But it doesn't stop there. This book explains why it doesn't have to be this way. This book explains why mobility, and particularly mobility across cultures, can be one of the richest sources of learning and personal growth that life has to offer. But these benefits are only likely to occur when mobility's massive challenges are managed well.

WHY MOBILITY SITS AT THE BOTTOM OF HATTIE'S LIST

The reason mobility emerges at the very bottom of Hattie's list is because comprehensive school-based programs for handling the challenges associated with moving rarely exist. There are several reasons why:

- general lack of awareness of the issues involved
- the adults involved are struggling with the exact same challenges
- fear and avoidance of the powerful emotions involved
- the notion that schools are not responsible for emotional issues
- the right programs are difficult for an individual school to build
- individual schools cannot build the requisite programs on their own

Hattie's landmark publication of *Visible Learning* should put mobility more centrally on the map of important educational issues, at least for any school dealing with a transient population. It is my hope this book provides readers with both a way to understand the challenges of mobility across cultures, as well as the tools for addressing that challenge.

This book represents an answer to what would otherwise be a disconcerting conclusion that educators and parents would logically draw after

Mobility emerges at the very bottom of Hattie's list is because comprehensive school-based programs for handling the challenges associated with moving rarely exist.

reading *Visible Learning,* namely that students should never be moved. As you will learn in the pages of this book, mobility across cultures can be, and deserves to be 'promoted' from its current ranking as the greatest risk factor for student learning. Mobility across cultures can be one of the greatest catalysts that exists for learning and growth for all people involved, and not just for students.

As with any overarching statement, this statement deserves to be qualified because it can be abused. Managers or CEOs or parents who put, force, or keep kids 'on the road' by referencing the above statement are abusing that statement's intent. They are putting the youngsters involved on course to experience 'mobility' exactly where Hattie found it, at the bottom of the list, as the factor most harmful to their learning and potentially traumatic

"I was offered a job as a CEO, and I said no."

  – Bjorn, Danish executive who didn't want to disrupt his family

to their development. The benefits of mobility across cultures only occur when sufficient attention is devoted to managing the challenges involved.

True to the aphorism "You get out of something what you put into it," what students derive from the experience of moving across cultures is directly proportional to what they, and in particular the adults responsible for guiding them, invest in managing that process.

A DEMOCRATIC STRESSOR

But children and young people don't know how to manage major challenges like this on their own. When children and young people don't know what to do, when they feel overwhelmed by a task, they logically turn to someone that John Bowlby, the father of the field of 'attachment theory,' described as 'stronger and wiser,' someone who hopefully knows what to do in such circumstances.

But that raises an even bigger issue than the one Hattie bumped into. Do the adults actually know what to do?

Hattie discovered the effect mobility has on children *because he was only studying children.* He found students did not learn as well when mobility was thrown into the mix. But what about teachers who had to move? How well did they teach? And what about parents who had to move? How well did they parent?

How well do parents parent when they feel left behind by dear friends? How well do teachers teach when they feel left behind by beloved colleagues?

It gets more complex, because anyone familiar with life at an international school with any degree of turnover knows that people move away too. And when people move, they leave friends and people who love them behind. How well do students learn when they feel left behind by best friends? How well do parents parent when they feel left behind by dear friends? How well do teachers teach when they feel left behind by beloved colleagues?

And it doesn't stop there. What happens when these processes keep happening to people over and over, as people in the international school circuit move every few years? What does that do to the way a student learns? What does that do to the way a teacher teaches? What does that do to the way a parent parents?

This book is grounded in the conviction – and, I would argue, the reality – that we are all in the same boat. By virtue of our humanness, by virtue of our being members of a social species, the experience of mobility across cultures levels the demographic playing field and challenges people with similar issues, whether they sit in the school's kindergarten or in the Director's chair. At schools with any considerable degree of turnover, students, parents, teachers, and administrators are all confronted with a situation where the social environment is in flux. Disruptions to the social landscape unleash similar reactions in people, whether they know it or not, and whether they show it or not, because of the way we are wired. This is why I refer to mobility in a school community as a 'democratic stressor.' We are wired to seek connection and a degree of predictability in our lives, so things feel safe and in control. Mobility across cultures wreaks havoc with these needs. We need only turn back to the 1950s, when the great psychologist Abraham Maslow provided us with a model for understanding why.

MASLOW'S HIERARCHY OF NEEDS

Maslow's hierarchy of needs provided a simple but powerful framework for understanding the order in which people seek the satisfaction of their human needs. The basic idea is that needs which are lower on the hierarchy require satisfying before a person can move up to the next level.

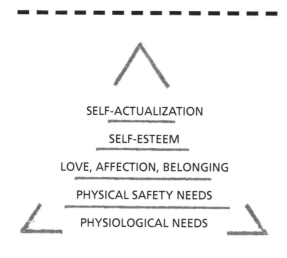

SELF-ACTUALIZATION

SELF-ESTEEM

LOVE, AFFECTION, BELONGING

PHYSICAL SAFETY NEEDS

PHYSIOLOGICAL NEEDS

FIGURE I: Maslow's 'hierarchy of needs'

The base of the pyramid has little to do with mobility and everything to do with staying alive. Nobody would dare question our physiological needs for things like oxygen, water, and food. Only if these needs are met can we pursue our basic physical safety needs. Again, in terms of transition, nobody would question a person's need to have adequate clothing, shelter, and basic physical safety.

It is at the level of love, affection, and belonging that things become interesting from a transitions point of view. While few would question the benefits of a child enjoying a loving home with sufficient attention and affection, the reality is that a child, over the course of his or her development, increasingly turns to sources beyond the parents for attention, affection, belonging, and, ultimately, love. Child and adolescent development consist

Over the course of adolescence, a teen shifts his or her primary attention from parents to the peer group, using peers as a 'transitional object' to migrate from the world of the child to the world of the adult.

of a continuous transition from one extreme, where parents are the primary source of love and attention and affection, towards another extreme, where people in the wider community, most importantly one's romantic partner, become the primary sources of emotional investment. Over the course of adolescence, a teen shifts his or her primary attention from parents to the peer group, using peers as a 'transitional object' to migrate from the world of the child to the world of the adult. Friends and peers serve as the primary target of affiliation over the course of adolescence, allowing the adolescent to loosen his or her dependence on the family, build bonds outside the family, and ultimately complete the arc of development by choosing a partner and investing attention, affection, and love in that partner.

To skip this reality is to skip the equivalent of what I would term the 'social oxygen' for a child – his or her surroundings. Where a child derives *some* sense of belonging from the places and people that are familiar, a teenager begins adolescence by deriving *much* of his or her sense of belonging from these places and people. And adolescence ends when 'much' has turned into 'most.' After a move, or after a dear friend moves away, a child may be struggling for emotional oxygen, but an adolescent may be gasping. Adults who label a teen's response to a Facebook incident 'exaggerated' or 'out of proportion' have perhaps put too many decades between themselves and their own teenage years.[6] The packaging on the interaction may look different (social media), but is it qualitatively any different from how we doted on the telephone as teens, or how our grandparents raided the mailbox in the hopes of receiving a letter?

This notion of 'gasping for social air' tends to be less for relocating employees as employees are generally older, but also because most of them *choose* their fate. For accompanying spouses, however, the sense of 'gasping for air' socially can be accurate. While the relocating employee has the identity associated with his or her new position, the accompanying spouse also loses the social surroundings that provided attention, affiliation, and belonging. Without such validation, the accompanying spouse needs to reestablish these sources of social oxygen in the new setting.

Despite the obvious importance of the factors at the lower levels of Maslow's hierarchy, many international schools proceed far too quickly up the

----

6   As a parent, I struggle with the ubiquitous presence of Internet devices, and the urgency of the latest Instagram, Twitter, or Facebook posting. The child psychologist in me, however, recognizes that such events are perceived by teens as more fundamental and essential in their Maslowian pyramids. Abraham Maslow did have children; had he exposed them to an internationally mobile lifestyle, and had he run his pyramid by them prior to publication, I'm sure they would have corroborated what I'm saying.

hierarchy, often focusing primarily or even exclusively on the level of 'self-actualization' and 'achieving your potential.' This kind of aspiring and inspiring rhetoric sounds remarkably similar to the type of language infusing many schools' mission statements.

> *Even though a student might have arrived physically from Australia, it may take months for his or her psychological self to fully arrive.*

How can a new student at school achieve cognitive and personal goals like this if he feels he has no real friends yet? What if he wakes up with a wrenching feeling of missing home? How can a long-term student at your school be expected to learn and thrive when she's lost her third best friend in three years, and the school has no provisions or programs in place to recognize or address this fact? What if a student – we'll call him a junior in High School, meaning he's in his last two years – was en route to becoming the president of the student government in his last school, the captain of his lacrosse team, and an academic star? His life was a string of successes, and everyone had assured him this next international move would 'add to his experience' and be a 'gem on his resume' for college. But, poorly coached and guided through his transition, he grossly underestimates the challenges of mobility across cultures, and now he's drowning in a school that feels far more demanding than his last one, and without a support network.

All these students are likely to find themselves sitting in classes and feeling, at times, as if they're living unreal existences. The teacher at the front of the class is talking about an English assignment or a period in history or the latest law of sines or cosines. The student in question has a feeling of depersonalization, as if he or she is not totally there. This is not a psychic anomaly or a harbinger of psychosis: this is true. He or she is not all there yet. As Harry Mulisch wrote in *The Stone Bridal Bed,* "the soul travels by horseback." Even though a student might have arrived physically from Australia, it may take months for his or her psychological self to fully arrive. And a school that attempts to proceed with 'business as usual' without programs to help students navigate these processes is a school attempting to – and arguably coercing students to – build castles in the sky, as depicted by the version of Maslow's hierarchy in Figure II.

The world does not work in ideal ways, and it is obviously not realistic to have all students feeling adequate affection, belonging, and self-esteem at all times so the business of education and self-actualization can proceed optimally. Hardship in the right dose builds character, and difficulty in the right degree breeds the confidence that one can overcome obstacles. This kind of confidence is the hallmark of resilience in the face of life's challenges.

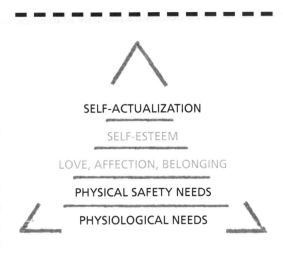

SELF-ACTUALIZATION

SELF-ESTEEM

LOVE, AFFECTION, BELONGING

PHYSICAL SAFETY NEEDS

PHYSIOLOGICAL NEEDS

FIGURE II: Maslow's hierarchy through the eyes of someone in transition

The point here is not to eradicate hardship, any more than it is to strive for some idyllic school or state where self-actualization is proceeding amongst lotus blossoms and chants of 'Ohm'[7] on the school loudspeakers. The point is to take our responsibility for the emotional and psychological realities we see forming around the swirls of mobility, just as sailors take precautions when they see the skies darkening over the Atlantic and the telltale signs of an approaching squall. If we can see challenges forming in predictable ways, shouldn't we establish the programs and processes we know will assist people in navigating those challenges successfully?

If we proceed thoughtfully, we can harness these forces and use them as levers for growth. Meaning in life, after all, is derived from how we respond to challenges. Challenges that overwhelm us are traumatic. Challenges that are managed, so they remain within the scope of what we can handle, become springboards for development. For everyone.

---

7   "Ohm" is the sound of the universe in Hindu mythology.

DRAMATIS PERSONAE

The right lenses for viewing the issues lead logically to the right tools for addressing them. If we accurately perceive the difficulties people experience during the processes associated with mobility, and if we possess the appropriate theoretical frameworks for understanding those difficulties, then the things we need to do will emerge naturally.

Who is doing the 'moving across cultures'? The clarity of perception we will need begins by accurately seeing the characters involved. As every play begins with the dramatis personae, allow me introduce you to the main characters in this story. Who is doing the 'moving'? What is meant by 'across cultures'?

Moving

The phrase 'moving across cultures' suggests there is a person who is moving, and everybody else around him or her is staying still. The phrase also suggests we are more focused upon the student or parent or staff member who is doing the relocating (the one *catching* the flight) and less focused upon the people in the life he or she is leaving or moving towards (the people *bringing* him to the airport, or the people *picking* her up).

Nothing could be farther from the truth.

Einstein's special theory of relativity states that the speed of light is the same regardless of the speed at which an observer travels, and it is the same for all observers everywhere. In practical terms, one of the upshots of this theory is that there is no longer a 'fixed point' from which events can be judged or measured.

Einstein's special theory of relativity pertains not only to bodies in space but also to bodies in international schools. Movement – or what I might call 'emotional movement' – cannot be judged relative to some fixed position we can all point to as some immovable origin. Rather, 'emotional movement' is relative to the people around us. Somebody may feel sad when they leave an international school, but the people they leave behind also feel sad and 'left behind.'

We have all experienced something related to emotional movement on a visceral level. Psychologists refer to this as the 'train illusion,' and you've experienced it if you've ever been sitting in a stationary train as the train next to you begins to leave the station. What happens? We naturally assume the train outside the window is standing still, and *our* train has left the station. Moments later we experience a feeling somewhere between humor and shock, as we realize we haven't budged, and it's the *other* train that's left the station. Our brains are wired to 'trust' our experience is built on terra firma. In other words, if the landscape outside our experience begins to move, it must mean that *we* are doing the moving. (There were no large moving objects or landscapes in our evolutionary history, so the conclusion our minds draw makes perfect perceptual sense.)

The loss the leaver feels when hugging her best friend goodbye is the mirror image of the gaping hole the best friend experiences on the other side of the embrace. One is flying away. The other is staying put. But if you step back and view these two people as two points in space, it is impossible to say who is moving away from whom. You can only say the distance between them is increasing. And that distance hurts them both equally.

In other words, if you are considering working on addressing mobility in your school, then the distinction between mover and 'movee' – to coin another new term – is not nearly as important as you might think. While it may seem logical to assume the needs of a person moving to a new country and school are substantively different from the needs of the person staying behind in the same country and school, one of the central arguments of this book is that such a distinction is unnecessary. The reason why is because of what I will call the 'Second Law of Transitions,' namely that:

- -

 For every connection, there is an equal and opposite connection *or* For a person to connect to somebody else, that other person must be willing and able to make the connection.[8]

- -

Though there are two people involved, mover and movee, there is but one connection linking the two. *Because of mobility, they are grieving the loss of the same thing.*

- -

8   *This Second Law of Transitions – and the very notion of suggesting the Laws of Transitions in the first place – was inspired by Newton's laws of motion.*

Across Cultures

What is movement 'across cultures'?

For the purposes of this text, 'culture' can be understood as a way of organizing experience. We are bombarded every minute with thousands of different stimuli. Culture gives us a framework for determining which ones we can afford to ignore, which ones we need to pay attention to, how to interpret the information we do attend to, and – perhaps most importantly – how to behave on the basis of the information received. Without culture, our brains would be overloaded. We would be attempting to pay attention to everything at once, and to choose an appropriate response.

Culture allows us to focus on some of the information, and then it gives us a correct response. When a stranger in Kansas says, "Good morning, how are you?" a USAmerican knows to say, "I'm fine, how are you?" What does that same USAmerican do when an elderly Japanese woman in Tokyo says to him, *"Atsui desu ne?"*[9] The need to digest incoming information without yet having mastered a framework for processing that information is arguably why visiting foreign cultures, and the accompanying 'culture shock', can be so disorienting and exhausting.

Culture gives us the basic tools for navigating the vast complexities of human social organization, an organization so vast and subtle it is now considered by many evolutionary biologists to be the reason why the hominid cranium underwent such a massive expansion between 500,000 and 100,000 years ago: to house a brain big enough to comprehend the society that was forming around it [1]. (See page 277 for notes on references.) We needed brains complex enough to navigate all the social interactions that occurred in such a society. In particular, we needed brains strong enough to restrain the basic, primal impulses that would otherwise disrupt society if they were given free rein.

Needless to say, when you move to an international school from whatever place it was you used to call 'home', some form of culture shock is likely to occur, particularly if you are making such a move for the first time. The way the local people organize their lives, experience, and relationships can

---

9   *It's hot today, isn't it?*

differ so drastically from what you consider 'normal' it can feel like you're being held upside down in a vat of soy sauce. The essence of culture shock is just that: a fundamental changing of the rules.

The way new students or parents at an international

A relocation has both a transitions aspect because of the grief and loss associated with moving, as well as a cultural aspect because of the shift in the societal rules and overarching framework organizing interactions.

school can feel is not necessarily fundamentally different from certain domestic moves. For example, a Chinese farmer who left his village for Beijing at eighteen would probably experience a similar sense of culture shock overload, even though he hasn't left his country. Everything would be new. And he would possess few frameworks for organizing the stimuli assaulting him.

A relocation has both a *transitions aspect* because of the grief and loss associated with moving, as well as a *cultural aspect* because of the shift in the societal rules and overarching framework organizing interactions.

To complicate matters further, in an international school, much is not what it appears to be. 'Moving across cultures' suggests the agent, i.e. the 'mover', is doing the crossing and entering something culturally new. But we have to remember there may be others who consider themselves 'members' of the mover's culture. What might it be like for the handful of Japanese students at the International School of Düsseldorf, Germany, to see another new Japanese student move into their midst? Or what it might be like for a quiet 9th grade boy originally from Texas, who spent much of his youth in Tokyo? How would he react to the realization there is a new Japanese student joining his class? When we are talking about 'moving across cultures', we have to remember Einstein and keep the relativity of the statement in mind. One person's experience of *moving away* (for example, the hypothetical new Japanese student above, who feels he is leaving his beloved Tokyo) is another person's experience of being *moved towards* (for example, the other Japanese students at the school, who are happy to welcome 'one of their own,' as well as the boy from Texas, with his invisible affinity for all things Japanese – and an ability to speak the language).

What about for the local Chilean students who attend Nido International School in Santiago, Chile?[10] To expat students who have just moved to Chile, these students might seem like locals. But what do these students themselves feel like when they return to their local Santiagan neighborhoods after school each day? How do the other local kids attending local public schools view them? To what degree are they viewed as 'one of us' by the rest of the neighborhood?

In attempting to understand what the dynamics of moving across culture feel like for those involved, the notion of 'cultural relativity' gets a new twist when viewed in Einstein's original meaning of the term. There is no fixed point. When it comes to culture, all we can do is be as aware as possible of our own cultural reference points, the reference points of others, and the reality that cultural reference points in international schools with transient populations are most likely not visible to the naked eye.

When nothing seems fixed anymore, including things that seemed clear in the past, a person can be described as grieving the loss of things that once made sense.

A move, then, involves a change not only to people and places surrounding a person, but also to the entire system of meaning surrounding the person's day-to-day interpretation of events. Transitions means 'moving across cultures' because it shifts a person's spatial, relational, and interpretational reference points. When nothing seems fixed anymore, including things that seemed clear in the past, a person can be described as grieving the loss of things that once made sense.

WHY I WROTE THIS BOOK – AND WHY YOU SHOULD READ IT

The purpose of this book is to motivate a broad range of readers from all walks of life in an international school community to become involved in establishing comprehensive transitions programs at their respective schools, and to empower these readers with the tools to develop programs that both work and last. If you are an interested parent, administrator, board

---

10 *Ruth van Reken refers to these students as 'Cross Cultural Kids,' or CCKs.*

member, counselor, teacher, prospective member of an international school community, or even a mature student, this book is for you. The reason for this may sound grand: the issues addressed in this book require attention if any international school with a considerable degree of turnover wants its students to have a chance to fully achieve their potential. In other words:

the issues addressed in this book require attention if an international school with any substantial degree of turnover wishes to achieve its mission.

If that's the reason why you should read this book, I have two main reasons for writing it. One comes from the heart, which I call my 'compassionate reason.' The other comes from the head, and is called the 'logical reason.'

The Compassionate Reason For This Book

The compassionate reason for pursuing the development of comprehensive transitions programs at international schools is because ignoring the challenges of mobility across cultures leads to real human suffering. Mobility across cultures exposes people to real threats to their attachments to important others, and it causes ruptures in a person's sense of identity. Identity is not an individual or atomistic construction, but something formed in connection and interaction with others. The loss of important connections confronts the individual with grief. And the only thing worse than grief is grief that remains unseen or unacknowledged.

This 'unseen' and 'unacknowledged' condition constitutes the unfortunate state of affairs in most international schools today, at least those with a substantial degree of turnover. A reality that already hurts (i.e. the loss of people important to you) is magnified by the reality remaining unvalidated by the surrounding community. The innocent victim suffers in a vacuum, contributing to the tragic conviction in the sufferer's own mind that his or her pain isn't real or warranted – a conviction which may hurt more than the losses themselves.

To make the existential conundrum tougher, international school students and families often come from more economically advantaged segments of society, meaning their entire experience of moving around and 'seeing the world' is viewed primarily as privilege. While the statements these students and families hear are certainly true – 'they are so fortunate' to be able to 'see the world' in a way 'most kids can only dream of' – it is also true that these privileges come with real challenges, which are often eclipsed by the simplistic and romanticized view of a 'life on the road.' This simplistic view is all too often held by those who have never lived such lives.

Moving jolts one's identity. 'Culture shock' is not an exaggeration in terms. And all too often the real pain people feel when they lose who they are is magnified one hundred-fold by the invisibility of the struggle. Add to this mix the fact that the person's degree of choice in whether or not to move is often severely or entirely constrained – certainly for children and often for partners – and you have the recipe for what can only be called a 'trauma of transition.' *A trauma of transition is a sense of one's identity being erased in a way that one had no control over, and in a way that no one seems to see.*

- -
The person's degree of choice in whether or not to move is often severely or entirely constrained – certainly for children and often for partners – and you have the recipe for what can only be called a 'trauma of transition.'
- -

Imagine being the victim in a traffic accident, laying in pain on the side of the road, and seeing people going about their business, and you get the idea. Trauma victims often report that the worst part of a traumatic experience had less to do with the accident or attack itself, and more to do with observers standing around and doing nothing.

We can, and must, do better than this in our schools. Schools are supposed to be safe places, for the simple reason that people grow and develop better when they do not feel threatened. For example, educators often teach children that watching somebody being bullied without doing anything about it is not qualitatively different or better than being the actual bully. In light of the issues described in this book, we cannot afford to become 'innocent bystanders' while mobility shoves people around, particularly children. The stakes are too high. Suffering is happening right in front of our noses. Some of the greatest potential benefits of international education are being missed.

The Logical Reason For This Book

The first part of the logical reason is based on hard data, and it has already been touched upon via the findings in *Visible Learning*. Moving *is* wreaking havoc with student learning. But it is also arguably wreaking havoc with parents' abilities to optimally parent, teachers' abilities to optimally teach, and administrators' abilities to lead most effectively. In other words, it is arguably wreaking havoc with the effectiveness of the entire school community of any school with a transient population. The attachment, neuroscience, and life-story arguments presented in the next two chapters provide ample evidence for believing that what is true for children continues to be true for the adults who parent, teach, and guide them.

The second part of the logical reason is based on cultural and demographic trends of the 20th and 21st centuries. In 1984, the sociologist Ted Ward made the famous statement that "TCKs are the prototype citizens of the future" [cited in 2, p. xiii]. His statement then predicted what is now a self-evident reality: globalization has shrunk the world, bringing people around the globe increasingly in touch with people with different cultural heritages. International schools were arguably at the vanguard of this development, as the children of parents whose work propelled them 'abroad' came to attend the same international school together, sitting in the same classroom – and at the same lunch table – with children from entirely different walks of life. Children's friendships traversed borders, cultures, languages, and skin tones. The obvious opportunities inherent in such educational settings for developing cross-cultural understanding quickly made their way into the mission statements of most international schools, captured by words like 'diversity' and 'respect for differences.'

Eventually, and more ambitiously, international schools began to be seen as potential incubators for the development of intercultural competence, which can be defined as the ability to communicate effectively and appropriately with people from other cultural walks of life. Goals associated with cultivating intercultural competence gained ascendency into the highest levels of thinking in the field, right up to the mission statement of the International Baccalaureate Organization (IBO). The IBO maintains as one of its foundational goals the hope of educating young people who understand that "other people, with their differences, can also be right." [3]

Putting people from different cultures in the same 'mixing bowl' does not in and of itself produce cross-cultural understanding or intercultural competence. Give a baby different faces to look at, and even a pre-verbal infant will tend to spend more time looking at the faces with a genetic code more similar to its own. In the roots of our biology are genes and processes that attune us to threats, and one of our primordial threats was anything, or anyone, who looked different. A gene for 'tourism' does not exist. When we lived in caves and tribes, he who looked different *was* different and may have been after your food, possessions, land, or loved ones. He or she therefore ought to be viewed warily.

We can convince ourselves that this fear of the other and this preference for the similar no longer reside in our biology, but it is reflected in the composition of societies around the world to this day, where like tend to reside close to like. And this preference for the similar and fear of the foreign pervades the hallways of cafeterias of most public schools the world over. Take a look, and you will generally see like clustering with like, where kids tend to socialize and sit with kids who look and behave as they do. Some are arguing that globalization itself is the reason for a shift towards more fundamentalist views we see in many places around the world today [4], rather than towards more cross-cultural understanding or intercultural competence.

Overcoming this default, fear-based response requires more than seating kids at a similar lunch table with similar sandwiches. It requires deliberate effort and the active maintenance of a school culture that countervails our biological defaults. A school's culture must *help* students cultivate a spirit of curiosity and openness towards one another. This does not happen by itself. Only with gentle but persistent help will students genuinely come to understand those who are different, thereby overcoming their biologically-based fears, making it possible over the longer term to achieve a stance of acceptance and validation towards the other and the other's experience. Few can argue, I believe, with the eloquent urgency with which George Walker, former Director General of the International Baccalaureate Organization, called on us to act:

> "*Against our contemporary background of a renewed sense of precarious isolation, the vocabulary of international education – responsible citizenship, compassionate thinking, tolerance, diversity within a shared humanity, cultural understanding – no longer sounds like high-flown idealism but seems, on the contrary, to offer the only practical hope for the future of humankind.*" [5, p. 209]

The Rationale That Emerges At The Intersection Of Head And Heart

My personal rationale for writing this book emerges at the intersection of the compassionate and logical reasons for addressing these issues. The human being, son, partner, father and psychologist in me has an instinctual wish to prevent and relieve suffering when I see it. I certainly wish to contribute to the relief of suffering for the students, parents, and staff members in the school communities which are the focus of this book. That alone is a worthy goal.

But it is not enough. The populations of international schools, particularly the children being educated by those schools, are in an ideal position to derive lessons from their experience that the world needs. *Safe Passage* seeks to assist them in thriving not purely for their own good, but for the good of the wider world they will inherit. In their thriving resides the seeds of the kind of hope Walker was describing, the kind of attitudes and skills needed to allow us to share and sustain our finite planet.

Bertrand Russell once declared, "From he to whom much is given, much is expected." I would nuance his statement: *As long as people are given the skills to cope with that which they're given, much can be expected.* This book seeks to assist parents, teachers, administrators, and especially students in managing and overcoming the challenges that come with mobility across cultures, so they learn to move in the world with confidence and intercultural competence. On our shrinking planet, where resources remain finite while population keeps growing, Walker is right. The vocabulary of international education is the only practical hope for the future of humankind.

ON THE HIGH SEAS
Why Moving Across Cultures is Challenging

Chapter 1

ATTACHMENT –
THE WIND IN EVERY SAIL

"It is in the shelter of each other that people live."
— Celtic proverb

Before devising a program to address transitions in a school, a framework is needed for viewing the challenge. Just as you'd rather have your physician make an accurate diagnosis before administering a treatment (or, more to the point, before making an incision), so too is it sensible to first develop a deep appreciation for the issues at stake for the students, parents, teachers, and administrators who attend, parent, and work at international schools with a high degree of turnover.

The purpose of Part I, *On the High Seas: Why Moving Across Cultures Is Challenging*, is to provide you with a vocabulary for understanding these issues. When the issues are understood, programs can be developed to address them. When the vocabulary this book will use is understood, the programs that are needed follow quite logically. *Part II, Finding a Safe Harbor: Building Programs To Match The Challenge*, demonstrates this principle. *Part II* puts the vocabulary developed in *Part I* to work, using it to generate the tools needed.

Three sets of vocabulary will be used throughout this book for understanding and addressing the core issues. We sail by them in sequence:

- grief
- attachment
- life stories

This chapter embarks from grief and arrives at attachment. The next chapter departs from attachment and arrives at life stories.

Let's sail.

WHY GRIEF IS RIGHT – BUT INCOMPLETE

In the groundbreaking text *Third Culture Kids: Growing Up Among Worlds*, arguably the first book that put the issues faced by globally mobile children on the map, David Pollock and Ruth Van Reken did exquisite work explaining what the experience of moving across cultures, at its core, is all about.

Loss.

Beneath the richness of experience a globally mobile life might provide, Pollock and Van Reken shed light on the loss that formed the defining emotional quality of a mobile lifestyle. Massive and regular waves of goodbyes and loss roll over third culture kids (TCKs) repeatedly, so often that Pollock

> *Pollock frequently made the unsettling statement in his presentations that "many TCKs have experienced more loss in their developmental years than most adults experience in a lifetime."*

frequently made the unsettling statement in his presentations that "many TCKs have experienced more loss in their developmental years than most adults experience in a lifetime."

Pollock and Van Reken's book has sold tens of thousands of copies and is now in its second edition. And still there are few examples worldwide of comprehensive transitions programs at international schools. Why?

Why have international schools worldwide been slow to establish the kinds of programs necessary for dealing with the issues Pollock and Van Reken described? Why are there so few comprehensive transitions programs in international schools when the issues at stake are so clear and pervasive? Is this merely an issue of awareness building and community education, so more education of more school communities is needed to help people finally 'jump on the bandwagon' and get involved? Or is there something more going on?

It goes without saying that establishing comprehensive transitions programs at schools with a high degree of turnover is difficult. This book addresses the challenges that make it difficult. But human beings are resourceful creatures, and there are plenty of difficult things in life that, with commitment and hard work, we successfully overcome.

What else could explain why comprehensive transitions teams at international schools worldwide have been slow to be established?

Might it have something to do with the fact that 'leave-taking' committees on many start-up Transitions Teams often struggle to recruit members, even when the rest of the Team is beginning to thrive? Might a hidden factor be at work?

The Repulsion Factor

In terms of their theoretical focus, Pollock and Van Reken dared to look into the depths of the experience of mobility and to name the dark beast nobody had named before.

Grief.

The word makes us uncomfortable. As I sit in my chair writing these words, I notice I've flinched and twisted several times. A seasoned psychologist who specializes, amongst other things, in grief therapy, the word still makes me catch my breath – particularly when it starts with a capital letter. I would like to surmise something I may never be able to prove, but which I sense is probably true: *it is the effect the word 'grief' has on people which contributes to inhibiting many transitions programs in international schools from getting off the ground.*

> *We are not designed to deal with making and breaking deep connections over the course of a single academic year, only to repeat the process again the next year, and then again the following year, ad infinitum.*

At the existential extreme, goodbyes remind us of death and the tenuousness of the connections we have in life. Mobility in an international school puts the normal cycle of life into warp drive, whereby people experience the cycle of connection and dissolution, arrival and departure, at an alarming rate. From an evolutionary point of view we are biologically designed to deal with grief over the course of a lifetime. We are not designed to deal with making and breaking deep connections over the course of a single academic year, only to repeat the process again the next year, and then again the following year, ad infinitum. The 'grief fatigue' that can set in for many people on the international school circuit exists because of the arguable overdose of grief that such a life exposes us to.

It is understandable that most people would turn from an overdose of unpleasantness by maintaining a strategy – at times – of avoidance. Who wants to get excited about implementing a program that helps us address things reminding us of endings, loss, and death? In choosing where to put one's free time or volunteer energies, most people don't spontaneously and excitedly think of volunteering at a hospice or a funeral home.

In fact, one could see the sluggishness of international schools to adopt effective comprehensive transitions programs as an ironic *confirmation* that Pollock and Van Reken were onto something. They *were* right. It *is* about grief. But because grief hurts so much, few people and organizations are hardy and steadfast enough to stick to developing the programs needed to deal with transitions for the long haul.

In other words, the very daring that made *Third Culture Kids* accurate from a theoretical point of view probably contributed to what I'll term the 'repulsion factor.' People may recognize the truth of the message cognitively, but they still end up averting their gaze emotionally. The issues come too close. It's akin to how many people react to the sight of blood – they know somebody needs help, but it's still hard to look.[11]

Responding to the repulsion factor by looking away is a form of coping. Other people cope with challenges they find unsettling by adopting a tough stance, making statements such as, "Our schools are places of learning, not places for group therapy." Issues of loss are better addressed elsewhere, right?

You Can't Escape Reality

Wrong. These issues underpin every single educational endeavor a school with any degree of turnover is attempting to achieve. If a school wishes to achieve its loftier educational goals, it needs to do everything in its power to avoid building on quicksand. And in terms of foundations, it doesn't get more fundamental than feelings of emotional safety and belonging.

One of the central ideas in this text is that it is relatively easy to harvest the value of Pollock and Van Reken's focus on loss without activating what I'm calling the 'repulsion factor' associated with grief. To do that, we're going to have to explore an underlying concept with more positive and hopeful implications, namely attachment theory. Once we've made that step, we'll sail in the next chapter towards an even more positive and practical idea, that of 'life stories.' In other words, we can supercede the 'repulsion factor' by putting the inherent 'attraction' of the concepts of attachment and stories to work for us.

Let's find out how.

----

11 *In his book* Optimism: The Biology of Hope, *Lionel Tiger discusses what he calls "perceptual defense," and points out that "words that evoke anxiety...require greater illumination before first being perceived." In other words, compared to neutral or positive words (like 'tree' or 'love'), words with negative connotations (and 'grief' would most definitely be one such word) must actually be printed or presented more clearly than neutral or negative words before experimental subjects will even report seeing them [6].*

ATTACHMENT THEORY

I once read somewhere that "we are leading lives for which we are evolutionarily unprepared." Our intelligence, creativity, and adaptability have allowed us to cope with that discrepancy. But the discrepancy still remains.

Let me explain.

In the 1950s and 60s, the psychologist Harry Harlow showed in a series of controversial experiments that a baby rhesus monkey would rather cling to a wire 'mother figure' shrouded with at least some soft cotton cloth than move to an adjacent wire mother figure with no such cloth, even when the second 'wire mother' possessed a nipple attached to a milk bottle that could provide nourishment [7, 8]. Only when absolutely forced by hunger would the baby monkey leave the comfort of the 'cloth mother' to quickly extract some nourishment from the relatively cold, metal-only counterpart. Once fed, the baby would quickly return to the cloth-covered 'mother.'

Residing behind the issue of grief and loss central to Pollock and Van Reken's *Third Culture Kids* is a psychological construct so massive and important it has redefined the landscape of psychology in the last several decades: attachment theory. This attachment revolution began with John Bowlby's studies of children separated from their parents during the Second World War [9, 10, 11, 12], followed by Mary Ainsworth's classic 'Strange Situation' experiments [13] taught in every introductory psychology and education course. Over the last half century, attachment research has crystallized into what is arguably the most researched and conceptually coherent field of modern psychology.

Attachment theory posits that a child's wish to survive fills them with a basic drive to maintain proximity to their caregivers. Considered in terms of evolution, those children who did not feel and act on this wish for proximity were at greater risk for accidents or predation, meaning their genes were less likely to be passed on via reproduction, meaning genes that failed to cue infants to seek proximity would disappear from the gene pool.

In the roots of our biology and brain stem – the origins of which go back hundreds of thousands of years – our bodies and minds developed in ways to help us survive in small groups or clans. Human beings spent their entire lives in these small groups, learning to trust and depend on a finite number of people, with new arrivals generally only occurring via birth, and departures generally only occurring via mating, migration, or mortality. What I will refer to as our 'attachment system' developed in seamless integration with other emotional systems, which evolved because of their utility for survival: fear, because it prompted us to flee from danger; anger, because it readied the body to fight off threats; sadness, because it signaled to our surroundings that we were in need. The attachment system evolved because it helped kinship networks to feel, trust, and use the mutual support that attachment could bring, with the resulting advantages in terms of survival, which all members of the network would enjoy. 'Attachment' is thus nestled neatly amidst the three survival feelings listed above, namely fear, anger, and sadness.

The fourth major human feeling, namely happiness, would seem to be the odd one out in the above lineup of unpleasant feelings. However, even happiness can be seen in attachment terms, because it allows the interconnected members of a kinship network to enjoy their attachment bonds, thereby maintaining and strengthening those very bonds during times of relative peace and harmony. Happiness therefore nourishes attachment bonds, better enabling these bonds to cope with the next threat when it arrives.

Working Models Of Attachment

Attachment theory is also able to make substantive predictions about the kind of attachment style a person will develop, depending on the experiences they have had with primary caregivers. Have they learned that caregivers are generally adequately responsive to their cries for help or assistance? Or are caregivers generally slow to respond? Or is the caregiver's response rather unpredictable? The basic convictions that a child develops depending on how attachment figures will likely respond in a given situation are referred to as the child's *working models* of attachment [see 14 for an overview].

These working models build and stabilize over time, allowing a child to predict how a given attachment figure is likely to respond in a given type of situation. Researchers have found that children can have different working models for different caregivers. For example, when frightened, a child might turn towards his mother because he has developed a working model that would be described as 'secure' towards his mother. But if frightened by something while in the presence of his father, this same child might work to deactivate his attachment response, because he has learned the father becomes angry when the child shows fear. This child would be described as having an 'anxious-avoidant' working model of attachment regarding his father.

This concept of working models will prove to be important in the discussion of an international school's role later in this book. I will argue that children – and, arguably, their parents and teachers – also develop working models of how international schools work with regards to issues associated with mobility, grief, and attachment.

The Human Drive For Connection

It is perhaps no coincidence Abraham Maslow was, for a time, a colleague of Harlow's at the University of Wisconsin-Madison. The need to belong and enjoy safe attachments also exists and continues over a human lifetime. In infancy and early childhood, the only essential attachments are to the child's primary caregivers – the mother, the father, and/ or the primary guardians. Relocations do not greatly unsettle children at this age, at least not from an attachment point of view, because they feel safe wherever their primary caregivers happen to be.

Fast-forwarding to early adolescence (10-14 years) and later adolescence (15-18 years, and arguably far later), the social surroundings take an increasingly prominent role in the teen's life because of the evolutionary reality that the child will have to find his or her way amongst these people in 'real life.' In other words, even though the teen might not think of the situation in these terms, his or her genetic self still knows their peer group forms the generation of people with whom he or she will have to interact if he or she wishes to survive and be successful in the future. In a very real way, the older generation stops mattering so much to the teens, because teens know they are going to inherit the world from – and most likely outlive – this older generation. Better to start investing more and more of their emotional energies into creating a place for themselves within the social fabric that is more truly 'theirs.'

We have been wired in this fashion over the last many hundreds of thousands of years of evolution. Modern life expectancies now easily double what they used to be only a few centuries ago, but that does not mean our genes and wiring have caught up with and incorporated this modern reality. (From an evolutionary point of view, the amount of time elapsed since the increase in life expectancy introduced by the Industrial Revolution is negligible.)

In other words, adolescence is around to stay for many millennia.[12]

What adolescence represents in attachment terms is a transitional period, where the teens' peers are used as a 'transitional attachment object' to help the young person separate from his or her early attachment figures – mom,

---

12 *I write this in the full awareness that I am the father of two teenagers, with another one knocking on the teenager door! I can also honestly say I genuinely enjoy even their most obstreperous moments.*

dad, or guardian – and move into the wider world as an independent adult. To understand what I mean, we need only take a brief departure over to the work of D.W. Winnicott, the renowned psychoanalyst who coined the term 'transitional object' to denote the teddy bear, blanket, or other such object a small child generally becomes attached to – to the point of being inseparable from that object [15].

He used the term 'transitional object' to describe the teddy bear or blanket as an attachment object that helped the child cope with moments when the mother or attachment figure was not readily available. The transitional object helps the child cope with anxiety and therefore, over time, it helps the child navigate those inevitable moments when his or her mother or care-giver is not readily available. In other words, the transitional object helps the child achieve the initial steps on the long road towards independence. After all, the mother or caregiver cannot be available 100% of the time. The child needs to learn these coping skills. The transitional object helps the child cross the psychological space involved in achieving that goal.[13]

A Drive For Connection That We Don't 'Outgrow'

However, the 'independence' of adulthood is now under widespread scrutiny by specialists in attachment, because it seems we never outgrow our need for safe attachments throughout our adult years. The attachment to primary caregivers gradually morphs over time, using teen social networks and early romantic relationships, into its final mature form, namely the safe romantic attachment to a partner. The romantic and sexual feelings involved in such an adult attachment might make it look very different than that between child and a caregiver, but the fundamental wish for proximity and affection in child and adult attachments are analogous. From an evolutionary point of view, it could be argued that healthy adult attachments increase the chances of survival for all involved, most importantly the children. Having two parents dedicated to mutually supporting each other in caring for their off-spring bodes better for the offspring (and the parent!) than the one-parent alternative – to say nothing of those children so unfortunate as to have been orphaned.

---

13 *I do not believe Winnicott was familiar in the least with the transition dynamics of life at an international school. Still, in terms of my use of his term for the purposes of this book, I find the coincidence in his choice of the term 'transitional' stunning.*

The fuses of the attachment system burn out, giving rise to a flattened, detached affect in the child.

It may come as a surprise to you to read about the importance of the attachment systems of adults and parents and teachers. Particularly in Western thought, independence, separation, and individuation are hailed as the hallmark of a fully mature adult. The need for attachment, safety, and connection is, by contrast, often portrayed as a sign of weakness, immaturity, or lack of individuation. Injunctions against the adult expression of attachment needs and vulnerabilities are quietly – and sometimes not so quietly – predominant in adult discourse, particularly in the West.

Learning From History's Mistakes: Attachment Has Been Ridiculed Before

Looking at the history of research on attachment [see 16 for a review of the history of the field of attachment research], an interesting trend becomes visible. The father of research into attachment, the psychiatrist John Bowlby, was initially maligned by the psychiatric establishment when he suggested children have a basic and fundamental need to perceive their caregivers as reliable, safe, and predictable. His early studies of London children separated from their parents during the London bombings in the Second World War, or children separated from their parents due to hospitalizations when they were young, revealed a prevailing, pervasive, and predictable pattern of responses, as the attachment systems of these children went into alarm mode.

Bowlby recognized that alarm as a desperate, biologically mandated and evolutionarily driven attempt to activate the attachment figure, so the attachment figure would return and provide the child with safety [9, 10, 11, 12]. Evolutionarily speaking, Bowlby recognized this system conferred a survival advantage for children, and that children who failed to sound the alarm were at higher risk in our evolutionary past of predation, getting lost, or any of a number of undesirable consequences.

The psychiatric establishment didn't want to hear it. Bowlby seemed to be pleading for parents to heed infantile wishes the Western medical establishment stamped as puerile and in need of outgrowing. Others gradually recognized the validity, whether popular or not, of what Bowlby was seeing. They recognized that these attachment systems *do* exist. Children *do* sound the alarm in predictable ways when they are separated from their caregivers. And if these alarms fail to produce the desired result after repeated attempts, the children eventually give up, as if to protect themselves from further pain. It is as if the fuses of the attach-

> *People are good for us, particularly people with whom we feel safe and supported.*

ment system burn out, giving rise to a flattened, detached affect in the child. With a burned-out child, the effect would stay flattened and detached even when the caregiver returned, as if it had burned out so badly it couldn't be reactivated. Many were baffled by these observations. Bowlby understood them perfectly. They constituted a desperate attempt on the child's part to protect him or herself from further disappointment – and further pain.

Over the ensuing decades, it became widely accepted that children's attachment needs are real and important. Nowadays, few people can believe there was a time when nurses and doctors didn't accept this as a self-evident truth. Most people today would profess their horror if they heard of a child being prevented from seeing his or her parents during a lengthy hospital stay.[14]

The Need For A Second Paradigm Shift

Many people continue to harbor the idea that attachment needs are all right for children, but they should ultimately be outgrown en route to the independence of true adulthood. There is growing evidence that such a view needs nuancing – at least as far as our genes and biology are concerned. If the first paradigm shift occurred during the second half of the twentieth century and involved the gradual, if reluctant, acceptance of Bowlby's attachment theory as universally true, I would argue that a second paradigm shift is currently underway and likely to span the first half of the twenty-first century. In this second paradigm shift, we are witnessing the further extension of attachment theory to include adult attachments, most importantly to one's romantic partner, but also to friends, communities, and even places.

Research across the board continually confirms a finding that psychologists started discovering long ago: *social isolation increases the chances of dying from any cause at any time* [17]. Phrased more positively, healthy

---

14 If Copernicus were here, I'm sure he would want to point out he was afraid of being jailed or executed for suggesting the Earth went around the sun, which is why his arguments to this effect were not published until after his death. But that's a different story.

attachments help us stay alive. The partners in a steady and long-term marriage[15] live longer than their divorced or unmarried counterparts [18]. People with large social networks also outlive those with a more restricted social network. In other words, people are good for us, particularly people with whom we feel safe and supported. Healthy attachments belong right where Maslow put them, if not at a lower and more fundamental level on his now classic pyramid.

It would seem we never outgrow our basic need for safe attachments, any more than an expanding onion can outgrow its inner layers. Thus, in much the same way as Bowlby's ideas were first rejected and then embraced, the notion that attachment safety is important for adults is gradually gaining credence and general acceptance.

A BRIEF EXPLORATION OF MODERN NEUROSCIENCE

Recent technological revolutions have allowed scientists to map brain activity in ways unthinkable only decades ago. The development of functional magnetic resonance imaging (fMRI) in the 1990s led to studies that have allowed us to see what various parts of the brain do during different kinds of activities. A technology unveiled in 2013 by Stanford researchers Kwanghun Chung and Karl Deisseroth allows postmortem brains to be made transparent, preserving all circuitry, so researchers can see the kinds of connections people developed in their lives, down to the synaptic level. Similar discoveries are likely to abound in the next decade, as the United States launches major initiatives such as the Brain Map Project, designed to map the activity of the human brain. The Brain Map Project is no less ambitious than the Human Genome Project, which ostensibly inspired it. Launched by the Reagan Administration in 1987, the Human Genome Project took only fifteen years to sequence and map all the genes of our species. The rapidity of such success suggests that, thanks to initiatives such as the Brain Map Project, we are soon likely to understand the workings of the brain in ways we cannot currently imagine.

One does not need a degree in neuroscience, however, to develop an appreciation of a few key concepts that are highly relevant to this book's discussion.

----

15   *This turns out to be particularly true for the men.*

Energy Can Only Be Spent Once

Philip Shaver and Mario Mikulincer, two leading theorists in attachment research, proposed a strikingly simple model of how attachment works. What their model essentially shows is that when a child is feeling threatened for any reason, he or she will devote energies towards eliciting a reassuring response from his or her attachment figures. Once that reassuring response is forthcoming, the child's attachment system calms down, and he or she gets on with the business of exploration.

In other words, a child needs to feel safe in order to explore. A child needs to feel his or her attachment figures are present and available before being able to launch into the world with confidence.

Shaver and Mikulincer's model [19] makes a simple but profound point for parents and educators: *energy can only be spent once.* When the attachment system is activated, a person *must* expend energy managing and responding to that activated system. My earlier statements have already likened our attachment circuitry to an alarm system, and the comparison is apt – it is difficult, if not impossible, to concentrate on anything else when an alarm bell is ringing. Similarly, it is difficult, if not impossible, to pay attention to anything but the need for safety when feeling fundamentally threatened. Energies normally flowing towards exploration have to be rechanneled towards the management of threats.

And learning is another form of exploration.

In other words, energies deployed towards managing a basic feeling of safety cannot be expended on personal development of any kind, be it exploration, learning, the development of one's personality, or building friendships. Here, I would argue, we encounter one of the fundamental explanations for Hattie's finding in *Visible Learning,* that mobility is the biggest risk factor for students' learning. Mobility yanks a person away from his or her trusted clan and roots – or forces a person to stay while trusted clan members leave – which bumps the person's attachment system into high alert and temporarily blocks any real interest in, or capacity for, exploration or learning.

Approach Versus Avoidance

Ronald Friedman and Jens Förster carried out an experiment which may illustrate how an activated attachment system affects learning [20]. Subjects had to help a mouse exit a paper-and-pencil maze. For half of the participants, an owl was pictured hovering above the maze. For the other half of the participants, a delicious block of cheese was pictured near the exit to the

We become more careful when our trusted attachment figures and safe places are not readily available. And our sense of caution isn't only reflected in the way we act. It's also reflected in the way we think. We're less able to explore new ideas and less able to creatively arrive at new solutions.

maze, waiting enticingly for the mouse at the finish.

The purpose of the research was to explore how the activation of our 'approach' versus 'avoidance' systems affects learning and creativity. Subjects had to take a test of creativity after solving the maze, and the findings were dramatic in terms of their implications for educators. Subjects who perceived the maze-solving problems as a search for cheese, which activated their approach systems, achieved scores on the subsequent creativity test that were 50% higher than those who perceived the maze as an escape from owl, which activated their avoidance systems.

In other words, the after effects of something as seemingly simple as solving a three-minute maze differed dramatically, depending on whether the conditions surrounding the exercise activated one's approach or avoidance systems, depending on whether one wanted to reach a tasty block of cheese or escape being tasted by a hungry owl.

The findings from this kind of research are readily understandable when viewed through an attachment lens. Whether we're focusing upon the mover or the movee, or somebody feeling alienated in an unfamiliar culture,the loss of familiar friends and predictable environments activates our biologically-based attachment systems, making our behavior tend in the direction of caution and avoidance. We become more careful when our trusted attachment figures and safe places are not readily available. And our sense of caution isn't only reflected in the way we act. It's also reflected in the way we think. We're less able to explore new ideas and less able to creatively arrive at new solutions.

In other words, we're less able to learn.

If you think of Friedman and Forster's research, and if you picture owls perched in the corner of every classroom, then you begin to understand why Hattie discovered that mobility hurts learning.

And again I tell you that it doesn't have to be this way. We can turn the owls of mobility into tasty blocks of cheese. It takes work, but it's possible. That's what this book is about.

The Wonder – And Costly Nature – Of The Prefrontal Cortex

Neuroscientists have now shown that what I've described above is not merely a metaphor. Modern neuroscience is demonstrating that these descriptive claims are true at the level of observable brain activity.

In a nutshell, when a person feels threatened for any reason, the frontolimbic regions of the brain become activated. We can see this when we place a person in an fMRI scanner and introduce things the person experiences as threatening. The regions that become active include the amygdala, the hippocampus, the hypothalamus, the orbital frontal cortex, the anterior cingulate cortex, and the insula. Call these frontolimbic regions of the brain the 'alarm center,' if you will. These regions fire when we feel unpleasant emotions such as fear, anger, or sadness.

When the 'alarm center' is activated, another part of the brain known as the prefrontal cortex (PFC) has to come 'online' to manage the emotions. The PFC is the emotion regulation center. It is active anytime we are struggling with strong feelings. Struggling with strong feelings feels like hard work because it is hard work – fueling the PFC is 'expensive' for the brain because the PFC requires a relatively large amount of glucose and oxygen to 'run.' We must remember that blood flow to the brain is relatively constant, meaning that any particular amount of glucose in the blood can only be consumed once, by one part of the brain. In other words, energy channeled to the PFC to manage emotion is energy that cannot be sent elsewhere –towards thinking about an arithmetic problem or an English composition, for example.

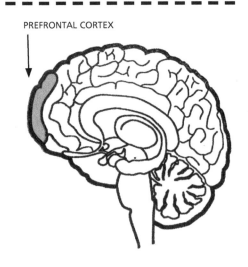

FIGURE 1.1: The prefrontal cortex

Hitting The Brakes

We have here an explanation for Hattie's finding that mobility hurts learning. This explanation is anchored in the hard facts of brain physiology. Moving across cultures, and having people move away from you, strains a person

----
One can literally conclude that
mobility causes pain.
----

and puts his or her attachment system on alert, which is reflected in the activation of the frontolimbic system. If the story were to stop there, the person would likely begin crying or screaming – something we see occasionally in small children during separations. What keeps that from happening is the emotional regulation coming from the prefrontal cortex. In a certain sense, we could consider the attachment system as firing up the frontolimbic areas of the brain with 'gas,' while the prefrontal cortex tries to keep control of our actual reactions by hitting the 'brakes.'

Children don't have very good 'brakes' when they're young, which is why their reactions are often more volatile and raw compared to those of adults. Within reason, such reactions from children are normal and as they should be. In contrast, adults who have not yet developed the emotional regulation circuitry to control their basic emotional reactions find themselves experiencing problems in all domains of life, be it in work or in relationships. As people become older, it becomes increasingly less appropriate to not have a good 'braking system.' In its most extreme form, a lack of braking ability from the prefrontal cortex is considered to be the neuroscientific reflection of something like Borderline Personality Disorder, one of the most difficult psychological disorders to cope with (both for the person in question and for his or her environment) because of the extreme emotional volatility involved, and the lack of impulse control.

Moving Hurts – For Real

It is fair to say that mobility across cultures 'hurts' for people, in exactly the same way as physical pain hurts. Naomi Eisenberger and her colleagues [21] have undertaken fMRI studies to show that social exclusion lights up the same parts in the brain as the experience of physical pain. This area, known as the anterior cingulate cortex, lights up in an fMRI in the same way when people are exposed to physical pain sensations and social exclusion.

Eisenberger and her colleagues had study subjects play a virtual ball game with several other 'participants' in the study. (There were no real 'participants' – the computer simulated the behavior of two other 'participants' but the study subjects didn't know this.) At first, the subject is included in the ball game, but in the second half of the experiment, the other 'participants' begin excluding him or her from the game. During the entire process, fMRI scans of brain activity are made. As the exclusion begins, pain centers in the brain get activated. In other words, the parts of the brain activated when somebody feels left out are the same parts of the brain that alert a person to physical pain, be it a finger burned or a leg broken.

Mobility is fraught with experiences of exclusion for all involved. Based on Eisenberger's research, one can literally conclude that mobility causes pain. When the alarm bells from the anterior cingulate cortex begin ringing, our reliable coping assistant in the right ventral part of the prefrontal cortex becomes active, allowing us (hopefully) to manage and cope with the associated feelings. While it is unquestionably positive that we have the PFC to help us cope with the ensuing feelings, it is also true that the energy being used to run the PFC is having to be rerouted from other things we could be doing or learning.

In other words, energy is a lot like money. It can only be spent once.

Energy Can Only Be Spent Once – And The PFC Spends A Lot

While weighing in at approximately 2% of the body's mass, the brain nonetheless consumes 20% of the body's available calories. Evolution would only have made such massive energetic investments in the brain if the dividends it generated were worth it. According to the line of thinking set out above, one of those dividends was the evolving PFC's ability to restrain and steer our basic impulses. If we were going to survive in the increasingly complex social arrangements emerging throughout human history, we needed to be able to control our basic impulses. We couldn't eat whatever food we saw. We couldn't hit or attack anyone who did something we didn't like. We couldn't attempt to mate with anyone we found attractive. Society wouldn't have it.[16]

If the brain is the body's prime real estate because of how energetically 'expensive' it is to run, then the PFC 'control center' is like a penthouse apartment on New York's Fifth Avenue. The PFC consumes a tremendous amount of glucose to do its work. As with any tissue, the PFC tires with use. Roy Baumeister and his colleagues were the first to point out that the notion of running out of 'willpower' is more than a metaphorical statement [1, 22]. Regulating our feelings takes willpower. Tired tissues require rest to recover. If they don't get it, they can wear out and burn out.

----

16 *Like any 'chicken and egg' line of thinking, the causal direction here can be reversed. One could just as well reason that it was our developing brains' increasing ability to restrain basic impulses that allowed more complex forms of social organization to develop.*

PFC Burnout

What happens if the PFC doesn't get that recovery time? What happens if people keep moving, if the strain of building and loosening relationships doesn't seem to remit, such that the person feels emotionally exhausted? This is arguably what occurs to people who deal with mobility repeatedly. The 'burnout' they describe, the oft-heard statement that "mobility gets harder, not easier, with time," can readily be explained now in neuroscience terms. These people are describing a prefrontal cortex that hasn't received enough support. These people are describing a prefrontal cortex that has had to regulate too much strong emotion, without receiving the time and space to recover.

In this regard, the kind of emotional burnout that can happen as a function of mobility is no different from the kind of burnout described in the employment literature, or the kind of burnout associated with depression. Have you ever heard a depressed person (or maybe even yourself) say that even the smallest acts seem insurmountable? Have you heard somebody describe the energy it seems to take to run a load of laundry, pay a bill, or even get out of bed? In many cases, they may be describing the consequences of having run their PFC into the ground. The PFC may have coped adequately for weeks, months, or even years with the troubles or sadness or threats they were facing in their work, relationships, or life, but the PFC cannot maintain this workload indefinitely [23]. Brakes do overheat. The prefrontal cortex can be so consumed in regulating the emotional signals emanating from the frontolimbic system's alarm center that it eventually burns out. The only solution appears to be total rest.

This type of 'burnout' likely does happen to people in the face of mobility across cultures too. But this need not be the case. The degree of suffering mobility sometimes causes is unnecessarily excessive. And when it is excessive, massive opportunities for learning and personal growth for all involved get missed.

A Thought Experiment

International schools have a lot to learn from our cave dwelling predecessors. Consider the following thought experiment.

Go back 20,000 years to the Lascaux cave region in France, and choose a cave-dwelling family to bring with you to the future, to an international school of your choice with a high degree of turnover. Drop this family in the center of a middle school cafeteria. Allow them to live there, in the middle of the cafeteria, for the next ten years, just watching as life occurs around them.

What would strike our ancestors the most?

You might think it would be the fabrics the kids are wearing, or the ringing, vibrating objects they're constantly pulling out of a hole in the side of the cloth they're wearing around their legs. You might think it's the food they collect on white flat circles. You might think it's the colorful paper each child exchanges for the food with the woman at the end of the line, or the shiny metal circles they get from the woman in return.

But, like I said, we are a highly adaptable species. Our cave-dwelling visitors get over their initial shock and begin to adjust.

Speed the film up, so that our ancestors watch the kids hugging each other and crying in the early summer. Speed the film through the first summer vacation for our visitors, and into the first week of the school's new student orientation. The cafeteria is flooded with new faces, and many of the faces that had become familiar to our cave dwellers are no longer there. The newness alarms them, and they clutch their spears more tightly. (Oh, by the way, in this thought experiment, the middle schoolers cannot see the cave dwellers. Let's not add that variable to a middle school cafeteria that's already noisy and chaotic enough!) But our cave-dwelling friends get used to these new faces too.

Time goes on, through fall, winter, and spring all over again.

As summer approaches, the hugging and crying begins again. The cave dwellers had learned to associate that crying with the last change, and they clutch their spears more tightly again. The school empties, and it is once again quiet.

And the next summer, there are new faces again, being greeted by people the cave dwellers recognize from the first year – but only a few. The entire population seems different. The cave dwellers know they're still in the same shelter they arrived at two years ago, but the clans who live here seem to have changed imperceptibly over time. They notice they miss some of the more familiar faces they had grown attached to, the ones they had grown to feel safe around.

Those faces are gone.

Speed the film up to maximum speed, so the springs and the summers tick by like ticks of the clock, and imagine the experience of our cave dwellers. They seem to ask themselves, "What are these people doing?" The speed with which they see the middle schoolers connecting to new people, and then separating from people they seemed to care for, is dizzying. By year five or so, some of our cave dwellers start to have a glazed look over their faces. They cannot keep up with the pace with which the middle schoolers are making and breaking connections.

Our cave dwellers can count on one hand the number of times they parted with a member of their kin network. But they have run out of hands to count what's going on in this cafeteria.

Lessons We Can Draw From The Cavemen

How did you feel as you read through that thought experiment? Did you notice any feeling of empathy or even pity for our cave dweller visitors? As time sped on, and as they watched life spin around them faster and faster, proceeding through the decade of their confinement, did you notice perhaps a sense of fatigue, even of defeat, settle upon you?

That thought experiment could be used to illustrate a number of ideas, ranging from how powerless it would feel to be transported someplace without being asked (many of our students and even parents can identify with such a sentiment), to how terrible it would feel to not really be seen, even though you're surrounded by people all day long (many members of an international school can also identify with this experience, including when people don't feel their culture or background is appreciated by those in their new 'place').

My main purpose in conducting that thought experiment, however, was to highlight the attachment ideas underpinning the statement cited earlier that David Pollock frequently made, namely that "many TCKs have experienced more loss in their developmental years than most adults experience in a lifetime." I do not know how familiar Pollock was with the attachment literature, but there are two potential implications in his statement.

The Rate Of Grief

The first and more obvious implication is that the human attachment system may have evolved to cope with grief and loss only up to a certain rate.

Beyond that rate of loss, the attachment system begins to get overwhelmed. This idea can now be readily understood in terms of the earlier discussion of the neurobiological basis for how

If attachment alarm bells are ringing, students will not be able to hear the teacher.

we cope with strong feelings and threats. Without sufficient care and protection, an attachment system repeatedly exposed to the challenges of mobility and loss arguably *could* be getting overwhelmed. Such a state of affairs could lead people to shut down their attachment systems preventatively, so as to avoid becoming hurt again, producing what is described in the literature as an 'avoidant attachment style

Is There A Limit To The Rate Of Grief?

The second implication is an extension of the first, namely that the human attachment system may have certain absolute limits to what it can handle. In other words, just as there is 'wear and tear' on the human body over the course of a lifetime, so too there may be only so much making and breaking of relational bonds a human being can handle over the course of a lifetime. An apt analogy would be with the mileage on a car. An automobile of the sturdiest kind can only drive a certain number of miles or kilometers before systems eventually give out.

Admittedly, this is conjecture and cannot (yet) be proven. However, if this second implication contains even a kernel of truth, then one can reasonably argue that our attachment systems can thrive longer – and endure more such 'kilometers' – if they are maintained and well cared for, as with a car.

What this all means is that the cave dweller's perspective may still reside in each and every one of us. We can dress ourselves up in Levi's or Ralph Lauren's, we can pocket a Samsung or an iPhone, we can pay for the food on our plates by waving the transponder hidden in a bank card, but we cannot override the basic architecture of attachment-based survival systems developed over the course of hundreds of thousands of years and tens of thousands of generations. Compared to the history of our species, our time on the planet and the number of generations that have come and gone since the Industrial Revolution do not span the blink of an eye.

It is therefore imperative we remember that the best of IB Diploma Programs, the best of teaching for understanding, the best of well-mapped curricula, the best of student-centered learning – any and all of these well-designed and well-intentioned initiatives are all built upon a biological substrate with attachment at its core. *If attachment alarm bells are ringing, students will not be able to hear the teacher.* The same holds true for parents and staff, neither of whom will be able to do their parenting or teaching jobs as well if the attachment systems in their lower brain stems are transmitting alert signals, activating adrenal glands to pump corticosteroids throughout their bodies.

MOVING TOWARDS MAINTENANCE OF THE ATTACHMENT SYSTEM

The solution, then, is that the attachment systems of all members of any school population facing a significant degree of turnover need attention and nurturance to allow those systems to calm down, so the person can again feel safe and secure and get on with the business of learning, parenting, or teaching. It is at this point we arrive at one of the central theses of this text, namely that:

it is incumbent upon the school to sponsor programs and processes that assist people in maintaining their attachment systems. The developing and maintaining of a comprehensive transitions program is the most effective way of doing so.

As with our bewildered cave dwellers exiled to that imaginary middle school cafeteria, the attachment systems of everyone involved in a mobile lifestyle – meaning the arrivers, the leavers, and the stayers – endure a massive emotional workout by virtue of the high degree of change and turnover that occurs in such a lifestyle. Who would not take their car to the garage for a checkup and maintenance at least every twenty or thirty thousand miles or kilometers? We get the ignition, transmission, and exhaust systems checked regularly. Shouldn't we treat our human attachment systems with at least the same care?

The Logical Extension Of Attachment Theory: Attachment To Place and Community

What might happen next in the field of attachment? I have long argued that attachments to place are an important dimension to our attachment systems [24], and one of the reasons why moving is so difficult is because we lose our attachments to the contexts for so many of our important stories. You could label this as 'place attachment,' but I prefer now to call it 'attachment to community.' As discussed earlier in this chapter, the field of attachment is expanding in ever-enlarging concentric circles. It began with the importance of a child's attachment to his or her mother. It is currently expanding to the domain of adult attachment, and the dawning recognition that our attachment needs continue into and throughout adulthood. Over the course of researching and writing this book, I have come to a realization that seems as unshakeable and self-evident to me now as it felt revolutionary when I first considered it, so much so it should be coined the Fifth Law of Transitions:

 LAW V **Humans need safe attachments to community. People in transition are looking for a community to attach to.**

There seems to be data emerging to support this idea from the most recent research on human attachment coming from Professor James Coan and his associates at the Virginia Affective Neuroscience Laboratory. Coan refers to their theory as 'Social Baseline Theory,' and this theory has some interesting applications to the world of moving across cultures [23].

Social Baseline Theory

Have you ever made a New Year's resolution and found it's easier to complete that resolution if you team up with a good friend or a loved one? Have you ever resolved to exercise more, to complete a diet, to stop smoking, or to eat more healthily? Or do you remember the days of studying for a difficult test or exam with a friend, or completing a difficult hike? Or, perhaps more to the point, have you ever had to move house yourself, compared to completing the moving process with the support of good friends or a good moving company?

If so, you may have noticed that doing difficult things with other people who you know well, trust, and maybe even love makes those difficult things seem a little bit easier [25].

"The ecology of a cheetah is the savannah. The ecology of human beings is other human beings."

– Jim Coan, Neuropsychologist

If you've had that experience, then you have a visceral understanding of what Social Baseline Theory is all about. Social Baseline Theory has emerged from a collection of psychological observations, both outside the laboratory and inside, that are relevant to this discussion.

Faced with threat, there is nothing worse than being alone.

For example, did you know that when people have to estimate the angle of a hill they're about to climb, they estimate the hill as being steeper if they know they have to climb the hill alone? And they estimate the hill as less steep if they believe they're going to climb the hill with a friend? Perhaps most intriguing, the deeper the friendship, the less steep the hill is estimated as being [26].

The same finding occurs when a person has to estimate the weight of a backpack he or she is going to have to carry up the hill. In the presence of a friend, the backpack is thought to weigh less. And again, the deeper and more long-standing the friendship, the less the backpack is believed to weigh [26].

Sue Johnson, Jim Coan, and colleagues put these findings to the test by using fMRI imaging to examine what is happening inside the brain during challenging moments. They first recruited *happily married couples* (that they were happily married is key, as we'll explore below) as volunteers to the study. They then explained the female member of the couple was going to be placed in the fMRI, and that if she saw an 'X' on her monitor, there was a 20% chance she would receive an electric shock.

What the researchers were interested in was seeing what would happen if the woman was alone when she saw the 'X' (indicating a shock may be coming), versus what would happen if she were holding the hand of a stranger or the hand of her husband.

We have already discussed that the frontolimbic system, including the anterior cingulate cortex (ACC) is activated during times of threat or strong emotion. The prefrontal cortex (PFC) is then enlisted to cope with and regulate the emotional response. Given the experimental setup, one would generally expect the ACC would actively fire when the 'X' appeared, indicating a possible shock, and the PFC would then fire as a result, to help the woman cope with the threat.

This is exactly what occurred when the woman was by herself in the fMRI, not holding anyone's hand.

What occurred next was baffling. When the women were holding their husbands' hands, their prefrontal cortex was hardly active at all. In other words, they didn't seem to be 'coping' with anything, even though the same chances of receiving an electric shock were present. The PFC wasn't actively coping because the ACC wasn't sending out alarm signals. No 'gas' from the ACC was getting pumped into the system, meaning the PFC didn't have to hit the 'brakes.' The women's brains were almost as quiet as when there was no threat of shock [27, 28].

Even more interesting, the happier the marriage was described as being (based on assessments before the fMRI scans), the quieter their brains remained in the face of a potential shock. The safer the attachment between husband and wife, the less the woman appeared to even *perceive* the possible shock as threatening. In happy marriages, the shocks hardly mattered, and the happier the marriage, the less the threat registered [27, 28].

This, then, was a laboratory confirmation of what researchers had already discovered through the hill slant and weight-of-backpack studies. Phrased as a rule of thumb, *the safer the attachment relationship, the less difficult something is perceived to be.*

What was perhaps most interesting for our purposes was what happened to the women when they held a stranger's hand. Part of the experiment entailed her holding the hand of someone she had only briefly met while undergoing the potential shock fMRI. While the effect of holding a stranger's hand was not as pronounced as that which occurred when the women held their husband's hand, holding a stranger's hand did have a moderate quieting effect on the ACC. In other words, even the basic sense of safety proffered by a stranger one only just met before entering an fMRI still provides moderate human comfort if one is about to undergo something distressing.

Our brains seem to be saying that, when faced with threat, there is nothing worse than being alone.

These findings have some obvious applications to the role that members of a transitions program at an international school can play for people who are 'enduring the scan' of an international and/ or cross-cultural relocation. Are we extending the hand of friendship to people who are undergoing the challenges of moving across cultures – both for those doing the actual moving and for those being moved away from?

If the experience of happily married couples seems slightly removed from the work of an international school, consider a similar study that reached the same results. Olivia Conner and colleagues investigated the degree of anxiety experienced by children and adolescents when they had to undergo an fMRI scan, depending on whether their mother was holding their hand or not [29]. (As it would have been unethical to expose children to actual shocks, the threat this time came in the form of mildly threatening or frightening words projected onto a viewing screen.) In cases where the mother was not holding the child or adolescent's hand, activity in the anterior cingulate cortex (ACC) was higher, requiring a commensurate amount of activity in the prefrontal cortex (PFC) to calm the feelings. In the cases where the mother did hold the child or adolescent's hand, activity in the ACC remained low, obviating the

People in transition are likely to experience their social surroundings as more of a threat than a buffer, as these social surroundings have changed and are no longer 'known.'

need for a coping response from the PFC entirely.

Once again, the proximity to an attachment figure provided regulatory resources to the child in question, making it unnecessary to fire up the coping regions in the PFC. Quite literally, in the presence of a safe attachment figure, threats seemed less threatening.

So what is the Social Baseline Theory that emerged from these kinds of studies? These studies showed that in the presence of trusted others, threats and challenges are perceived as less threatening or challenging. Coan and his colleagues surmise this is because the social environment is the natural environment of our species. According to this theory, we evolved amidst the baseline assumption that other trusted clan members are in our immediate vicinity, helping to share the challenge of looking out for threats and dealing with the demands of life. When trusted clan members are nearby, our brains reflect this reality by quieting down. Even in the face of mild threats, the anterior cingulate cortex (ACC) produces little or no 'gas,' because we know we're amongst the safety of our own people. And because there's little or no 'gas,' the 'brakes' from the prefrontal cortex (PFC) don't need to work.[17]

The net result? A massive savings in individual energy. While most of the readers of this book may, like me, enjoy the owning of a fully-stocked refrigerator in a home that offers reliable shelter from storms and bandits, our forefathers were not so fortunate, and our biology evolved to reflect it. Anything to economize our activity provided an advantage to survival. And sharing in the social baseline was one great way to acquire just such an advantage.

From The fMRI To Our Schools

What does this mean to people in transition? Whether they are the ones doing the moving or the ones being moved away from, whether they are the students doing the learning or the teachers doing the teaching or the parents doing the parenting, it places all people in transition in the same boat. Their

---

17 *You can see this phenomenon in any species that lives in groups to share demands. For example, if you observe a flock of any bird species at rest, you will see many of the birds are resting, and some are sleeping with one eye open and one eye shut (allowing one half of their brains to rest at a time). In this way, the group distributes and shares responsibility for looking out for predators. Biologists refer to this kind of behavior as 'load sharing', and it is a key feature of Social Baseline Theory.*

social baselines have been threatened – or erased. In the face of threats and challenges, the biological buffer system that would usually have made the challenge seem smaller and more manageable has been removed, making the threat seem larger. In what would seem to be an irony of evolution, people in transition are likely to experience their social surroundings as more of a threat than a buffer, as these social surroundings have changed and are no longer 'known.' People find themselves surrounded by new clan members. The anterior cingulate cortex fires up, necessitating an 'expensive' process of emotional regulation from the prefrontal cortex. This process is 'expensive' because it redirects psychological resources – and the glucose to fuel them – towards the management of the attachment system, which has been set to 'high alert' mode.

No wonder Hattie discovered that mobility has a negative effect on learning outcomes.

So what can we do about all of this at international schools with a high degree of mobility?

Working Models Of Schools

We've already learned how a person's 'working models' of attachment develop from the person's basic experiences with attachment figures and how such figures tend to respond in times of need.

One of this book's central arguments is that *people who experience mobility also develop working models of the mobility experience and how international schools deal with it.* These working models are fundamentally shaped by the philosophy and priorities of the schools involved, both the school from which a person departs and the school to which a person moves. Without necessarily realizing it, people involved with mobility have feelings that become churned up around questions like:

- what is happening to me?
- what am I feeling?
- why am I feeling this way?
- does anybody know how I am feeling?
- does anybody care?
- will anybody help me when I feel this way?

These are the exact same questions a child grapples with any time he or she feels threatened or in pain. And just as a child will develop a working model for how a particular caregiver tends to respond during critical moments of need, I would argue that a person in mobility also begins to develop a working model for how a school tends to respond to the feelings associated with mobility:

- do people at this school know what's happening or what I'm feeling?
- do people at this school understand why I'm feeling this way?
- do people at this school know how this feels?
- do they care?
- will anyone at this school help me make it through these challenges?

Different Working Models For Different People And Situations

The literature on attachment provides reason to believe that 'working models' for an international schools do exist. The reason is simple: children develop different working models for different caregivers [14].

Suppose a child has an insecure working model of attachment towards his father, based on the unpredictability of the father's availability (for example, the father drinks heavily, and he is frequently absent from the household). That same child may have a very secure model of attachment to his mother if she is predictable, available, and nurturing in the regularity of her care.

Suppose that child, now aged 10, has to make his first international move because of Dad's job. He's moving to another country, to a school without any form of a comprehensive transitions program. The child is slightly timid by nature and is dropped into a 4th grade class, which – because mobility issues haven't been addressed at all – has experienced an almost traumatic degree of turnover in the last three years. One third of the class has left each year, one third of the class is new each year, and the young teacher – new to the school herself – is feeling relatively unsupported in what is her first year in international education.

However much security the mother may have provided in the past or be attempting to provide in the present, she now feels as if she is paddling up a torrential river. She finds it difficult – even excruciating – to see her son struggling like this at his new school, especially as she is barely holding her head above water too.

What kind of a working model of a relocation experience is this child developing? Returning to the questions cited above, the child, without knowing it, might be unconsciously arriving at these kinds of answers:

- I have no idea what is happening to me or what I am feeling
- I have no idea why I am feeling what I am feeling
- nobody seems to know what I am feeling
- nobody seems to care
- nobody is stepping forward to help me

When this poor child sits sadly at the dinner table, he is yelled at by his father for being 'a wimp' and told he needs to "get out there and make some friends." However much security the mother may have provided in the past or be attempting to provide in the present, she now feels as if she is paddling up a torrential river. She finds it difficult – even excruciating – to see her son struggling like this at his new school, especially as she is barely holding her head above water too.

She knows what she is feeling and why, but nobody else in her new school community seems to know. Nobody seems to care. And nobody is stepping forward to help.

In her first international relocation, this mother is also developing a working model of how these kinds of moves work, and how international schools and communities tend to deal with issues like hers.

What would her working model look like and sound like?

We can only speculate. But it wouldn't be pretty.

Working Models Work In The Other Directions Too

Skeptics could argue the experience of a positive and effective transitions program at one school would only prepare people for failure in the real world, by 'softening them up' and not readying them for how the real world works.

The ethical question of whether a 'survival of the fittest' mentality belongs in schools, and whether people charged with the education of young minds should allow their decisions to be guided by such values, will be addressed in the next chapter. Such skepticism also ignores – and perhaps helps to cause – the hugely negative effect mobility can have on educational outcomes, as described earlier on the basis of John Hattie's research in *Visible Learning*.

Most importantly, such skepticism allows the detrimental effects of negative working models of attachment to continue eroding the quality of human life. In study after study social support emerges as a crucial factor to a fulfilling, healthy, and long-lasting human life [18]. Let's explore the implications of this fundamental truth, because it will reveal that international schools can no longer ignore their role in shaping the kinds of expectations young people develop regarding human relationships.

The Importance Of Being Able To Believe In Other People

In any given year across the life span, people with more social support are more likely to survive the year than those with less social support [17].

This statement is so important it deserves restating, but in reverse. *People with less social support are more likely to die of any cause at any time than people with more social support.*

In other words, social support protects our very lives. This fundamental truth occurs right at the intersection of public health and psychology, and has been confirmed in study after study. People who are less integrated into the social fabric are more at risk for every ailment. Whether it is heart disease or diabetes, depression or schizophrenia, people who enjoy less social support enjoy less 'shelter' from these ailments. The quality of their lives is diminished, and the length of their lives is shortened.

What does this have to do with people's experience at international schools? If we focus on the young people involved, namely the students at international schools, then their formative years are occurring in settings where human beings are in flux. On the basis of these formative years, what will they learn about human relationships?

At the positive or 'secure attachment' end of the spectrum, students could begin to incorporate positive statements into their 'working models', statements which would include the following:

- saying goodbye to people is difficult, but my life has been enriched for knowing these people
- saying goodbye is hard, but at least I know how
- life's challenges are really disguised opportunities for growth
- I can make new friends, and I know how to do that
- although it might be hard to say goodbye to them, it is *knowing people deeply* and *being known deeply* that makes life worthwhile
- I will never lose the important connections I have felt to important people

These kinds of conclusions are only likely if international schools with a high degree of mobility have comprehensive transitions programs in place.

Conversely, in the absence of effective programs capable of meeting and mastering the challenges of mobility, students are likely to end up drawing conclusions from the negative end of the spectrum. These kinds of conclusions begin to characterize their working models as insecure:

- people you begin to care about will leave
- it's better not to let people too close
- the only person you can really depend upon is yourself
- other people will ultimately disappoint you
- life's challenges are things you have to make it through on your own
- if you don't care too much about people, it's not so hard to say goodbye
- if you're leaving anyway, what's the point in making friends?

For the reader familiar with Joseph Conrad's classic *Heart of Darkness,* such students are at risk for agreeing with Marlow, as he mutters under his breath, "We live as we dream, alone."

Students who develop negative, insecure working models of attachment are being placed on a trajectory that questions whether other human beings really are sources of support. Social Baseline Theory teaches us that a perceived lack of social support deprives people of a biologically mandated craving to share loads and distribute risks.

But what if others actually aren't available? What if the reason a person believes they're not available is because of

If a student's experience at an international school exerts an important shaping influence upon how that student thinks about and approaches human relationships, and if these 'working models' will affect the student's entire way of interacting with the social landscape for the rest of his or her life, then what should schools be doing about it?

real life experiences she actually had – some of which may have occurred at international schools? What if she learned she can't rely on others?

Then she will conclude she must do it all herself. The resulting sense of vulnerability requires that people 'run' their 'expensive' prefrontal cortex (PFC) in order to regulate the ensuing feelings. But as we learned earlier struggle to pay the bills or to adhere to the treatment protocol for their diabetes or high blood pressure, all these 'difficult things' require self-management and self-regulation. The self-management that emanates from the PFC is energetically costly, and at a certain point, something has to give. People let go, lose track of, or give up on what would be best for their bodies and souls.

The net result is a negative health outcome, be it physical, psychological, or both. And so we have an explanation as to why people with less social support live shorter lives.

If a student's experience at an international school exerts an important shaping influence upon how that student thinks about and approaches human relationships, and if these 'working models' will affect the student's entire way of interacting with the social landscape for the rest of his or her life, then what should schools be doing about it?

PUTTING THEORY TO WORK

The first step in addressing any problem is to recognize the problem and develop a vocabulary for dealing with it. The purpose of highlighting the challenges associated with the stress of mobility across cultures has not been to highlight the problem for the problem's sake, but rather to move towards solutions.

And the most obvious solution is to help people redevelop their social baseline. They can only do this if:

- they know they need to
- the social baseline makes itself available
- the social baseline maintains itself, so it can provide this service over time without burning itself out

Conjure up the following image, and I believe you'll see what I mean. People in transition are arriving with a suitcase in one hand and a bundle of roots in the other. They are looking for soil in which to gently plant those roots, so they can begin again. This process feels vulnerable and frightening.

Or consider this image. People leaving a place have a suitcase in one hand, and with their other hand they're having to pull up the roots they've laid all around them. You can hear the strain in their voices and see the strain in their arms. This process hurts.

Or consider this image. People staying in one place feel as if their hearts have been turned into soil. Those arriving are trying to plant roots in these hearts. Those leaving are trying to pull roots – down to the tiniest capillaries – out of these hearts. This process can feel agonizing, exactly because 'stayers' have to support both arrivers and leavers, while they themselves don't appear to be going anywhere. They feel they're simply undergoing the process. Constantly.

If part of the challenge of transitions comes from the fact that mobility across cultures threatens people's social baseline, then I would argue we can logically conclude that international schools have an obligation to assist people with recreating their social baselines. Their very ability to function well depends on it. Stated more clearly, I would argue this gives rise logically to a Sixth and final Law of Transitions, namely:

LAW VI

The international school should conceive of itself as a transitional attachment object for its clientele.

As people arrive with their roots in their hands, an international school can appropriately see itself as a *transitional object* or a *transitional social baseline* for a vulnerable family, student, or staff member. The school can provide programs, services, people, and emotional warmth that authentically convey to the person, in both word and deed, "We care. We are here. You can hold on to us."

A FEEDBACK LOOP: IT TAKES SAFETY TO ASK FOR SAFETY

We must remember people do not generally name and verbalize their attachment needs. People do not generally show up to their teachers, parents, or spouses with language like, "I am feeling vulnerable and exposed. I need some love, reassurance, and a hug. Can you help me?" People may not even be aware of these feelings. But more to the point, when people are feeling this way, they're generally not inclined to say so. This is because exposing one's vulnerabilities requires a basic sense of safety.

How in the world is somebody supposed to untie this logical loop, this paradoxical reality that *a sense of safety is required before acknowledging the vulnerability somebody feels when they don't feel safe?*

The answer is quite simple. School personnel should assume feelings of vulnerability are there. Such a conviction becomes the default starting point. The need to attach to a community is a given at all phases of the transition cycle, and the prudent and responsible international school sees its own role and responsibility in being the community and 'transitional object' people can attach and hold onto, both when they're new, and after they leave – during the process of feeling vulnerable at their next place.

Where The School's Responsibility Stops

D.W. Winnicott was also the theorist who pointed out that mothers, or any caregiver, need not strive to be perfect mothers or caregivers. Life is fraught with challenges and setbacks. Children must learn to cope with challenges and setbacks and things not working exactly as they would have them work – starting with a mother or caregiver *not* being available at all times and whenever the child would have it. Winnicott emphasized the importance of being a 'good enough' mother or caregiver [30].

Availability and predictability need to be solid enough that a child isn't traumatized by absence or unpredictability (like the children in Bowlby's studies whose attachment systems 'burned out' when their cries for their parents were not responded to for extended periods of time), but not so available that a child never learns to be alone or to soothe him or herself in a parent's absence (like the child whose every need is promptly attended to, known in lay terms as 'spoiled').

As people arrive with their roots in their hands, an international school can appropriately see itself as a transitional object or a transitional social baseline for a vulnerable family, student, or staff member. The school can provide programs, services, people, and emotional warmth that authentically convey to the person, in both word and deed, "We care. We are here. You can hold on to us."

Extending the analogy to schools, a school also only needs to be a 'good enough' transitional object. They need to have a good enough transitions program, so enough support is available to help the large majority of families and individuals find their way.

The reason why is because those same families, individuals, staff, and even students have their own responsibilities too, responsibilities to develop their skills and their networks to cope with and navigate the challenges inherent in mobility across cultures. This is a personal growth opportunity for all involved, but growth only comes if there is sufficient willingness and motivation to navigate the challenges. This brings us to an important topic not touched on until now, namely the limitations of what transitions programs can do.

Challenges and hard things happen to people.
But people are also agents in their own lives.
Both sides of the coin are true.

It Starts With Schools, Just Like It Starts With Adults

The philosophical starting point of this book, however, is to attend to our own schools' responsibilities first. Just as I tell parents in my practice that they are the adults, and they must attend to their own behavior and management at home before they can ask and reasonably expect their kids to adjust their own behavior, so, too, are the teachers, staff, and managers of a school the 'adults' in the metaphorical community family. If a school isn't taking its responsibilities in assisting the community with these very real, and large, challenges, it is difficult to bring pressure to bear on students and parents to take their responsibilities for managing mobility well. Conversely, once we have gotten our affairs in order, we *can* appropriately hold people accountable to how they choose to manage their mobility.

The only way a school's transitions program can lend itself to such a function is if it takes good care of itself. It is not easy to be the transitional soil

People who help others regulate their feelings must also regulate their own.

into which people attach themselves, en route to creating their 'real' life in their new place. People who help others regulate their feelings must also regulate their own. In neuroscience terms, they have to be careful not to burn out their regulatory PFC brakes through years of caring for others' emotions, without attending to their own. *Chapter 5: Sustaining the Harbor* looks more closely at this important reality.

WRAPPING UP: ATTACHMENT THEORY MAKES IT EASIER TO ADDRESS GRIEF

Attachment theory provides a positive framework for viewing and talking about the issues involved in mobility across cultures. Unlike the 'grief and loss' paradigm of Pollock and Van Reken – however true to the reality of the TCK life it may have been – the attachment paradigm is not likely to engender a repulsion factor in an audience. The term 'attachment' carries connotations of warmth, enclosure, and attraction, making it a more 'user-friendly' paradigm than language steeped in 'grief and loss.' It is universal and inclusive. The wish to feel safe and included is part of our genetic inheritance. Every human being participates in attachment because of our shared biology. Best of all, the concept is accessible to the layperson. You don't need a PhD in psychology to intuitively grasp the importance of safe and reliable human relationships.

For all these reasons, an attachment-based paradigm might be the logical 'missing link' needed to finally lift the inspiration infused by Pollock and Van Reken's *Third Culture Kids* into actual widespread use throughout international schools worldwide. An attachment paradigm could help shift the work on mobility across cultures to a new level, from what is currently a 'hit or miss' application by pockets of professionals at some international schools, towards widespread, school-wide, systemic application that is finally recognized as a 'must' in terms of best practices.

> *"I am interviewing new best friends."*
> – Amy, mother of four

By explaining to people that they have lost their attachments to their previous communities, and by naming the hurt and anxiety that such losses naturally create, a comprehensive transitions program can offer to be a transitional buoy for people to hold onto, a temporary attachment object for people to cling to and feel safe with until they have built or rebuilt their own networks and found their way.

This sounds good, I can almost hear you asking. *But how do you do it?*

Let me start to answer that by telling you some stories.

Chapter 2

FINDING THE SHIP'S LOG – THE IMPORTANCE OF LIFE STORIES

"People are people because of other people."
  – African proverb.

*"I'm not dead. But when I am, it's like…
I don't know, I guess it's like being inside a book
that nobody's reading."*
  – Tim O'Brien, *The Things They Carried*

LET ME TELL YOU A STORY

The Jewish tradition is infused with stories that convey important messages for important situations. These stories are known as parables, and *The Maggid of Dubno* is one such parable.

THE PARABLE OF THE TELLER OF DUBNO

Truth is bemoaning the fact that nobody wants to listen to him. He goes from home to home and from gathering to gathering, but nobody wants to be with him or socialize with him, despite Truth's conviction that he knows valuable things about life and that the people really need to hear what he has to say. Still, nobody will listen.

Along comes Story to the village, and everyone wants to be with Story. Story is surrounded by visitors who want to hear his tales. Never is a seat beside him left unoccupied when he is in town.

One day Truth manages to have a word with Story. He explains how it saddens him to want to help the villagers, when none of the villagers seem to want his help. They pass him and his wisdom by, rarely sitting with him, rarely wanting to listen to what he has to say, even though they seem to recognize its importance.

Story hears this and decides to help Truth. Story tells Truth that he will start accompanying him on his walks and visits through the village.

From that day forward, Truth and Story walk side by side through the village, and never again is a seat left unfilled next to Truth at the tavern, in the square, or at the park. Accompanied by Story, the villagers want to hear everything Truth has to say. They begin to follow his each and every word, as though their lives depended on it. Truth realizes he is in inseparable from Story, that he cannot thrive in the people's hearts without Story [31].

Rather than being a collection of stories with a fixed purpose for use at fixed, pre-ordained times, the meaning in these stories and the lessons they convey seem to depend on the time and circumstances in which they are used. The meaning can depend on the listener, and may differ from one person to the next. The point is that such stories are often a more powerful means of transmitting – and receiving – a life lesson than a more direct statement, which can often induce a spirit of defensiveness and threat in the listener.[18]

Sailing Around The 'Repulsion Factor'

In *Third Culture Kids: The Experience of Growing Up Among Worlds,* David C. Pollock and Ruth E. Van Reken told the unflinching Truth, namely that grief is rampant in the lives of the globally mobile. But to this day, townsfolk have either been daunted by the bald Truth or not known what to do about it. In *Chapter1: Attachment,* I referred to this effect as the 'repulsion factor.' People may have recognized the Truth of what Pollock and Van Reken were describing, but they may have needed a Story to help them digest it and understand what to do about it.

Why might this be?

We all love stories. Most of us grew up with stories. Anytime somebody said, "Let me tell you a story," we were inclined to want to relax, to curl up,

----

18   I might emphasize that the Maggid of Dubno could be described as a meta-story, a story about the power of stories.

to listen. Stories seemed safe. They made us want to drop our guard, in the knowledge that nothing is expected of us. We only needed to listen. If you were read to as a child, the next thing you likely did after the story was sleep.

I would argue most of us carry this basic trust in stories with us throughout our lives. We let people launch difficult or challenging stories at us because the message (whatever it may be) is not necessarily obvious, allowing it to 'fly under the radar' and enter our airspace. Whatever lesson needs to be learned is veiled and indirect, allowing it to land in our own time. The indirectness of stories renders our defensive artillery useless; there is no need to shoot at something lacking clear form or substance. These characteristics of stories perhaps explain why they continue to engender feelings of safety across the lifespan.

The Story Of This Chapter

Some would say every good story has a hero, a villain, some kind of conflict between the two, and a resolution.

In what follows, I will explore three reasons why 'Story' is the hero in our discussion of mobility. We will examine:

- how we are wired to discern stories in our surroundings
- how we all strive to create and maintain the coherence of our own 'life stories'
- how life stories provide the vehicle for translating attachment theory into practical applications for school communities to use in addressing mobility

After understanding these three core characteristics of our 'hero,' we will turn to an examination of our 'villain,' namely mobility. The villain moves into the scene, disrupting our basic human drive to tell stories that flow and make sense, disrupting our sense of a coherent life narrative, and robbing us of the people who know our stories.

What to do?

Happily, this story has a happy ending, because Story – our hero – can prevail. Story is capable of generating all the tools needed to overcome the villain of mobility, rescuing the townsfolk from desperation and helping them find a place of resolution and meaning.

It's not an easy tale. But nothing worthwhile ever is. Let's get on with the telling.

MEET THE HERO: STORY

As in any traditional story, let me first introduce you to the hero of our tale, Story, and the three main reasons why stories are essential in human lives.

First Reason Why Stories Matter: We Are Wired To Tell Them

Since the beginning of time, humankind has had a need to tell stories as a way of making sense of experience. Oral traditions kept stories and traditions alive, as they passed from generation to generation prior to the written word. Ancient cave drawings such as those at Lascaux, in the south of France, attest to the need felt by our ancestors 20,000 years ago to create records that would last longer than the spoken word, records that others could see and appreciate. And with the development of written symbols, the printing press, modern day online journals and blogs, and certainly phenomena like Facebook, Twitter, and Instagram, one can witness the human drive to express our experience and to have others read, see, and validate it.

This is more than just talk. Experiments repeatedly show we have an innate drive to turn our experience into stories. We may be literally wired to tell stories. One of the most compelling examples of this reality was a study undertaken in 1944 by Fritz Heider and Marianne Simmel [32] using a simple animation involving lines, two triangles, and a circle.

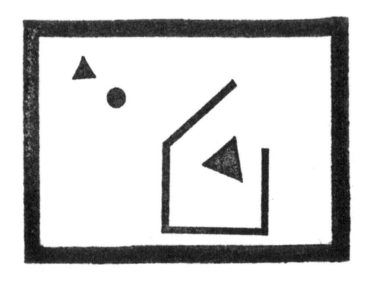

Before reading on, I would suggest searching YouTube for a video clip from this study. It's easy to find.

What do you see?

The visual material in the study simply shows two triangles and one circle moving amongst several lines assembled into a box-like shape. For a little over a minute, that's what happens.

Almost without fail, viewers begin creating a story about what they see. As the big triangle moves in towards the smaller triangle and the circle, both of which seem to be hiding in the box-shaped figure, viewers invariably see a bully trying to intimidate the smaller figures. And as the smaller triangle moves in front of the small circle, eventually 'helping' this circle escape from the larger triangle, viewers unfailingly invoke terms such as 'protection' to describe what the smaller triangle 'is doing' for the circle. When the larger triangle is eventually foiled in his attempt to capture the smaller triangle, it bangs against the lines, suggesting to many viewers it is smashing the room in a rage of frustration.

In reality, the video only shows this – several lines and geometric shapes are moving around on a screen.

What Heider and Simmel wished to demonstrate was how the mind arranges the information it encounters by searching for the hidden meaning organizing the information. *The most efficient and natural means of organizing information is into a story.* We are wired to look for the hidden storyline in any set of ambiguous information.

As Daniel Kauffman shows in *Thinking, Fast and Slow* [33], his monumental masterpiece on this very topic, our minds – at least when we're relaxed – aren't critical about what story is chosen. Our minds want a story that makes sense, one that seems to account for the data. If they have that, our minds relax and engender feelings of ease.

As it turns out, this is more than just metaphor. Our minds might actually *be* happy when they discover a story that makes sense. This drive to find logical connections between things appears to be wired into our deepest unconscious. We could label this wish as our 'drive for coherence' – we want stories that work. Stories that don't work – chaotic, disorganized, unfinished, or opaque – somehow leave us cold.

One of the most remarkable demonstrations of this fact comes from a study in 2009 by Sascha Topolinski and colleagues [34]. The 'Remote Association Test,' or 'RAT,' is a test of creative potential originally developed by Martha Mednick in 1962. Subjects are presented with three words or triads, and they have to discover the word or idea linking the words in the triad.

Some triads are relatively easy to find the linking word or concept:

cream   skate   water[19]

others are more difficult, such as:

sense   courtesy   place[20]

others are extremely difficult, such as:

fence   card   master[21]

and still others are impossible, because there is no known connection:

desk   sand   brain[22]

Topolinski and her colleagues presented subjects with various triads, and asked them to press the spacebar on their keyboards after they had read each triad. They were to move through the triads quickly, affording them enough time to read each triad, but certainly not enough time to solve them.

Using electrodes located on the faces of the subjects, the researchers were interested in what would happen every time subjects were presented with a coherent triad. In other words,

A life story is the tale we tell about ourselves. A life story is how we tie together all that has happened over the years. A life story is therefore never finished.

although subjects would not have time to solve the triad, would they be able to sense on some intuitive, 'gut' level that the triad had a solution?

In fact they were. Every time subjects saw a coherent triad, researchers were able to observe slight activation of the sygomaticus major muscle (one of the main muscles involved in smiling) and a slight relaxation of the corrugator supercilii (one of the main muscles involved in frowning), *even though the participants in the study didn't have time to think consciously about the actual solution.*

It would appear we have mechanisms of recognizing coherence that operate outside of consciousness. This 'coherence detector,' as we might call it, is constantly scanning the world at large for things that belong together, things that fit, things that make sense. And when it finds those things, this 'coherence detector' begins to put a smile on our face.

Literally.

Second Reason Why Stories Matter: Mental Health Requires A Coherent 'Life Story'

Not only do we have an innate drive to search for a coherent story in any collection of ambiguous information, we also experience that same drive with regards to the stories we have about ourselves. In other words, we all have a drive to develop and maintain a life story that makes sense.

But what is a life story?

A life story is the tale we tell about ourselves. A life story is how we tie together all that has happened over the years. A life story is therefore never finished. It must incorporate new events constantly, providing the foundation for reinterpreting the past while also offering a launching point to envision the future. Dan McAdams formulated a 'life-story model of identity' in which he contended that:

> "People living in modern societies begin, in late adolescence and young adulthood, to construe their lives as evolving stories that integrate the reconstructed past and the anticipated future in order to provide life with some semblance of unity and purpose."
> [35, p. 243]

We need and seek a story that makes sense. The father of narrative therapy, Michael White, once expressed it like this:

> "In striving to make sense of life, persons face the task of arranging their experiences of events in sequences across time in such a way as to arrive at a coherent account of themselves and the world around them... This account can be referred to as a story or self-narrative. The success of this storying of experience provides persons with a sense of continuity and meaning in their lives, and this is relied upon for the ordering of daily lives and for the interpretation of further experiences." [36, p. 10]

Writers and thinkers through the ages have had different ways of expressing this goal of a coherent life story. Maslow wrote of achieving 'self actualization.' Erickson wrote of achieving the phase of 'generativity' versus 'stagnation' during middle life. Positive psychologists like Seligman talk about achieving a state of 'flourishing.'

----

19   *The linking word is: ice*   21   *The linking word is: post*
20   *The linking word is: common*   22   *No known solution.*

In one way, shape, or form, what it comes down to is perhaps best expressed by Viktor Frankl, the founder of logotherapy, a therapy focused on discovering the *logos*, or meaning, of one's life. If one can ascertain a meaningful logic to one's life story, such that all the disparate events of one's life somehow

> *If one can ascertain a meaningful logic to one's life story, such that all the disparate events of one's life somehow have their place and function in the flow of that evolving story, then one's story could be said to be coherent.*

have their place and function in the flow of that evolving story, then one's story could be said to be coherent. And as an individual's life continues unfolding until his or her last breath, there is no such thing as a coherence that has been lastingly 'achieved.' Coherence is something that must be maintained and constantly recalibrated, the events involved constantly reinterpreted, because life constantly inserts new significant events into the flow of one's story. At times when people do feel as if their life story makes sense, they sometimes express it by saying they're 'in a good place.'

Although there might be many numbers of ways people over the millennia have described this outcome of a coherent life story, there is some philosophical convergence on the idea that coherence – or something like coherence – represents the pinnacle of what might be called 'the good life.' Coherent life stories are important because we all feel better, deep in our gut, when we have them.

Third Reason Why Stories Matter: They Make Attachment Theory Tangible

If I made my case clearly in *Chapter 1: Attachment,* then you grasp the basics of attachment theory and understand why a school needs to make itself available as a 'transitional attachment object.' People readily accept attachment is essential, but it's less clear what to do with that fact on a practical, day-to-day basis. Given a real school in a real community, facing the real challenge of real mobility, what should be done with the ideas of attachment I've discussed?

If we move from attachment theory to the notion of life stories, the essential concepts become far easier to work with.

What happens when people hear, read, and therefore know our stories? Answering this question produces the essential link between attachment theory and the study of life stories:

We feel attached to those who know our life stories.

The more people truly know our story, the safer we are likely to feel with them. The safer we feel with people, the more we are inclined to gradually feel attached to them. And this works in reverse too: the more others know our stories, the more likely it is we know theirs, meaning they feel safe and attached to us, too. In other words, attachment develops hand in hand with our knowledge of people's life stories.

You can confirm these statements from your own experience. Think about the people who really know you, the people who really know what you've been through, the people who've heard your tale. And think about how you feel about them. Now, consider people you feel little or no connection to, and ask yourself how much they really know about who you are and where you've been. With the exception of relationships tainted by current or long-standing conflicts, I would expect the people you feel close to are the people who really know your story.

MEET THE VILLAIN: MOBILITY

Let me say at the outset that the heading of this section is misleading because I don't see mobility as a villain. But the reason why is because I have studied it for decades, and I know how it moves, twists, and turns. This awareness has made me comfortable with understanding what to do about it. It also positions me to share what I've learned with the people and schools I consult with, helping them convert mobility's twists and turns into growth opportunities.

If you're not aware of how mobility operates, it can feel like a creeping, lunging, suffocating villain. All too often, I have encountered people who are caught off guard. When mobility strikes, they feel overwhelmed.

Let me illustrate how this works with a story from my time as a high school counselor. Picture the first day of orientation. Stand in my shoes, as you watch the auditorium fill with new and apprehensive faces.

THE VILLAIN STRIKES

As they walk into the auditorium, I can see it in their eyes. Only faintly at first, but it grows more apparent as the opening presentation gets underway. The way they are sitting back in their chairs, as if to increase the distance. The way they don't look at those around them – their eyes point straight ahead or down at their laps. Fifteen minutes into the presentation on the opening day of orientation, the dull ache in their eyes says their ears aren't switched on. They're not completely here. Their minds, their hearts, are elsewhere.

After introducing who's who and walking through the program for the week, I fall silent. I count to five. People look up, wondering if something's wrong. Then I announce something that nobody's dared say to them before.

"Some of you don't want to be here."

Eyes flash open, suddenly riveted on mine.

"Some of you never wanted to make this move." You can hear some shuffling in chairs, as if to sit up straighter.

"Some of you are really mad at your parents, or at your mom or dad's boss – or even at your partner – for making you come." Awkward glances, knowing looks, uncomfortable grins.

"Maybe what makes our school special is that we know it. And we're not afraid to say it."

This first dose of validation gets followed quickly by another, a massive one, and one I have heard kids tell me years later that they never forgot. "Well, don't worry. It's okay. If you're mad or sad about coming here, you need to be as mad or as sad as you need to be, for as long as you need to be. You may have built up a total life in your last place, and you may have been very, very happy with it! Your life might have felt like this, like the Dow Jones index on a good year."

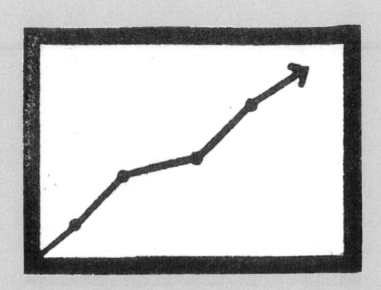

In the middle of this presentation on the first day of welcoming new families to the High School, I put up a slide that graphically depicts a lifeline moving upwards. As the dots move upwards and to the right, the line climbing ever higher, there is recognition and relief, and a sense in the audience that the slide has captured something about what it might feel like to be them.

"And then," I interrupt the upward vibe, "maybe a few months ago, or maybe only a few weeks ago, you find out you're going to have to move. And this is maybe how you felt."

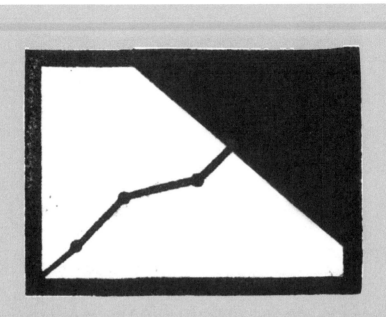

The line gets chopped off by blackness.

"And even though you might be doing your best to try to make the most out of this move you find yourself making, it hurts. And you're stuck with a really hard question: How do you pick up the storyline again, when you feel like it's been cut off?"

Every time I would show these slides, you could hear a pin drop. That chopped off life storyline captures something about people's experience at a visceral level. I once had a woman in her mid twenties tell me that one slide had been seared into her memory nearly a decade earlier, as she sat in the audience as a new 11th grader. That black 'psychological cliff' seems to capture an experience everyone recognizes at the bottom of their gut.

This sense of dropping off into a void after a move repeatedly surprises people. Many people do not see the chasm coming. They may have heard of 'culture shock' or 'homesickness,' but they rarely expect to be visited by severe adjustment problems and even depression.

In what follows, I will discuss why this 'psychological cliff' both hurts and surprises people so badly. Understanding what produces the cliff provides a starting point for devising a plan for how to keep 'the villain of mobility' from nudging us towards its edge.

FIRST REASON FOR THE PSYCHOLOGICAL CLIFF: AN ASSAULT ON OUR DRIVE FOR COHERENCE

Imagine a young woman who is an honor roll student in the 10th grade of her Texan High School, playing varsity soccer, aspiring to be the captain of her team by the time she's a senior, and occasionally babysitting her two younger brothers. Her father is the CEO of a telecommunications startup begun after college in his garage in Houston and is now a global player being scouted for a potential buyout by Bouyges Télécom. Her mother was an advertising executive at Proctor and Gamble, but stopped working four years ago after the twins were born. All the members of this family have formulations of their individual identities, which are determined by what they do, what they're good at, and what 'hats' or roles they wear. Their 'life stories' are constantly unfolding and evolving, as pages are added every day, bundled into chapters, and bound by a tone or tenor so that the authorship makes sense, so there is a story line, so the events connect.

The personal sense of continuity that one's self-narrative affords undergoes a massive rupture when the majority of the strands that make up 'who you are' get cut. The face in the mirror looks the same, but it is gazing back at you from a different mirror, in a different bathroom, in a different home, with different furnishings, on a different street, in a country where the language is different, where people look different, where everything is different.

While the tenor of this family's life stories might be characterized by upward progress and outer success, these people may never have considered themselves as having life stories. Until they move, that is. In line with the aphorism 'you don't know what you've got till it's gone,' members of a family that moves may feel an unpleasant rip when their life stories get torn by a discontinuity like moving.

The personal sense of continuity that one's self-narrative affords undergoes a massive rupture when the majority of the strands that make up 'who you are' get cut. The face in the mirror looks the same, but it is gazing back at you from a different mirror, in a different bathroom, in a different home, with different furnishings, on a different street, in a country where the language is different, where people look different, where everything is different. As our Texan family wakes up in

Paris and Dad heads to work, the daughter wakes up struggling to feel like the successful soccer star she used to be, the mother tries making breakfast with ingredients she can't read,

But for the writing of a life story to have any meaning, it also needs to be read.

and the twins scream that they can't find their toys.

And we have to remember this doesn't only happen to the movers. What about this 10th grade girl's best friend back in Houston? How is that student feeling as she sits in IB Spanish or AP European History class? The attachment system of those left behind are also activated by international mobility, lending credence to the notion that this challenge – and arguably the points made in this book – are not only for international schools with a high degree of turnover. Mobility, particularly in this global age, reaches into most domestic schools around the world as well.

SECOND REASON FOR THE PSYCHOLOGICAL CLIFF: AN ASSAULT ON THE 'READERS' OF OUR LIFE STORIES

The individualistic, author-focused strands of a life story are only one half of the equation. Of course a life story needs to be authored, and it stands to reason our Texan family members will struggle when they are not sure how the next pages of their stories should read – or even where to find the pen and paper in their new Parisian townhouse. But for the writing of a life story to have any meaning, it also needs to be read.

Life stories need audiences. When a person moves, she loses the audience she was accustomed to. In boarding an airplane and taking flight, she loses the face-to-face connection to the many people who regularly 'read' and therefore reinforced her current 'draft' of who she was. Our Texan mother loses her peers who saw her as an extremely competent professional-turned-full-time-mother, those women who saw her as somebody who was only on a break from her advertising career while her twins were small, those friends who 'read' her as somebody who would return to professional life as soon as her circumstances allowed. Her teenaged daughter lost the teammates who expected her to take the lead on the soccer field, the friends who could read her moods in a glance, the classmates who understood her wry wit the first time she cracked a joke (and not after the explanation). The twins knew the best places to play, and kids throughout the neighborhood counted on their invitations to join whatever was being played. In boarding an airplane, all of these family members lose vast portions of their readership.

What about our Texan father?[23] The father has the easier task, at least when considered through this 'life story' lens. The reason is simple. For the father in the traditional role described above, the link between the two lives in question (pre-move and post-move) is his job. His employment is the *raison-d'être* for why the relocation occurred, the rational 'link' that supplies a sense of continuity and meaning between what he was doing before, and what he is doing now.

For the father in the traditional role described above, the link between the two lives in question (pre-move and post-move) is his job. His employment is the raison-d'être *for why the relocation occurred, the rational 'link' that supplies a sense of continuity and meaning between what he was doing before, and what he is doing now.*

In a way our traditional Texan mom and her children likely do not enjoy, this identity of Dad's is reinforced throughout his new office. Just as everyone saw, 'read,' and reinforced him in his previous employment role, so too is it likely his new personnel see, 'read,' and reinforce him in his new role – he's the "new fellow from Houston" who is "heading the GPS-9 project" because "Bouygues Télécom wanted a leader from the American market." Micro-dialogues around his upcoming role existed before he arrived. Dad lands in a bed of reinforcement that leaves no question a to who he is in his new position – his sense of identity continues to march forwards and upwards, just like the Dow Jones visual metaphor on page 47.

----

23 *For better or for worse, a majority of the families I encounter in my work in international schools are still structured along lines often described as 'traditional,' meaning the father occupies the 'breadwinner' role while mother takes primary care of the children and the home. As in our Texan family, the emergence of such a traditional family structure is often a recent development. In fact, it is often spurred by the very relocation in question: in taking the large promotion overseas, the family had to choose one career over another. More often than not – at least in my experience – the career that seems to get the 'right of way' is the father's. The purpose of this divergence is not to launch into an analysis of social demographics, earning power, or gender lines. All are beyond the scope of this book and are deftly analyzed else where. [See 37 for a deft discussion of the topic.] The purpose is mainly to highlight that many single-income families at our schools weren't always that way – until recently.*

At least in the beginning. As truth would have it, and as our experience with mobility tells us, it is impossible for the members of a family system to get too out of sync with each other's rate of adjustment. In keeping with the fiscal allusions to the Dow Jones on page 48, sooner or later a 'correction' takes place. Sooner or later, the rates of adaptation are pulled towards one another. Sooner or later, those who are struggling are pulled 'up' by those who are thriving, or those who are thriving are pulled 'down' by those who are struggling. In other words, the moods of family members exert a gravitational force on one another. And as relocation specialists in companies are coming to understand and appreciate, gravity pulls 'down.' In other words, it is not possible for Dad's new identity – or anyone's, for that matter – to thrive if a member or a portion of the family is in shambles. If every member doesn't find ways to continue the threads of who they are in their new setting, their sense of identity will strain, and they will struggle.

And there is plenty of data to underscore the reality that a failed relocation is extremely expensive for a company. This book emphasizes the less tangible emotional costs, and the recently 'discovered' educational costs highlighted by Hattie's *Visible Learning*. There is also ample data on the financial cost of sending a family on an international assignment, only to have that assignment fail. More often than not, the failure can be traced not to shortcomings in the employee, but to difficulties experienced by his or her family members, and the resulting strain and interference these familial difficulties created in the employee's ability to function well.

THIRD REASON FOR THE PSYCHOLOGICAL CLIFF: WE FORGET THAT READERS ARE IMPORTANT

The crucial importance of the 'readers' of one's life stories often surprises people, particularly those who locate their cultural roots in the West, especially in the United States. As mentioned earlier, I grew up in Southern California, at the far reaches of what was 'the American West.' I came to appreciate at a cellular level that people in individualistic, Western societies such as the USA feel quite comfortable with the notion that they are in charge of writing *their own* story. USAmericans even take pride in a certain fierce individualism, born of generations who had to survive on their own if they were to survive at all.

In his 1960 classic *Travels with Charley,* John Steinbeck chronicled the landscape of the lives of his fellow USAmericans as he traversed the continental United States, accompanied only by his poodle, Charley. Throughout the book, he repeatedly meets people who can manage alone –

as could Steinbeck. Whether it was repairing a car or fixing a roof, people believed they could get things done using one focused mind and two willing hands.

And they were proud of it. So it came to pass that people in the West – and arguably particularly in the 'Wild West' – came to believe a person's identity becomes invested in, and even synonymous with, the story *they* create about themselves as an individual. Readers of these stories were less important, if only for the reason that, from a pioneer's or settler's point of view, there were few of them around. The notion that outside forces determine anything about one's story is a notion inherently repulsive to many USAmericans.

The Limitations Of Space

That the strongest form of individualism anywhere in the world arguably arose in the United States is no coincidence. That the most rugged strain of this individualism arose in the 'Wild West' of those same States is also no coincidence. The 'West' of the United States provided something the European settlers of the 19th century had largely run out of on the European continent: space. The vastness of the space available in the uncharted West was on an unimaginable scale, a scale never experienced by large numbers of people on this planet ever before – and one that will never be experienced again – at least on this planet. With new space came new possibilities, including *the ability to move on.* This possibility for people to move to new lands, whether due to population demands, conflict, or the pursuit of novelty or adventure, had likely not been seen on this scale since our species' hunter-gatherer days.[24]

The limitation of space, together with higher levels of population, contribute to developing a collectivist approach to society. This is logical. If there are more people around, there are more people whose interconnecting needs need consideration if society is going to function.[25] When people have unlimited space to move into, on the as-needed basis that was the reality of the United States until early in the 20th century, then the natural shift is away from collectivism and towards individualism. Although space to expand has run out, the United States continues to this day to live proudly with its individualist values. Individualism could be described as the most fundamental of the United States' cultural exports.

----

24 *The rightness or legality of this appropriation of space is a different matter altogether, one far beyond the scope of this book. For a succinct history of the United States' treatment of the Native Americans, and the rampant violations of the Oglala Lakota people in particular, whose treaties remain violated to this day, see the "Life After Wounded Knee" article in the August, 2012 edition of* National Geographic.

25 *This, too, I learned at a visceral level, when I traded the wide spaces of the West I associate with rugged individualism for the small streets and cramped houses that are a reality in the Netherlands. The Netherlands is still an individualistic country, but far more socially regulated than the United States.*

A New Frontier?

The reason for this brief departure into USA history and the individualist-collectivist spectrum is because of a reality few may have considered. The advent of the global world economy, with the associated rise of international mobility, has created a way of life and an international school system where 'moving on' is again a real possibility. *Though there may not be new physical space to move into, new psychological space is only a move away.* Moving may not be sparked by population pressures as in the past, but it can be sparked – or even become – a way to cope with interpersonal pressures, strains, and even conflicts.

As this book has repeatedly emphasized, this dynamic can – and must – also be viewed from the stayer's point of view. In the absence of appropriate transitions programs to manage these challenges, those who stay and are re-peatedly moved away from are likely to gradually develop a default belief that others, whether you care about them or not, move away. In other words, to coin a new term, 'unmanaged mobility' creates a steady and cumulative drag on people's ability to sail into personal relationships with confidence. When too much drag is placed on people's natural inclination to build relationships, when enough of these relationships have been dissolved by mobility without suffi-cient emotional coaching and guidance, then the logical result is for the person to pull back, hold back, or withdraw from connecting.

> "*I expect my friends to have a shelf life.*"
> – 19-year-old TCK

Is this what we want for our schools?

Individualism Versus Collectivism

Contrast this Western, individualistic way of thinking about identity with more socially embedded ideas of identity found in many other areas of the world, and you discover one of the fundamental ways of differentiating cultures. Is a culture more *individualistic* or *collectivist* [38]? If individuals in individualist societies are largely expected to take care of themselves, then collectivism is "a tightly-knit framework in society in which individuals can expect their relatives or members of a particular in-group to look after them in exchange for unquestioning loyalty" [39]. Within collectivist societies, you are not an atomic or separate self. You are your position in a larger, indissoluble web of interconnected selves.

This individualist-collectivist distinction makes it likely, in my opinion, that people from more collectivist (i.e. Eastern) walks of life would be less likely to be caught off guard by the shock of mobility than people from more individualist walks of life (i.e. Western), because a collectivist mindset places more value on social relatedness than an individualist mindset. For this reason people from collectivist walks of life are less likely to be surprised by the shock of transition. To a certain degree, although it may be at a subconscious level, people from more collectivist walks of life may be expecting the shock. They know they are leaving the networks that so much define who they are.

By contrast, take the individualist Westerner who cherishes socially-sanctioned ideas of self-determination and self-reliance. However valuable that mindset might have been to surviving on the frontier, it could arguably prove to be a liability during mobility because it obscures the importance of attachments. With a Western, individualist mindset, a person is inclined – and even encouraged – to downplay the importance of attachments in his or her definition of self. While such an individual can get away with this while all of his or her attachments are readily available – be those attachments to individuals, places, communities, or cultures – things get dramatically trickier when these sources of reinforcement get taken way.

The upshot of this discussion is that life stories require not only authorship but also readership. No story exists in a vacuum. And this is reflected in our attachment architecture; we have an innate wish to connect and to trust. Every other personality structure that deviates from secure attachment is an attempt to cope with having missed out on something our healthy core naturally seeks.

As with most true things in life, the truth is likely 'in the middle' with regards to 'what's best' on the individualistic-collectivistic continuum. The experience of mobility shows those from individualist societies they *do* need readers for their life stories to have any meaning, that a person cannot write a story on his or her own and expect to feel healthy and whole. In analogous fashion, the experience of mobility shows those from

FIGURE 2.1: Chinese yin-yang symbol

collectivist societies they cannot rely entirely on the wider society to tell them who they are. When that social fabric is torn away in the process of a move, when collectivist-minded people find themselves in a new school and a new community, many find they must take a more active role in re-authoring their lives than they are accustomed to.

In other words, as in the Chinese yin-yang symbol, each half is only whole by virtue of the existence of the other. Each half contains within itself the seed of the other reality.

Take away either half of this important reality, and you'll be left with a large apostrophe.

FOURTH REASON FOR THE PSYCHOLOGICAL CLIFF: CULTURE DETERMINES WHICH STORIES ARE VALID

The fourth reason why people identify with the image of the cut-off line depicted on page 48 is because of the importance of culture.

Many theorists have defined culture differently. Milton Bennett says "culture provides us with the tendency to perceive phenomena that are relevant to both physical and social sur-

Different cultures have vastly different notions about what a good life story would be.

vival" [40]. In other words, we notice things that are important to succeeding and staying alive. Implied in this definition is something equally important – culture also tells us what we can afford to *ignore*. Every second of every day, our sensory channels must process a massive amount of information coming from without and within, from both our surroundings and our own bodies. To pay full attention to all of this information is impossible – any attempt to do so would tax our systems and leave us with no energy to do anything else.

Culture provides us with frameworks for viewing and thinking about what is happening. Perhaps in its simplest definition, culture tells us what is normal. If we know what's normal, we know what's abnormal, and therefore what we need to pay extra attention to. That which is unexpected could, after all, be a source of threat.

In terms of the topic of this chapter, namely life stories, culture has an analogous affect. Culture tells us which stories are the ones most worth listening and aspiring to. Just as musical notes can be arranged into an infinite number of compositions, so too can words be arranged into an infinite number of stories. Culture provides us with guidelines to answer questions like:

- what is a story?
- what are the qualities of a good story?
- how should a story be structured?
- what kind of qualities does the hero of a story have?

For example, one of the USAmerican founders of the burgeoning research movement into life stories, Dan McAdams, has distinguished between two dominant strands in life stories, which he describes as 'contamination sequences' and 'redemption sequences.' A contamination sequence is characterized by a movement away from a time that was good, rewarding, and hopeful, towards a time when that goodness and hope gets lost. These types of passages feel tragic to read and even worse to live, and those who emphasize contamination sequences generally score lower on measures of well-being. Redemption sequences, on the other hand, tell a tale of overcoming disadvantages or challenges, such that the protagonist rises above misfortune. People who emphasize redemption sequences tend to score higher on measures of well-being.

McAdams emphasizes how the love and fascination with redemption sequences is a typically USAmerican phenomenon.

> "Evolving from the Puritans to Emerson to Oprah, the redemptive self has morphed into many different storied forms in the past 300 years as Americans have sought to narrate their lives as redemptive tales of atonement, emancipation, recovery, self-fulfillment, and upward social mobility. The stories speak of heroic individual protagonists – the chosen people – whose manifest destiny is to make a positive difference in a dangerous world, even when the world does not wish to be redeemed. The stories translate a deep and abiding script of American exceptionalism into the many contemporary narratives of success, recovery, development, liberation, and self-actualization that so pervade American talk, talk shows, therapy sessions, sermons, and commencement speeches" [35, p. 255].

Redemptive sequences describe a type of story that is understood, sought, and exalted by USAmericans. But are these kinds of stories held in such high esteem elsewhere?

The answer is no. Different cultures have vastly different preferences for what makes a good story. By extension, different cultures have vastly different notions about what a good life story would be. What is 'the good life'? How would a story of that good life read from a more collectivist society in an Asian culture, where

By moving, a person loses not only the flow of his or her story, and not only the readership who used to read that story – by moving, the person in question loses the very cultural norms that supported the value of the kind of story he or she had to tell in the first place.

success is often defined more in terms of how well one fulfills his or her social obligations, and how successfully one honors the family name and family ancestors?

The 'good story,' therefore, would depend on where you are, who you ask, and the cultural values and lenses being used to read and evaluate the story.

The loss of one's cultural frames of reference forms a fourth reason for the experience of the psychological cliff in depicted on page 48. By moving, a person loses not only the flow of his or her story, and not only the readership who used to read that story – by moving, the person in question loses the very cultural norms that supported the value of the kind of story he or she had to tell in the first place.

Consider the boy from Saudi Arabia whose family moves to New York City. In Saudi Arabia he was praised by his teachers for being obedient and diligent. He memorized his rote passages perfectly, never asked questions, and always had his homework done. Described by his teachers as the ideal student, he was a paragon of Saudi educational virtues. In Saudi Arabia, he felt confident about his identity as a student.

What happens when his father accepts a position at the UN in New York City? In moving to an international school there, he is suddenly asked to make presentations, to participate in group debates, and to offer his own opinion spontaneously in classroom discussions. At the end of the first semester, this boy and his parents are disoriented and confused. On his first school report, his teachers have written comments about the boy being 'too passive' and 'needing to take a more active role in his learning.' And at the first parent-teacher conference, the teacher tells the parents their son seems "more interested in saying what he thinks I want to hear, rather than in deciding what he thinks himself." The boy receives the lowest marks he has ever received in all his years in schooling. The value placed on memorization and doing what you are expected to do, so important in this boy's home school in Saudi Arabia, has evaporated, leaving him with a way of being that holds little value in his new USAmerican classroom. Once the star Saudi pupil, he sits in the back seat of a cab en route to the Upper East Side, feeling devastated and useless.

Similarly, what counts as a story of a 'good parent'? Or a 'good teacher'? Or even a 'good administrator'? The answers vary across cultures. Value is subjective and relative, and anything but absolute. The moral of the story seems to go back to the picture on page 47. Just as there is no 'storyline' in this picture without people to 'read' it, there is no storyline without some cultural agreement about what kind of *frame* to put around it. If you change the *frame* on an image in some significant fashion, the entire feel of the image changes too. Culture provides the framing for our story lines.

FIFTH REASON FOR THE PSYCHOLOGICAL CLIFF: THE COMPLICATIONS OF POSTMODERNISM

'Postmodernism' is a word that scares people. Any word with five or more syllables, ending with an 'ism,' has often been conjured up inside academic walls. And many would argue such *isms* should stay there.

After grappling with this concept for decades, let me offer a definition that will hopefully make this concept understandable for the reader – assuming you have ever been as baffled by this particular 'ism' as I was.

Postmodernism is the world we live in now, where everything gets questioned and is up for debate.

Is that brief enough? I can elaborate, but I'll only do so briefly, so I can quickly move towards what postmodernism has to do with mobility across cultures.

One could argue that postmodernism is the very opposite of how things worked in the Middle Ages. In the Middle Ages you lived where you were born. Period. Most things were determined for you – the village you grew up in, what you believed, and your station in life. Religious edicts, establishments, and personnel were not questioned. Power was respected. The nobility was the nobility, and the peasants were the peasants. If the priest said it was true, it was. Traditions and establishments were sacred. The individual was negligible.

Then the Enlightenment occurred.

Then the Industrial Revolution.

Then modern science, including the advent of modern contraceptives.

Then the Computer Revolution.

Throughout this process, the gradual secularization of society has been accompanied by the gradual dismantling of social structures that used to be 'givens.' The result has been the inverse of the Middle Ages – the individual has become central, and many traditions and establishments have gradually vanished.

Many would emphasize the progress that has been gained in the modern world in terms of civil liberties and individual freedoms. Many would celebrate that the individual can now decide what he or she wants to believe, and how he or she wants to infuse his or her life with value and meaning. But have we only made gains? Has anything been lost?

How Much Choice Can A Human Being Handle?

The arguments from the proponents of progress can be flipped over. It is equally true to say that people now *have* to decide what they want to believe, and largely on their own. Since many social structures people would normally have inherited from their elders have shrunk or even disappeared, many people have to infuse their lives with meaning and value *on their own*. Though people generally think that 'choice' is undisputedly good, many experience difficulty with the process of *choosing*. In the *Paradox of Choice*, Barry Schwartz [41] reviews the Western conviction that more choice in-variably leads to greater well-being. He then goes on to provide a compelling argument as to why an overdose of choice – right down to 175 different salad dressings at the local supermarket – is beginning to rob people of a sense of meaning in their lives. We seem to have confused having choices with having happiness.

While not having choices arguably can limit life satisfaction, the addition of more choices to a person's plate does not lead to more happiness in some kind of linear fashion. It may only lead to what Baumeister and others have referred to as 'decision fatigue,' the gradual erosion of our mental and emo-tional energies by little decisions that don't really matter, but still require energy to make [1].

According to the World Health Organization, depression is now the most prevalent and costly disorder on the face of the planet [42, p. 117]. Given that depression often arises in response to a sense of failure in finding meaning in one's life, the astronomical rise of rates of depression around the world could be an indirect indication that members of the 20th and 21st centuries cannot handle the freedoms they think they want.

The point of this supersonic flight through history is not to evaluate the rightness or wrongness of the process that has led to our current state of

---

According to the World Health Organization, depression is now the most prevalent and costly disorder on the face of the planet. Given that depression often arises in response to a sense of failure in finding meaning in one's life, the astronomical rise of rates of depression around the world could be an indirect indication that members of the 20th and 21st centuries cannot handle the freedoms they think they want.

---

postmodernism, but rather to point out what this has to do with people coping with mobility. The point is this: Life is hard enough. Adolescence is arguably one of the trickiest phases of life, as a child pushes off from the safety of family without (yet) having a fully articulated sense of who he or she is. Amidst all the things people have to figure out now that so little is 'given' in our postmodern era, the reality of also having to both reauthor a life story and recraft a readership for that story is another massive challenge overlaid upon a life already challenging enough. Having to figure out how to manage such challenges during childhood and adolescence only makes the difficulties of these developmental phases grow exponentially.

I believe this is why entire audiences go silent and 'gulp' when I show the slides on pages 47 and 48. They are looking at a reflection of their own experience. Their life stories just flew off this postmodern cliff.

THE HERO MEETS THE VILLAIN: HOW STORIES CAN RESOLVE THE CHALLENGE

If the foundational layers of Maslow's hierarchy of needs (see page XLIII) pertained to basic requirements for survival and basic well-being – food, shelter, and belonging – then the pinnacle of his hierarchy had to do with the more abstract and 'pie in the sky' ambitions often summarized as 'self-actualization.' The composition and maintenance of a coherent life story is admittedly one of these higher ambitions. Such pursuits are not essential for survival. But does that make them any less worthy? The human condition would seem to be about moving as high up the hierarchy of needs as one can. This is in no sense a quest for material improvement in life (plenty of studies have shown that once you clear the poverty line, there is no connection between material well-being and actual happiness), but rather for 'meaning making' in life. Ultimately, people want their lives to feel meaningful. When one's life story feels as if it has broken down, one's sense of meaning scatters in the wind.

The point here is not about the right way to make meaning, but the importance of attempting to make meaning.

And this is where all of the strands of thinking and theory presented so far in this book begin to converge – at the place of meaning. We have talked about the challenges of mobility across cultures and the associated grief. We have talked about attachment, how taxing it is to have our attachment systems 'revved up,' and how relieving it is to be able to rely on other people as a 'social baseline' to help us regulate tough feelings. We have explored how the sharing of stories provides a path for building attachments to other people – and letting them build attachments to us.

THE FIRST INGREDIENT IN MEANING: CHALLENGE

How do we then create meaning? This is a massive question each person on this planet either attempts to answer or avoid in his or her own personal way. *Any* attempt to answer this existential question (i.e. by doing work that makes a difference in another person's life) leads to a better psychological outcome than any attempt to avoid the question (i.e. by fleeing into an addiction). The point here is not about the right way to make meaning, but *the importance of attempting* to make meaning. And I would argue that every attempt to make meaning has a similar entry-point:

Challenge.

Things that come easily, or at little personal cost, generally do not become meaningful or important to us.

Things that are challenging, or difficult, or things that come at great personal cost, often become – over time – the very elements of our lives most saturated with meaning.

I am confident an examination of your own experience will confirm this for you. How easy was it for you to complete a university degree? How easy was it for you to remodel a particular house into a place you loved, a place that felt like 'home'? How easy was it for you to give birth to a child?

Closer to the point, how easy was it for you to move, internationally or otherwise? If you read the stories in my *Preface* to this book, you know my first international relocation to the Netherlands tumbled me into a depression so dark I couldn't find the light switch for years. This terrible time of feeling utterly 'erased' by Life was made worse by there being no book like this to describe the contours of an experience I could only vaguely trace.

And yet I am thankful for that experience. I am thankful for the years of frantic swimming that brought me back to the surface. I am thankful for the many years of sailing experience since then that have taught me how to navigate the psychological waters and currents swirling above and around the trench that swallowed me.

In other words, the challenges I have faced – and the suffering they have involved – have taught me my greatest lessons.

All it took was a willingness to be taught.[26]

And I would venture to say, or at least to suggest, that the readers of this book are no different. In other words, the challenge of mobility across cultures provides a massive opportunity for personal growth for all involved. The reason this challenge sometimes doesn't show up as 'growth' or as something positive (the results of Hattie's meta-study being but one good example) is because it is poorly understood and poorly managed by the individuals and organizations involved.

It doesn't have to be this way. Challenges seen for what they are and re-alistically assessed can lead to the mobilization of resources appropriate to the situation, leading to a 'success experience' and the growth of personal confidence.

To stay with this book's maritime metaphor, if you deny the reality of a 20-meter swell rolling your way at 50 knots, you do run the risk of getting broadsided and toppled, with all the associated dire consequences. Conversely, if you follow the weather reports, know which way the swells are coming from, warn your crew to head below deck and hold on while you turn your bow *into* the wave, your ship will do what ships are designed to do.

Float.

Hattie discovered the negative consequences of mobility on educational outcomes not because mobility across cultures is bad. *Mobility isn't bad. It is neither good nor bad. It is simply a massive challenge.* As long as they are not too massive or too frequent – in which case they can be traumatic – massive

---

26 *Let me stay honest. I wasn't always willing to be taught. There were many years I wished the lessons would leave me alone. 'Willingness to be taught' is a final outcome that can take a long time to reach.*

challenges can lead to massive growth, as long as they are managed well.

And massive growth lives just down the street from massive meaning.

THE SECOND INGREDIENT IN MEANING: RELATIONSHIPS

To achieve psychological health, a person has to integrate the events of his or her life into his or her life story. To maintain psychological health, a person has to attend to this process of integrating new events constantly, as life is continuously occurring and unfolding. But as the previous discussion has revealed, a story only acquires its ultimate meaning in the tell-

> *To achieve psychological health, a person has to integrate the events of his or her life into his or her life story.*

ing. It is finding an audience for that story that leads one to feeling seen and heard, because a story has to be seen and heard to be – and to stay – real.

A Brief Return To The Attachment Literature

Returning to the discussion of 'working models' of attachment discussed in the previous chapter, securely attached people are lucky enough to believe their attachment figures will respond in a generally adequate and timely fashion to their needs. As discussed in *Chapter 1: Attachment,* the literature unequivocally demonstrates that *people with more secure models of attachment outscore those with insecure models of attachment on every single measure of human functioning* [14].

Insecurely attached people do not believe their attachment figures will be available. Insecurely attached people have two ways of coping with this disconcerting belief, leading to the two forms of insecure attachment. One option is to 'up-regulate' their attachment needs, as the so-called 'insecure-preoccupied' types do. Those who 'up-regulate' their attachment needs tend to amplify their attachment calls, in the hope that if they cry a bit louder or longer, that will activate their attachment figures to respond. John Bowlby always emphasized that a person's 'working models' of attachment figures were 'reasonably accurate' reflections of how things worked, so it would be reasonable to surmise that insecure-preoccupied types learned that increasing their cries worked. *Cry, ask, or demand more forcefully, and the person will respond.* This is what life taught them.

The second option, implemented by the 'insecure-dismissive' types, is to draw the opposite conclusion. Rather than up-regulating their attachment cries, which has likely *not* led to the desired results in the past,

People with more secure models of attachment outscore those with insecure models of attachment on every single measure of human functioning.

insecure-dismissive types 'down-regulate' their attachment needs, meaning they attempt to downplay and ignore the warning signals their internal attachment systems emit. Down-regulators have found this is the best long-term way of coping with these signals. *If people aren't going to respond adequately or appropriately to our cries, we might as well not cry out.* This, too, is what life has taught them.

People with less secure models of attachment have to divert resources to managing their attachment systems, which leaves them with less energetic 'cash' to devote to other healthier pursuits. In other words, our attachment systems behave much like real economies. Growth creates new revenue, which fuels further growth; whereas fear scares people, which only pinches spending further, leading to recession. In commerce and the human psyche alike, both positive and negative feedback loops exist. One could argue that the trick in life is to find ways to create and maintain positive feedback loops.

International schools with any significant degree of turnover find themselves the stewards of families and young minds subject to postmodern forces most people never have to contend with. Amidst all the challenges of normal life, the members of such communities also face unmitigated turbulence in their human attachments.

People come. People go.

People come. People go.

Over, and over, and over again.

The point I am making here is that, in the face of unmanaged mobility in these school communities, the natural tendency of people will be away

"It affected all of my marriages. At a certain point, I was just ready to leave. Or she left me. And in both cases, I never really understood why."

— Mark, lawyer in New York who grew up as a TCK before the term existed

from secure models of attachment. As forces beyond their control place steady pressure on them to experience human relationships as mercurial and unreliable, members of communities where there is no transitions program or plan will logically slide towards insecure-avoidant attachment styles. *If people aren't going to respond adequately or appropriately to our cries, we might as well not cry out.* Just as the American West likely 'shaped' an attachment style that was logically avoidant in its down-regulation of attachment needs, so too is a down-regulation of attachment needs the logical result for children at schools where mobility experiences are not properly managed.

Note that it does not matter if one is a mover, a stayer, or a mixture of the two. In a setting dominated by unmanaged mobility, where people are constantly on the move and you feel you're the only one you can ultimately count on, doesn't it make sense to conclude that it's better not to make your happiness depend too much on others?

Modern research is beginning to demonstrate exactly how a strained attachment system drains energy, interferes with our ability to listen, and impedes our capacity for learning.

INSIDE A 5TH GRADER, WHERE MIND IS NOT ALWAYS OVER MATTER

Crawl inside the mind of a 5th grader, a 5th grader who's just had his third best friend in four years move away, and you can logically empathize with the conclusion that he might draw in a school with unmanaged mobility. *I'm not going to try anymore. It hurts too much. And my next best friend will just leave anyway.*

The problem with this conclusion, however understandable, is that it does not change this student's basic human architecture. He still has a need to establish and maintain safety within his broader social networks. This mandate is written into his DNA. And modern attachment research now confirms this.

John Gottman's research with couples, for example, shows that partners who down-regulate their emotions during conflict may appear to be unemotional, but inside they still exhibit all the signs of intense physiological arousal. In other words, though one partner may appear stoic in an argument, he[27] is often intensely agitated inside. The partner in question may appear indifferent or withdrawn, but his heart rate is elevated, his blood pressure is heightened, and his galvanic skin response (a measure of how stressed somebody is) is off the charts.

All of these physiological signs show that the prefrontal cortex (PFC) is working overtime to regulate the brain's emotional centers. The down-regulation of the attachment system is not occurring for free, and energy spent there isn't available for other purposes.

Let's return to our fictitious 5th grader. Even though he may appear disinterested, we cannot sidestep two realities:

1. He is wired for attachment.

2. If his attachments are strained, he will be spending energy managing the associated feelings, regardless of how it looks on the outside.

Behind our fictitious 5th grader's disconnected gaze, he is likely relatively consumed by an elevated state of physiological arousal. *Will I make another friend? Is it even worth trying? Forget it; he'd just leave anyway.* 'Running' his prefrontal cortex to manage this sense of persistent anxiety is consuming his energy.

The teacher asks our fictitious 5th grader, "Are you listening?"

He probably isn't. And he might not be able to.

Allan Schore's work on brain physiology and affect regulation demonstrates that people in a heightened state of emotional arousal are actually not able to listen to what somebody is saying [43, 44]. In other words, when we are emotional, we cannot even hear! Is our fictitious 5th grader hearing 90% of what Mrs. Rodriguez is saying? Or 50%? Or, on a particularly bad day, is he hearing anything at all that Mrs. Rodriguez is saying?

To make matters worse, our fictitious 5th grader gets sent by Mrs. Rodriguez to the Principal for 'staring out the window' and having a 'bad attitude' when spoken to about this recurring problem.

Our fictitious 5th grader is also very perceptive. He feels like saying that Mrs. Rodriguez is a local teacher who has never moved in her life, and has no idea what he's going through in this school with 'unmanaged mobility.'

But he's a born diplomat. To himself, he wishes his school had a comprehensive program for addressing the challenges of mobility across cultures.

To the outside world, though, he simply keeps his mouth shut.

---

27   *Research also shows that the withdrawing partner is more often male.*

A Summary Of A Large Portion Of The Psychological Literature

In a sweeping review of large swathes of the psychological literature entitled *Polarities of Experience,* Sydney Blatt [45] distills the research in personality psychology down to one core idea. Every model of human personality and functioning can be traced back to the *interdependent* need to develop both self-definition and relatedness. In other words, the ability to ultimately shape one's identity as an individual is dependent on how comfortable and secure one is in depending on others.

But this psychological 'truth' operates in exactly the opposite direction too – the ability to truly rely upon others is dependent upon how well one has shaped and defined one's own self.

In other words, at the foundation of the entire field of psychology, we seem to encounter a paradox, a circular line of thinking reminiscent of the Chinese yin-yang symbol depicted earlier. A true 'self' depends on the ability to deeply relate to others. But the ability to deeply relate to others depends upon feeling as if one has an authentic sense of self.

Extended to this chapter's main argument, the conclusion could read like this: *the ability to really author a life story depends upon the ability to truly relate one's life story to another. But the ability to truly relate one's life story to another depends upon how successful one is feeling as an author of one's story.*

If the line of argument above is sound, then this chapter's closing is clinched. International schools with a significant degree of mobility cannot in good conscience shirk their portion of responsibility for shaping the kinds of working attachment models students develop 'on their watch.' Without knowing it, students are wondering:

- what is happening to me?
- does anybody see it?
- does anybody care?

What is your school saying to them?

RECOMMENDATIONS THAT LOGICALLY FLOW FROM THE LIFE STORY ANALOGY

The life story metaphor is not only accessible and readily graspable, it also readily produces the additional vocabulary we need for the concepts addressed in the text – *stories* need to be *written* by *authors,* but to have any real *meaning* and *survive,* a story also has to be *read* by an *audience* that *understands* and *validates* it.

Proceeding further, 'life story language' begins to generate many of the very tools needed for addressing the challenge of mobility across cultures in our schools.

> *Stories need to be written by authors, but to have any real meaning and survive, a story also has to be read by an audience that understands and validates it.*

Moving erases large parts of a person's story, because it *erases the audience* who used to read and understand the person's tale. Movers don't automatically know this, so they need *help understanding where their story went*, and why that hurts so much. Movers aren't aware they don't have to go anywhere to be a mover. Even without moving, you can have vital members of your readership move away, leaving your story with the feeling of *no longer being read. Authors* who have undergone such shifts will need a chance and the space to begin *rewriting their stories* when they're ready. But because a mover lost his or her former audience, the supporting community must also see to it that *audiences get reinvented* so the person's *revised story* can be *read anew*.

The interventions that flow from the 'life story' analogy enjoy what psychologists refer to as 'face validity.' They simply make sense. Just as with the attachment paradigm, audiences exposed to the life story paradigm generally don't require convincing or elaborate theoretical arguments. They recognize the paradigm from their own experience. And two key types of interventions logically flow from this life story analogy:

- People whose stories have been disrupted by transitions will benefit from opportunities and assistance in resuming the writing process.

- People whose stories have been disrupted by transitions have also lost the audiences they once had for their stories, meaning they will benefit from opportunities and assistance in recreating and discovering new audiences.

Together with the attachment paradigm described earlier, the dual focus of story resumption and audience recreation form the theoretical backbone on which the programs and interventions in this book are built.

The task for any transitions program in any international school, metaphorically speaking at least, is to help people find ways to pick up the pen and keep writing, and then to create audiences where the story being written can be shared. One of the greatest gifts that can be offered to any member of an international school community – whether they be arriving, leaving, or staying – is an audience for their unfolding stories. One of the greatest gifts an international school can offer its community is a framework and a context in which that growth can occur. This means developing a comprehensive transitions program that can employ the right vocabulary and tools to create the validation people need to feel if their life stories are being seen.

A MORAL IMPERATIVE

Aristotle is credited with first pointing out nature's distaste for empty space. He believed nature would not tolerate a vacuum, and would rush to fill it before it could arise.

Life stories would seem to be no exception: when they feel emptied, our natural human tendency is to do something – anything – to rectify the situation. Without the benefits of a comprehensive transitions program, more and more protagonists in our mobile communities – including the arrivers *and* the stayers *and* the leavers – would feel as if their challenges were happening in a vacuum, without anyone watching, without anyone validating their experience as it unfolded, leaving them feeling like they're gasping for air.

The strongest will grow through these most severe of relocation circumstances. The question, however, is whether we want to contribute to vacuum-like school climates which support 'survival of the fittest' mentalities. The question is whether we think our schools can 'afford' the relocation casualties that occur when such an approach is put into or – perhaps better said – left in practice. The question is whether we consider it wise at our respective schools not to maximize the vast opportunities for (inter)personal growth, social-emotional development, and cross-cultural literacy that issues of mobility across cultures afford for every member of a school community.

I would argue that schools with any degree of turnover have a moral obligation to do better than 'survival of the fittest' policies or practices surrounding mobility across cultures. Schools can, and should, provide the safe havens where students can acquire the abilities to cope with a world where 'survival of the fittest' is the norm. But it would seem to me schools should also be places where that standard gets raised, where people aim for a 'thriving of all students' approach, where a commitment is nurtured in each student to make the world a better place, each in his or her own way, inch by inch, contribution by contribution, drop by drop. Instilling that commitment starts with a community caring for itself. If we disregard the importance of this care, we tacitly model for our students that some people miss the boat. This is a toxic message anybody who considers themselves an educator would not wish to send.

This book is grounded on care for the people doing the learning, parenting, and teaching. When they feel they are allowed to develop a safe attachment to the school to which they belong, they are enabled to grow towards their best. Then, and only then, can schools truly get on with the rest of their core business – teaching well, so that students have a chance of learning well.

FINDING A SAFE HARBOR

Building Programs to Match the Challenge

PART II

Chapter 3

LAND HO!
DESIGN CONSIDERATIONS
FOR HARBORS

"Ultimately it is the sense of being understood in our experience that is most healing."
– Viktor Frankl

If you wanted to build your dream home, what would you do first? Suppose I had the resources to buy you land anywhere you wanted in the world, and all the building materials you could wish for. You'll have to arrange your own personnel, but I'll give you a generous budget to fund the process. All you have to decide is where to begin. And what you will do after that. And so forth.

In other words, you're in charge of the process.

While each of us would approach this task in different ways, the most successful building projects would start with a brainstorming process that enables people to discover what they might want in their home, followed by a planning process. Wishes are important. So are practical plans. All of this would happen before anyone picked up hammer and nail.

In a similar fashion, any approach to dealing with transitions in international schools should appropriately start with what it is that you *want* to achieve, followed by a practical *plan* for how you want to go about achieving it.

IDENTIFYING WHAT YOU WANT TO ACHIEVE IN ADDRESSING TRANSITIONS

The least common denominator in any transitions program at any school probably includes the goal of *helping people more successfully navigate the challenges of moving across cultures.*

This very general departure point can be nuanced once you have formed a team to address the challenges specific to your school, most notably in the form of the mission statement your team creates for itself. I will have more to say about teams and their missions in the next chapter, but I mention mission statements here because an identification of what one wants precedes the devising of any plan of how to get it. Development does not often occur in straight lines, and a general understanding of needs that will come later has implications for practices which need addressing earlier.

Though it might sound like a confusing proposition, when it comes to transitions we need a plan for how to make a plan. Knowing some best practices for planning the building of your school's program may shape what you end up wanting in the first place.

Let me explain.

IDENTIFYING WHAT YOU NEED TO PLAN FOR IN ADDRESSING TRANSITIONS

Even after decades of working on and thinking about transitions, I struggle to devise a comprehensive and efficient picture of what a successful Transitions Team is trying to accomplish. Many different pictorial metaphors exist to convey something about how the process works. In my opinion, no single image fully captures all the complexities.

This chapter is structured as a tour of the major images I have encountered, used, and developed in my work with Transitions Teams. All of these images attempt to succinctly capture what a successful comprehensive transitions program must entail – and all of these images, on their own, fall short. Taken as a whole, however, the images begin to convey many of the main considerations involved in building a successful transition program.[28]

My purpose in presenting these images to you at this point is to provide the conceptual tools you will need to fully grasp the nature of the challenge facing an international school with any degree of turnover. I consider these images the 'tools of the trade.' They provide you with a framework for

---

28 *If you should ever devise a single two-dimensional image that does capture all of the core variables involved in transitions work, I would be grateful if you would share it with me.*

visualizing what is happening and what your school is doing – and not yet doing – about it.

IMAGE #1
THE STOOL: HELPS VISUALIZE THE NEEDS OF EACH POPULATION

The most fundamental of images, first provided by Barbara Schaetti in the trainings she originally did for international schools in the 1990s, is 'the stool.' Each of the three legs of Schaetti's stool represents the needs of the three fundamental populations within the school, namely students, parents, and staff. Please note that 'staff' includes administrators, as administrators in the face of mobility experience the same human strains the other populations endure. A successful transitions program has to address the needs of each of these populations. A balanced, three-legged approach constitutes a successful transitions program, which arguably is the seat from which any school can pursue its main goal, namely the education of its students.

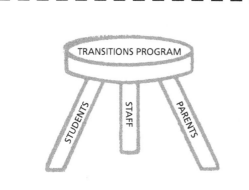

FIGURE 3.1 The stool: three essential legs of any comprehensive transitions program

Parity

If we unpack this image, a number of other important things become clear. Firstly, each of the legs must be proportional. A successful transitions program cannot occur if one of the legs grows ahead of the others – or if one lags behind. Such imbalances can occur, for example, if a school has an excellent program for students but neglects the needs of parents or staff. The struggles of parents or staff would likely have a negative impact on whatever positive things were happening for students. The legs of the stool would be disproportionate, making the stool unbalanced and wobbly. The adage "you can only really do something for another person that you're capable of doing for yourself" proves true in transitions work too. If the parents and/ or staff who are guiding the transitions work for students are not themselves feeling secure and well adjusted, they will be unlikely to guide anyone in the provision of services that are authentic and truly meaningful for the recipients. It is worth noting – however uncomfortable this might make us as adults – that adults can struggle with resentment towards youngsters when the youngsters' transitions-related needs are being well serviced while their own needs are not. A neglected, shortened leg of the stool breeds resentment towards its longer, better-served counterparts. Extending the metaphor to its dramatic conclusion, the whole stool will ultimately fall down in the direction of the shortest member. 'Parity' emphasizes the importance of keeping the legs equal.

This graphic is not only true to the importance of balance amongst the programs a transitions program sponsors, it is also true to the importance of balance in the composition of the team. Successful teams maintain proportional representation of parents, students, and staff. Administrators are an essential part of the staff leg. And the essential importance of having and maintaining student representation on the team cannot be overstated. If you haven't read my 'Message in a Bottle' addressed to students on page 236, please consider doing so now.

Crosshatching

Over the course of my experience with transitions, a logical addition to Schaetti's stool began to form in my imagination and it looked like the figure to the right.

In the same way a stool with stabilizing bars, known to carpenters as 'spindles,' would be far more capable of bearing a significant load than a stool lacking spindles, so too would a transitions program with spindles be far more effective and solid than a transitions program without them. What does this mean in a concrete sense?

FIGURE 3.2 The 'crosshatched' stool

I devised the term 'cross-hatching' to describe the provision of transitions-related services by one population for a population other than their own.

Parents are in the ideal position to provide services to parents, just as staff is the logic primary provider of services for other staff, and just as students are best positioned to provide services to their fellow students. But what happens when one population provides services to another population? In certain cases, we expect nothing less, just as it is the job of staff and teachers to provide services for students and for parents. But other forms of cross-hatching provide novel sources and directions for services that add a tremendous amount of stability to the stool, while being extremely rewarding for all parties involved.

For example, what effect does cross-hatching have on parents and teachers alike? More specifically, what happens when parents provide services to the teaching staff? Later in the text we will explore examples of these kinds of activities, such as ASH's 'Cultural Awareness' program described in *Chapter 6: An Exemplar Harbor*, where parents from various cultural areas of the world are placed in a position of training the teaching staff to understand the educational process, and everyone's role in education, from that culture's point of view. To see a largely Western group of teachers enjoying Korean food while being taught by a group of South Korean mothers about the way their children view their teachers, and the way the parents conceive of an appropriate parent-teacher relationship, is extremely gratifying for all parties.

Such cross-hatching moments level the playing field, once again demonstrating the democratic principle involved in transitions, namely that it affects all of us not by virtue of our age or position, but by virtue of our being equal stakeholders in the human condition. It is for this reason a kindergartner can address the board of directors with authority, explaining to them in a presentation on 'What Moving Does to Us' exactly what it feels like to move to a new school, or to not understand certain cultural rules, or to have a best friend move away – again. Such cross-hatching initiatives unveil one group's lived experience before the eyes of another group, fostering a culture of mutual understanding and a collective sense of striving to thrive in the face of transition together.

Returning to the life stories metaphor, such cross-hatching experiences create unexpected 'readers' of stories that would otherwise remain invisible. When important stories get 'seen,' validation occurs, an experience gratifying to the teller and eye-opening to the reader.

Thus begins our graphical understanding of the issues involved in mobility across cultures. The stool helps distinguish the separate 'identities' and needs of the three target populations. It also effectively implies why these three populations' needs are interdependent, and how they must be addressed proportionally. Lastly, the image of the stool shows what can be done to create further program stability, via the development of cross-hatching initiatives that allow one population to help another.

But population is only one important dimension in grasping what makes a comprehensive transitions program. A dimension I will call one's 'emotional vector' is equally fundamental, and this dimension is best captured by the umbrella.

IMAGE #2
THE UMBRELLA: SHOWS THE VECTOR WHERE PEOPLE'S HEARTS ARE 'POINTING'

The umbrella allows us to split the needs of each population out across subpopulations, so it becomes clearer what a group's needs are, depending on their future plans. In physics, a vector is something with both size and direction, such as the wind (it's not just blowing 25 kilometers per hour, but rather 25 kilometers per hour in a southwesterly direction). For our purposes, an 'emotional vector' describes where a person's energies are flowing. Are they primarily investing in arriving, or in staying, or in leaving?

Somebody with an 'arriving vector' is generally hoping to make new friends, get involved in activities, and build a new life (unless they are still heavily invested in their last place, and refusing to relinquish their old emotional investments, which would mean they're still highly invested in a 'staying vector' aimed at their *last* place). Somebody with a 'staying vector' aimed at their *current* place has successfully navigated the arrival process, and is now committed to building a life in the here and now. And lastly, somebody with a 'leaving vector' is in the process of extracting emotional energies that were invested in the current place, so these energies can be packaged and shipped to the next destination, in the same way as books, china, and furniture also need to be boxed and sealed. David Pollock used to say, "You need six months to pack up your heart before leaving, and six months to unpack it after you arrive" [46]. He was right.

Once again, the following graphic combines administrators into the 'staff' column. When the three resulting populations are plotted against these three emotional vectors, a 3x3 grid emerges which I have referred to as the 'umbrella':

Arguably, the comprehensive transitions program should address the needs in each of the 9 sectors, and plotting what one's school does in each of these sectors can be a good first step towards auditing one's current services and seeing where any obvious gaps exist. As you map what programs your

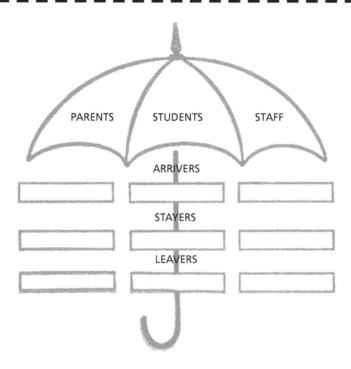

FIGURE 3.3 The 3x3 umbrella: a simple means to view a complex program

school has in each of these various areas, the squares that are 'thin' become immediately apparent.

The Leak In The Umbrella

As useful as this graphic is for further differentiating the needs of various subpopulations in a target school, it still has a serious shortcoming: *it is static.* This is because a person's emotional vector is not fixed. It shifts over time. The new parent who starts the school year with an arriving vector begins to shift – hopefully – to a staying vector. The student who has been a backbone to so many student programs – a highly invested 'staying vector' – finds he or she is leaving, and has to painfully begin shifting towards a leaving vector. The shortcoming of the umbrella graphic, in other words, resides in the fact that there is no interaction with the annual calendar over time. What is needed is a three dimensional graphic, where the third dimension would depict something of where one is on the annual school calendar, whether that be in the beginning of the year, the middle, or the end.

> *By paying attention to what happens to different people's emotional vectors over time, we arrive at a powerful interface for conceptualizing the issues related to transitions.*

Why is this an important detail? For the reason that real processes at real schools often do not fit nicely into clean boxes. While the majority of students might be arriving at the beginning of the year, students can end up arriving much later in the year, at a time when only a minority of students would have an 'arriving vector.' These late arrivals must take the plunge into a sea of 'staying' and even 'leaving' vectors. What does this do to a student? In life story terms, it is tantamount to making one's 'arrival story' invisible – everyone is so busy reading and participating in 'staying' or 'leaving' stories that this poor student's tale of arrival doesn't get read, because nobody is looking for it.

Or what about the mother who has to leave at the beginning of the school year, when she is surrounded by people showing up on the scene with 'arriving vectors,' and everyone in the community is tuned in to that kind of 'arrival story.' What does this do to a parent? As with the student, this parent is likely to feel her 'departure' story is invisible, that people are looking for other kinds of stories, that she's got the wrong kind of story at the wrong time of year.

That doesn't feel good. And it doesn't feel good because it isn't.

IMAGE #3:
THE 3x3x3 CUBE

What happens when we do cultivate an appreciation for how the 3x3 grid of the umbrella interacts with the real calendar, as that calendar turns slowly in the background? By paying attention to what happens to different people's emotional vectors over time, we arrive at a powerful interface for conceptualizing the issues related to transitions.

It is necessary to move to three dimensions like this to truly start to split out the shades of grey that exist in any school population at any time of year. The general progression in any school population is from the top front edge of the cube, down through the far bottom edge of the cube. In other words, a transitions program generally needs to focus upon and follow the shaded

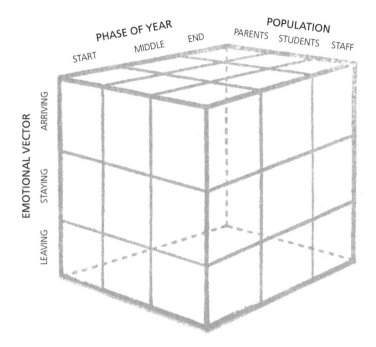

FIGURE 3.4 The 3x3x3 cube: a comprehensive way to conceptualize mobility

row of three cubes down and into the distance over the course of any given school year, as depicted in Figure 3.5 on the following page.

The advantage of the cube depiction is that it calls the viewer's attention to other segments which might otherwise be overlooked. Said differently, it calls attention to those people whose experience does not fit into one of the more traditional types of experiences depicted by the shaded rows. For example, what about the student who is arriving at the end of the year? Or the mother who is leaving at the start of the school year? These types of experiences are 'off the beaten path' of what a transitions program is normally trying to cope with, but to be a comprehensive program, one could argue that no person's story should be overlooked, and that everyone's story has a chance of being addressed. To fail to do so would be to reinforce the invisibility of someone's experience, which is exactly what makes something that is already painful hurt even more.

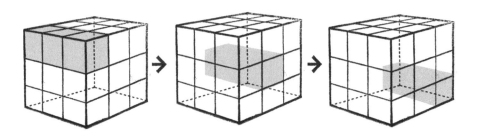

FIGURE 3.5 The general progression of the majority of the population through the 3x3x3 cube over the course of the school year

Unfortunately, thinking in a three-dimensional space is cumbersome. While the above graphics begins to do more justice to the complexities of what the different populations are in any given school community at any given time of year, the resulting 27 sectors are so detailed that the model is difficult to use.

Isn't there an easier way? Fortunately, I believe the 'fountain' image provides an elegant solution to conceptualizing the comprehensive program in a way that makes intuitive sense. The fountain has the added advantage of making strong suggestions about the best way to activate a mobile community to combine forces in building and maintaining the kind of transitions program that will be safe for all, and stand the test of time.

IMAGE #4
THE FOUNTAIN: A VISUAL DEPICTION OF A COMPREHENSIVE TRANSITIONS PROGRAM

You've all seen a tiered fountain before. A three-tiered fountain looks like the image below: it draws up water from the pool at its base, and as the water flows into the top tier, it spills downwards, into the middle tier, and down to the bottom tier. When it flows out of the bottom tier, the water returns to the larger pool, and the cycle begins anew.

The three-tiered fountain provides a powerful visual metaphor, which combines many of the earlier visual metaphors into a single idea.

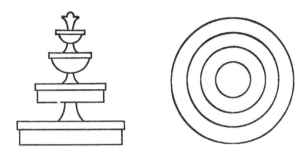

FIGURE 3.6 The fountain viewed in profile and from above

As suggested earlier, people first come into the school community as 'arrivers,' so let's label the top tier as the 'arriving' tier of the fountain. The water gradually flows downwards into the 'staying' tier, and eventually into the 'leaving' tier. When the water flows out of the 'leaving' tier, it returns to the source pool, and the cycle starts over.

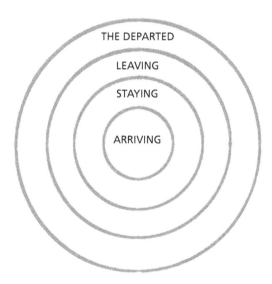

FIGURE 3.7 Progression through the fountain over time, when viewed from above

If we add the dimension of time to this overhead view, the visual metaphor begins to become even more complete and powerful.

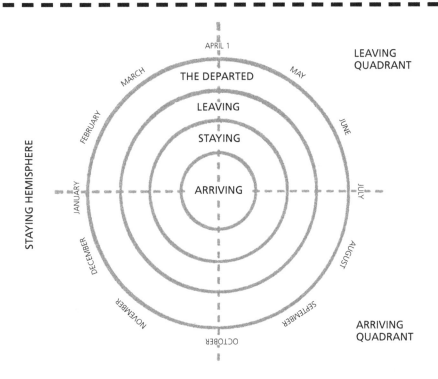

FIGURE 3.8 The fountain with the annual calendar

A number of important things are happening in this overview of the fountain. (Please note – these elements have been framed from the perspective of a Northern Hemisphere calendar. They would need to be adjusted accordingly for academic calendars that deviate from an August to June cycle.)

The key elements depicted in this graphic are:

- Time – The calendar has been added around the perimeter of the fountain, starting in April and progressing through all twelve months.
- April – In keeping with the First Law of Transitions, which states "you have to say a clear 'goodbye' in order to say a clear 'hello'," the start of the emotional calendar is appropriately pegged not on January 1st, but on April 1st. It is at this time goodbye-related activities throughout the school community should be getting into top gear.

- Quadrants – Certain portions of the year are more focused on certain processes. For example, from the months of July through the month of September, international school communities are focused upon things related to arriving. This quarter of the year is therefore called the 'Arriving Quadrant.' April through June are naturally focused upon departure, which is why these months are labeled the 'Leaving Quadrant.' And the remaining half year, from October through the month of March, entails two quadrants together, where school populations are generally stabilizing and consolidating. Hence the term 'Staying Hemisphere.'

Fountain 'Congruence' And 'Incongruence'

That certain portions of the year lend themselves more naturally to certain portions of the transitions cycle brings with it the inverse of that idea – that certain portions of the year do not lend themselves naturally to certain portions of the transitions cycle.

Figure 3.9 on the following page is a variation on the annual calendar fountain, introduced in Figure 3.8. The dotted areas in Figure 3.9 depict areas of what I will call 'congruence.' Students, parents, and staff who arrive, stay, and leave in these dotted zones are arriving, staying, and leaving when it feels most natural to do so.

This version of the fountain with congruence zones makes the following fundamental points. Again, the perspective used is from the academic calendar typical in the Northern Hemisphere, where the school year begins in August:

- Relatively speaking, it will feel more natural to move into a new community (for the one doing the moving) and to receive a new member of the community (for those who have stayed) if this process happens during the 'Arriving Quadrant.' Inversely, it will be more difficult for all parties involved if the arrival occurs at a different time in the year.

- Relatively speaking, it will feel more natural to leave a community (for the one doing the moving) or to be left (for the one who is being left behind) if this process happens during the 'Leaving Quadrant.' Inversely, it will be more difficult for all parties involved if the departure occurs at a different time in the year.

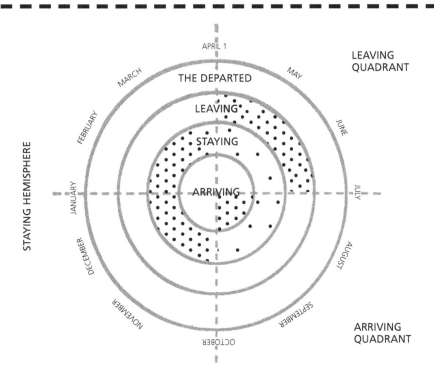

FIGURE 3.9 The fountain showing areas of congruence

It makes one additional point regarding the stayers, which is worth noting:

■ While it is certainly natural to 'Stay' throughout the year (we should hope so, otherwise all our schools are in trouble), the density of the dots in the above graphic is intended to convey the fact that life for the stayers can feel fairly tenuous in the months between April and October. Stayers are the backbone of any transitions program, and potentially having to repeatedly say goodbye to dear people during the Leaving Quadrant, while subsequently having to welcome new people during the Arriving Quadrant, takes its emotional toll on the Stayers. This is why the density of the dots is thinner for the Stayers throughout this phase of the year. Just as somebody might struggle for breath during a trek through the mountains, the air gets thinner for the Stayers throughout this period of time. It is natural for them to have stayed. But having said goodbye to many potentially important people in the Leaving Quadrant, and having welcomed many new people in the Arriving Quadrant, their emotional reserves may feel thinner during this portion of the year – and they may not even know why.

Turning The Fountain On – At The Right Time

When you combine all of the information above into a working fountain, where we turn the fountain 'on' to see what happens, you can see all the information coming together, as shown in Figure 3.10. Let's say a new student arrives in the month of August, in time for the new student orientation. She stays at school for three enriching and enjoyable years, and then finds out in January she will be leaving at the end of her third year. There is time for her to participate in all of the goodbye rituals the school has planned, and after three years she flows out of the fountain and back into the wider pool, producing a total three-year trajectory as shown in Figure 3.10 below.

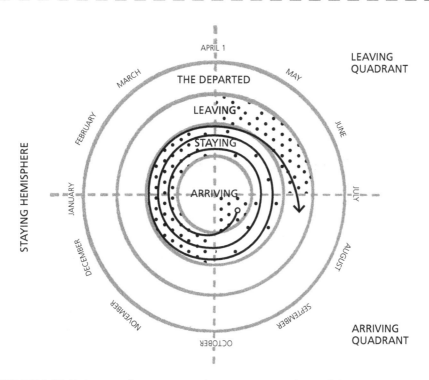

FIGURE 3.10 Trajectory of someone moving at congruent times of the year

Figure 3.10 shows a typical trajectory for a student at an international school. More importantly, it is the typical trajectory for anyone at an international school, be it student, parent, staff member, or administrator. On the other hand, people are adversely affected by not arriving at a new place or leaving an old one at a time that feels natural.

Turning The Fountain On – At The Wrong Time

This means any trajectory that deviates from the one above is exactly that – deviant. It will feel less natural for the individual involved. Whether the person is a student, parent, or staff member doesn't matter.

Let's look in Figure 3.11 at an example of somebody who arrives at the start of February, and also stays for three full calendar years. He finds out at the beginning of his third academic year that he will be leaving, and his last day of school is December 1.

Several things stand out for this person's experience. Again, it doesn't matter whether we are describing a student, parent, or staff member. In all cases, the following challenges would be present:

- He arrives 'out of phase' with his surroundings, disembarking during the Staying Hemisphere. His surroundings are not tuned to his experience. He is looking for an environment that will welcome him, but these wider systems are naturally 'shut down' and dormant during this portion of the year. People have made their friends for the year, activities and organizations have their membership set, and students know their teachers and vice versa. A positive arrival and integration into the school – already a challenging prospect – will be even more challenging.

- He learns he will be leaving (where the line leaves the second tier of the fountain, entering the third tier) at a time which is 'out of phase' with his surroundings – September. People have just said their good-byes during the Leaving Quadrant, and are now focused upon those flowing *into* the fountain – not those getting ready to flow out of it.

- He leaves at a time that is also out of phase with his surroundings. The goodbye traditions and systems the school might have in place during the Leaving Quadrant are not primed and running in December. People may even be becoming preoccupied with the upcoming holidays, exams, and trips home. To leave now is to leave at a time when

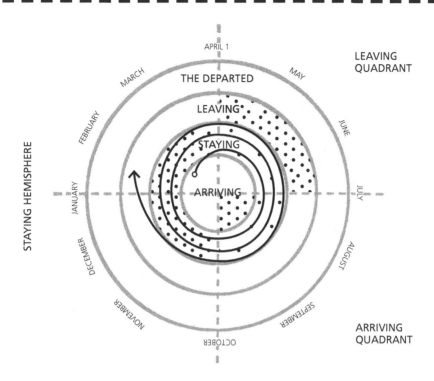

FIGURE 3.11 Trajectory of someone moving at incongruent times of the year

nobody is focused on leaving. Nobody is reading his story because nobody is looking for it.

- He flows into the wider pool at risk of violating the First Law of Transitions, "You need to say a clear goodbye in order to say a clear hello." His ability to move forward well in his new place may well be compromised, which is likely to make an already difficult process even more challenging.

What If The Fountain 'Goes On' At The 'Wrong' Time?

A word of encouragement is probably appropriate here, as there are people who have to move at less than ideal times, and for reasons that feel beyond their control. Of course my purpose in describing the dynamics above is to encourage people to move at times that put them 'in sync' with wider school processes, and to encourage their sponsoring organizations and companies to facilitate this optimal kind of timing.

But if that is not possible, wouldn't you rather be forewarned? "Forewarned is forearmed," they say, and being aware of the following factors can ease the challenge of moving at a time that puts you out of sync:

- Plan your own positive leaving rituals with the people who matter to you. Parties, dinners, get-togethers, and (for your kids) sleepovers can all be ways to mark the beginning of a positive ending.

- Ask the school for assistance in activating the school's goodbye rituals for you, if the school has these rituals. Or try collaborating with your son or daughter's mentor to provide food and an activity for the whole mentor group, so everyone can say goodbye.

- For a departing staff member, organize a goodbye gathering for the entire department or grade-level-team.

- Create a soft landing for yourself and your family at the future destination. Ask the admissions office at the new school to assist you in arranging a student ambassador, and/ or a colleague, and/ or a fellow parent you or your child can be in touch with, get to know, and ask questions of before getting close to packing your moving boxes. See if a physical visit to the new site before 'really' leaving can be arranged.

- Consider *asking* that a fellow student, colleague, or fellow parent take you 'under their wing' when you get there. It is amazing how helpful people can be – and want to be – when they are asked in an authentic, straightforward way.

Wrapping Up: A Sculpture Garden Of Stools, Umbrellas, Cubes, And Fountains

Now that I have introduced you to these four visual metaphors, let me situate them in your imagination, as though you were walking through a sculpture garden on a cloudy day.

You pause before a bronze three-legged stool, with supporting spindles 'crosshatched' between the legs, and you're reminded of the importance of a transitions program that attends to all three populations in a proportionate fashion, students, parents, and staff. (You also remember that staff includes everyone who works at a school, including administrators and support staff, not only the teachers.) The legs are balanced in length and girth, and the stool radiates stability. This same stability is reflected in the Transitions Team, you've heard, where there is proportional representation of parents, staff, administrators, and students on the Team.

As you walk on, the clouds begin to groan and lose their restraint, and drizzle descends earthward. You pop open your umbrella, and you're reminded of how the umbrella shelters the three different populations depicted by the stool. The rain increases, pelting the umbrella's cone, and it creates a cylinder of dryness around you, making you consider how the umbrella shelters your head, your body, and your legs, just as it shelters the various populations along three phases of time, from arriving, to staying, to leaving. You notice a sizeable leak in your umbrella, though, and as you peer through the gaping hole at its edge, you see a cubical structure in the distance. You walk towards it.

You stop before a massive clear cube, composed of 27 smaller cubes lined up in a 3x3x3 fashion, and you think about the cube metaphor. Not only are there three populations (students, parents, and staff), and not only three vectors in how people view their relationship towards times (as an arriver, stayer, or leaver), there are also three phases in the academic year (beginning, middle, end). You try to picture what I was saying about the cube, and what that could mean for the practice at your school. However, the consequences are so complex you begin to develop a headache. You shake your head and resolve to move away from the cube.

Without thinking about it, your feet gravitate towards the sound of running water. You are reminded of the opening chapter of *Moby Dick,* where Melville writes:

> "*Take almost any path you please, and ten to one it carries you down in a dale, and leaves you there by a pool in the stream. There is magic in it. Let the most absent-minded of men be plunged in his deepest reveries – stand that man on his legs, set his feet a-going, and he will infallibly lead you to water, if water there be in all that region.*"

Your feet lead you infallibly to water, to running water cascading downwards from a massive three-tiered fountain at what appears to be the center of the sculpture garden. The water explains it all. Without having to think about things in the complex and rigid form of the cube, the three-tiered fountain conveys the essence of transitions in a simple, elegant fashion.

Moving pumps us to the top, and arriving can be so exhilarating, so adventurous. The water flows down into the middle layer, a layer that is neither arriving nor leaving, a layer that can feel stable and grounded but also staid and static. From this middle existence, the water pours into the leaving layer, lowest of the three tiers, the largest and heaviest layer of the fountain. This tier is full of tears, you think to yourself, as the water flows out of this layer too, down into the basin, the inevitable gathering point from which no molecule of water escapes.

And the cycle begins again.

Water explains everything, you muse to yourself. And, as if prompted by your aquatic meditation, the clouds grumble and drop the water they'd been carrying in a dramatic deluge. Drops as big as marbles splatter all around you and rattle your umbrella, making it buckle under the weight. Squinting, you look out at the fountain and see each downward drop double into a splash that ricochets upwards. You manage to stay dry under your umbrella – just barely – but you wish to your warm self that you had an umbrella big enough to protect the whole fountain.

You don't. But now that you have some tools for thinking about what's happening, maybe you can build one?

Chapter 4

BUILDING THE HARBOR – CREATING AND SUCCESSFULLY LAUNCHING A TEAM

*"We create the story, and at the same time
the story is what sets us in motion."*
  – Haruki Murakami, *1Q84*

The key to a successful Transitions Program at any international school is the development and maintenance of a successful team. This chapter focuses on how to develop such a team. *Chapter 5: Sustaining the Harbor* focuses on how to maintain the team once it is developed.

Have you ever created a website, blog or a Facebook page? Have you ever put any thought into posting something on the Internet, if only a curriculum vitae or a LinkedIn page? Then you know how good it feels to get the information 'out there' (hopefully good). You may also know how it feels after some time has passed, and you know the information needs updating – or is out of date (probably bad). Teams and programs work the same way: it feels great to get them started, but they also require maintenance to produce lasting improvements over time.

Let me repeat – *the only way to address challenges as complex as those described in the opening chapters of this book is by creating and maintaining an effective team to address the challenge.* But the challenges of creation are different than those of maintenance. This chapter focuses on the first challenge.

THE CHALLENGE OF CREATION

In the course of my work with transitions teams at international schools around the world, I have distilled a number of golden rules that describe the best practices of teams that lead to success. While there is no recipe for success for all schools, there are some key ingredients I would argue transect all types of schools and situations, the observation of which will improve the effectiveness of the Transitions Team – both in terms of the programs the Team creates as well as the effectiveness of those programs. I have distilled the list into the 'Top Ten Tips To Tackle.'

The Top Ten Tips To Tackle: From Preparation To Launch

1. See the process as the product
2. Form a core group
3. Get full administrative and board support
4. Establish a budget and find funding
5. Create a representative team
6. Arrange training
7. Make your start clear
8. Foster team identity
9. Establish evaluation measures and procedures
10. Plan follow-up

To a degree, the Top Ten list describes things I would recommend occur in chronological order. There is a logical flow to this list. You can also consider this logical flow to be composed of the following phases:

- preparatory phase
- pre-launch phase
- launch phase
- sustaining phase

This chapter deals with the first three phases. *Chapter 5: Sustaining the Harbor* focuses exclusively on the fourth phase, as we look at sustaining the

Transitions Team and Program over the medium range.

To begin with, let's turn to the preparatory phase for launching a Transitions Team and a Transitions Program at an international school.

THE PREPARATORY PHASE

Tip #1: See the process as the product

Were you ever told as a child during a long trip to "just try to enjoy the journey"? As a parent yourself, have you been asked, "Mom, are we there yet?" Have you ever said "just try to enjoy the trip" to your own child, in the hopes the constant questions or complaining would stop, that they would look out the window, be quiet, and let you try to enjoy the start to the vacation too?

Working with Transitions Teams means working with people. If, in your enthusiasm, you focus exclusively on all the programs you'd like to establish, you risk losing sight of the people involved, and therefore of the goal itself. Transitions Programs are run *by* people *for* people. To be meaningful – and therefore effective –such programs must emerge from processes infused with genuine meaning and commitment. You get genuine meaning and commitment by attending to the process. This means staying in the moment, and making sure you care about each step of the journey. "The journey of a thousand miles," says a Chinese proverb, "begins with a single step." A meaningful journey of a thousand miles, I would counter, consists of millions of meaningful steps.

Yes, it boils down to *care*.

If care is your starting point, your program cannot go wrong. And this is the essence of *intrinsic* enjoyment – as opposed to working at a program like this for any of a number of extrinsic reasons that people might pursue.

I am not guaranteeing your program will succeed if you and your team members simply care. More is required. But care is an essential departure point, fundamentally necessary for any program to move forward with a chance of doing well.

When care infuses and informs each step of your journey towards building a successful transitions program, you remain mindful of each step your team takes. You pay attention to the quality of the wood selected for your vessel, to the placement of each beam, to the beveling of every edge and the gluing of successive seams. As in the world of real boat building, when care infuses every single move and consideration, the result is a boat that sails straight and strong and is also beautiful to behold. This means focusing on the process. If you assemble your transitions team from the right materials, and if genuine care is your primary adhesive, then your vessel has the right starting trajectory for a successful journey.

Tip #2: Form a core group

The challenge of transitions at international schools with a high degree of turnover is so massive that no one or two individuals can address it in a meaningful and sustainable fashion. You need a team, a fully-fledged and highly functioning team so no one or two individuals are responsible for the whole. Such a team will not appear overnight, any more than a healthy apple tree can sprout overnight. The process of developing a team must be broken into steps that are navigable and accomplishable.

One of the first steps is to find the people at your school who care about this issue and who are likely already doing things to address it in their classrooms, with their friends, or in their respective networks. These people exist. They're in your midst. The trick is to find them.

One of the main reasons school-wide transitions programs do not get off the ground is that the individuals who care about this issue do their good work in relative isolation. In the absence of coordination, people miss opportunities to share and receive inspiration and support. More importantly, these caring individuals take their programs with them when they leave. Many such inspired individuals would welcome a chance to collaborate. They just need help doing so.

You may be one of these people, and picking up this book essentially represents a concerted attempt to break your isolation and move your efforts to the next level. Congratulations! You, by definition, are part of the core group.

A large group is not needed, but four to eight inspired individuals can generate the critical mass, the varied expertise, and the network base to begin to ground the hopes and dreams of a fledgling Transitions Team in reality. I suggest setting a cap of eight people because larger groups begin to experience group dynamic processes that make decision-making and progress unwieldy. That said, if you have more than eight inspired and enthusiastic individuals, you have what the Dutch would call a 'luxury problem'! Make sure you keep interested parties aware you'll want to call on them when the actual Transitions Team gets launched.

In summary, the core group will become the nucleus around which the actual Transitions Team forms and should ideally:

- Have at least four people, but not more than eight.

- Show the early markers of good representation from the school's various populations, with members who come from the ranks of staff, parents, school leadership, and board.

- Show the early markers of good representation from the school's cultural composition, with members from the various cultures represented in the school.

While I would unequivocally argue that students are essential in the Team once it forms, I would also argue they are not needed at this early macroplanning stage. The political, financial, and logistical issues the core group needs to tackle are likely to be utterly new and overwhelming for all but the most mature and politically minded of teenagers. Having said that, if a potential future senator or member of parliament exists in your midst and is interested in transitions issues, by all means invite him or her on board. Otherwise student involvement can wait.

What are the issues the core Team needs to address? They need to get administrative support, find funding, and invite people to the formation of a definitive starting Team.

Tip #3: Get full administrative and board support

I cannot overstate this enough: only attempt to establish, build, and maintain a comprehensive transitions program if you have the full and unequivocal support of your school's leadership. I don't mean to discourage, but if you do not have this support, wait until you do.

The Philosophical Support You Need

Why? Because what a transitions program begins to question and modify tends to reside close to the core of a school's identity. For example, a transitions program might ask these philosophical questions:

- How far does our responsibility to educate and care go?

- How comfortable are we as a school talking about and helping people with their real feelings?

- How much do we really believe a person's emotional well-being is intimately tied to their performance, be it as a student, a teacher in the classroom, an administrative or support member of staff, or as a parent?

- How comfortable am I as an individual with the kinds of things the Transitions Team people are encouraging me to think about?

Many find these large questions daunting. This fact deserves respect. Nobody likes to have large questions crammed down their throat. We all like to deal with things when we feel ready for them, and not before. The early core Team described in Tip #2 can perhaps bring in the visiting speakers to foster the dialogue that begins to get people considering the issues. But the organization as a whole cannot move towards working on these issues until the people at the top are ready to allow and encourage employees and participants in the organization to embark on such a journey.

The Practical Support You Need

On a practical level, some of the things the developing Transitions Team will need in terms of administrative and/ or board support are as varied as:

- support for staff to get substitutes to participate in training and team meetings – without feeling guilty

- support for students to miss class to participate in training and team meetings – without being criticized or questioned by their teachers

- a location to meet

- basic funding for things such as refreshments, lunches during meetings, etc.

- funding for training, visiting speakers, etc.

The above list, which is very partial, includes only a few of the ways a school leadership can withhold support for, and therefore prevent the successful growth of, an emerging Transitions Team and program. You need the school's leaders to have your back. Solidly. If you don't have that yet in explicit terms, don't go on! Work on Tip #3 more first.

If you haven't by now, I strongly encourage you to read the *Messages in a Bottle* in *Appendix A* of this book that are addressed to the Head of School and to board members. (See page 226.) Doing so will help you appreciate how mobility issues might be relevant to the people who occupy these key positions.

THE PRE-LAUNCH PHASE

Tip #4: Find funding and establish a budget

To put it bluntly, your team is not real until it has financial means to support its goals and a budget line to lend it credibility. Until such time the team will have to ask – and potentially beg – for every financial crumb of support it gets.

The real task for a nascent Transitions Team is to identify what its budgetary requirements are per year, and to submit a proposal through the Team's administrative representative (see Tip #5) as part of the school's regular budget cycle. Budgetary needs can range from tea and coffee to training, from book and material purchases to gifts for departing Team members. Certain programs the Team sponsors are likely to have budgetary requirements. Consider the t-shirts you might like to order for your Student Ambassadors or Parent Welcomers, not only for theoretical reasons such as the building of team spirit, but also for practical reasons, so that these individuals are easily recognizable for new families during the school's orientation process.

> *The real task for a nascent Transitions Team is to identify what its budgetary requirements are per year, and to submit a proposal through the Team's administrative representative as part of the school's regular budget cycle.*

I am frequently asked if teams should aim primarily for a Team-wide budget covering all program-related needs, or if these budgetary costs should be housed under the programs that more directly sponsor them. (In the above example, financing for t-shirts for Student Ambassadors could be included in preexisting guidance and counseling budget, and the t-shirts for the Parent Welcomers could be budgeted for under the Admissions Office budget.)

The answer depends on the politics of your particular school.

In general I would suggest doing both – have a Team budget for activities clearly related to the Transitions Team and the Transitions Program, and gradually subsume activities that can be brought under the headings of existing programs under those programs' budgets. Doing so accomplishes two things. First of all, the costs of the improvements the Transitions Team is making to the school get sponsored quickly by those programs or departments where the improvements are being delivered. This helps the Transitions Program avoid the uncomfortable scenario where it appears to be becoming more and more costly. Improvements to a school's culture do not come for free, but it is important to avoid providing skeptics with easy ammunition for shooting down a Team's early work. Unfortunately, the emotional costs to unmanaged mobility are harder to measure than the relatively straightforward bottom-line costs. If we are not careful, people who are skeptical about the value of these kinds of programs can turn this reality to their favor.

The second reason why it is wise to gradually shift Transitions Program initiatives to existing school programs and departments is because it bolsters the durability of the initiatives. The goal is to effect a shift in perception, away from seeing these initiatives as new programs the Transitions Team spawned, towards seeing them as programs the school owns. Quickly housing Transitions Team initiatives within existing school departments moves them more quickly into the fabric of the school. This needs to be reflected right down to budgetary planning.

And the sooner the better.

Tip #5: Create a representative team

Democratic principles of representation exist because they are the fairest model of governance human beings have been able to develop.

What constitutes the sense of 'fairness' created when governing bodies are actually 'representative'? The answer boils down to one word: credibility. 'The people' generally do what their elected officials decide, because these elected officials enjoy the credibility of a widely-shared conviction, namely that nobody knows a better way of doing business than democracy. If the decisions of these elected officials stray too far from what 'the people' are willing to tolerate, they get replaced in the next round of elections.

> *The Team will need administrative support to have a chance of being successful throughout its long-term work, which is why it is of paramount importance to have a willing and motivated member of the administration sitting on the Transitions Team.*

Don't get me wrong – I am not arguing for the need for a democratically elected Transitions Team. (Though when this does occur at some school around the world, it will usher in a new time period, namely one in which that school community considers its transitions-related activities important enough to elect people to do the work, rather than having them self-appoint.) But democratic principles lead to credibility exactly because of the representation on which they are based. In simpler terms, *representation* means everyone in the wider community feels they can identify with some person or people on the Team. And this leads to two pragmatic realities. To begin with, it means the programs the Team develops, and the way these programs are run, have a greater chance of being relevant to people in the community, and therefore actually helping people. And secondly, it means everyone in the community will have the greatest possible chance that their particular transitions-related needs are addressed by the Team.

To be truly representative, Team composition must capture all of the following factors:

- staff, parents, students, and administrators

- males and females

- members of all, or most, cultural walks of life at the school

While I suggested a core-group size of between four and eight, the actual start-up Transitions Team needs to represent all of the variations of the above constituencies, while also being able to absorb departures of Team members in the future, without 'wiping out' that constituency. Ideally, a start-up Transitions Team will have:

- several students from each division, with broad cultural representation

- several parents from each division in the school, with broad cultural representation, including at least one member of the board

- several teachers from each division, representing a broad range of disciplines and cultures

- several members of support staff, representing varying cultures and tenures (long-term, new arrival) at the school

- two administrators, to avoid the relative fragility of single representation, should this administrator leave the school

Staff, Parent, Student, and Administrator Representation

Students, parents, and staff obviously need to be represented on the Transition Team. But hopefully you will also recall the metaphor of the stool from *Chapter 3: Land Ho!*, where the Administration was also emphatically described as a part of the 'staff' leg. As stated, the Team will need administrative support to have a chance of being successful throughout its long-term work, which is why it is of paramount importance to have a willing and motivated member of the administration sitting on the Transitions Team. But Administrators also have transitions-related needs that mobility across cultures creates. A 'meta-level' organization like a comprehensive Transitions Team is broad enough to provide long-term shelter to all members of the community, including these administrators. Such a Team needs the help of all constituencies in order to get started, so it can accomplish this function over time.

While I suggested students need not be involved on the early core Team, it is of paramount importance to mobilize a few visionary student leaders to participate on the Team as it is getting launched. Leaving students out of the process of forming the early Team places the entire program at risk of not being student-owned, and therefore ineffective. Students belong at the table, and – with the exception of the caveat offered in Tip #2 above – it would be better to get them there sooner rather than later.

Furthermore, it's important to have a few members of each 'type' of person on the Team, to shield and buffer the Team against departures of one of these members in the future. For example, it would be wise to have more than one teacher, and more than one administrator.

Gender

Many of the helping professions – education, nursing, psychology – continue to attract more females than males. The gender stereotypes that support notions of 'caring' as feminine and 'toughness' as masculine continue to reinforce this gender discrepancy. But vicious circles get their viciousness via imitation – if boys and girls see more females doing the caring around society, they implicitly get the message that it's normal – and okay.

If a Transitions Team and its resulting program are to be truly representative, then I would

If a Transitions Team and its resulting program are to be truly representative, then I would argue we need to be aiming for a 50/50 mixture of males and females on such a team.

argue we need to be aiming for a 50/50 mixture of males and females on such a team. Unless your community deviates significantly from the norm (in which case you should be alerting *National Geographic* or the Discovery Channel), half of the community you are serving is male, and the other half is female. This is certainly true of the student portion of the stool.

The unfortunate reality in most of the Teams in which I have been involved is that the overwhelming majority of members are female. The majority of these women tend to be highly educated and highly qualified 'trailing spouses' who gave up their careers to accommodate their partner's promotion, an international move, the raising of children, or all of the above. Not only does the predominance of women on Transitions Teams skew the representativeness of the programs the Team sponsors, but resulting programs may be more relevant or fitted to female needs. It also sends an implicit but insidious message to all involved: *caring comes more from women.* And it's not only the students who will consciously or subconsciously notice this implicit message – male staff members and parents will notice this compositional trend of the Transitions Team, and may conclude "work like that isn't for me," meaning they do not opt to get involved in volunteering for the program, which means potentially rich contributions get missed altogether.

I repeat: vicious circles get their viciousness via imitation.

And let me say a word about men, as this section is focusing closely on gender. Even if they are at work for the majority of the week, men need effective transitions programs too. Office walls do not insulate them from shifts in identity and pangs of grief. Men need effective transitions programs to understand their own emotional responses to change and – perhaps more importantly – those of their children and spouse. Men who work need effective transitions programs so they can comprehend what's happening at their own dinner tables when they get home.

If you strive to create a gender balance from the beginning of your Team's formation, you will accomplish two things. First, you will resist slipping into the vicious circle of more females and fewer males being attracted to the Team in the future. And secondly, you will be contributing to a political statement worth making around the world and in all walks of personal and professional life: men can be role-models for caring too.

Our boys and girls are watching us. When it comes to role-modeling, what we do is more important than what we say. Returning to the narrative metaphor at the core of this book, a boy's story must be 'seen' and 'read' by men (and not only by women) en route to that boy becoming fully a man, just as a girl's story must be 'seen' and 'read' by women en route to that girl becoming fully a women. It's key to get these 'readers' at the table from the outset.

Cultural Composition

The narrative metaphor continues to hold sway as we turn towards culture. How can a Transitions Team assist people with the ongoing development of their own cultural identity if the Team does not 'see' and 'read' a person's cultural background?

A story will elucidate this point. In its early years, the Transitions Team at the American School of The Hague had gotten well underway, and people throughout the community were excited by a number of programs it had sponsored and launched. A number of Team members had moved on or stepped down from the Team, necessitating the recruiting of our first batch of 'second generation' members.

Gera Klijnsma, a Dutch parent who had recently relocated back to her 'home' country from the Middle East, sat at the table and got introduced to the other members of the Team she had just joined. I remember her eyes roaming the oval table, and the disarming smile on her face. That smile made it impossible to be offended by one of the first phrases she uttered. "It's absolutely wonderful what you are all doing here," she said. "But it's also very American."

It took probably five years for the full import of Gera's first words to settle into my brain and to the bottom of my gut. She was right – as one looked around the table at the fifteen or so members of the Team at that time, every person besides Gera located their cultural sense of home primarily in the United States of America.

An impossibly complex and important question rose on the horizon, and loomed increasingly larger in the years that would follow: *how on earth is a Team that does not include a broad mix of cultural backgrounds ever going to address the cultural needs of a school community with a broad mix of cultural backgrounds?* The American School of The Hague prided itself on serving the educational and developmental needs of students from more than fifty cultural walks of life, but its Transitions Team was populated by well-intentioned people predominantly from one. Was this cultural composition 'representative'? Absolutely not! Could an unrepresentative Team claim to be fully credible and optimally effective? This was an uncomfortable question which I, for one, felt we needed to address.

It is impossible, and I would argue unnecessary, to represent the totality of cultures represented at an international school on that school's Transitions Team. The point is to beware of cultural dominance. Most schools have a dominant culture. By methodically populating the Team with adults and students from other walks of life, cultural dominance on any Team can be kept in balance, and space can be cultivated and protected for other ways of thinking, or – in terms of life stories – for other types of stories. In this way, space can be cultivated and protected for the idea from the mission statement of the International Baccalaureate Organization (IBO), cited in the opening chapter of this book, where the goal is to educate young people with the ability to understand that "other people, with their differences, can also be right" [47].

Returning to the narrative metaphor again, a plurality of cultural backgrounds on the actual Team will also increase the chances that people from various cultural walks of life feel 'seen' and 'read' by the programs the Team creates and sponsors. Depending on their cultural frame of reference, people respond very differently to questions like these:

- how much feeling is it okay to show in public?

- what is the 'right' way to behave when you are new in a group?

- how are women to behave in the presence of men outside the family?

- how involved should a parent be in the life of a school?

- as a parent, what is the proper way of relating to a teacher?

- as a student, what is the proper way of relating to a teacher?

- how do 'good students' behave in class?

- what's the right way to participate in class?

These are just a few of the many questions to which people from various cultures might respond in drastically different ways.

If your Team can recognize, understand, accept, and validate these differences, it can contribute to programs to help people negotiate them.

If your Team unconsciously slips into a composition that reflects the dominant culture, it loses its ability to even see these potential differences. By definition, a Team cannot do anything to effectively address differences it cannot even see.

In this latter, less-ideal, case, the chances increase that many people move through the school community feeling their experience is *not* seen, read, or adequately understood. Opportunities for cross-cultural learning are lost. And who would want that?

Tip #6: Arrange training

The start-up Team has a number of considerable issues to contend with. Here are some of the questions a new Transitions Team must address in order to get off to a good start:

- creation of a Team that feels emotionally safe and inclusive

- formation of a durable team spirit and identity

- learning, developing, and practicing rituals from the beginning that will contribute to an inclusive climate and a durable team identity

- acquiring a deep understanding of the role of grief in an international school community, including a deep appreciation and acceptance amongst each Team member for how he or she copes with grief – and for how others might cope

- acquiring a deep understanding of the role of culture in an international school community, and a personal understanding of what each person's own sense of cultural identity is

- learning and mastering the vocabulary associated with the narrative metaphor, and brainstorming programs to address the associated challenges of 'identity erasure' and 'identity rewriting'

- performing an inventory of programs already in existence

- brainstorming programs the Team wants to consider addressing

- prioritizing the Team's focus upon the essential programs it wants to address, and avoiding spreading the start-up Team too thin

- checking for parity (page 193) and gaps in the programs being focused upon, as a final check prior to strategic planning

- performing strategic planning on the targeted programs

- developing evaluation measures for Program success

- writing an effective mission statement

- creating a Team logo

- addressing practicalities like leadership, a meeting schedule, record-keeping

These are just a few of the issues a starting team must bear in mind. The successful addressing of these issues requires several days of training by a person or team of persons with at least these three qualities:

- a deep understanding of the dynamics of grief

- a deep understanding of culture

- a deep understanding of team building and organizational dynamics

The reason it is helpful to have an outside individual do the training is because it ideally provides the team with an injection of inspiration and a sense of external accountability, particularly if this train-

Allow two years to launch a Transitions Team properly!

er returns for one or more periodic checkups over the course of the launch period (which I define as the first two years of the program). In many presentations over the years, I have described the external trainer's role as the 'visiting father or mother' – that nurturing individual with all the requisite expertise to which the 'fledgling Team' can turn for affective or practical nutrition.

That external expert can also constantly remind Team members to be patient, and to allow two years to launch a Transitions Team properly!

THE LAUNCH PHASE

Tip #7: Make your start clear

Before embarking on how to start a Transitions Team, let me dip briefly into some historical, psychological, and philosophical considerations.

Historical, Psychological, And Philosophical Considerations Before Launching

You can't negotiate with the seasons. No matter how much you like spring, it won't come in October (unless you move to the Southern Hemisphere). You also cannot argue with the circle of life. All living things are born, and all living things die, and the atoms that make up existence move through the organic and inorganic world in an endless cycle of creation, death, and renewal.

The cycle of transitions can be compared to both of the above cycles, because the phases of the year move through a prescribed cycle reminiscent of seasons and the circle of life. New people arrive. Old friends go. And the cycle rolls on and on in a way that can feel relentless, inexorable, and unforgiving. While life on the international school scene is exciting and invigorating, many have also described it as emotionally draining, where the 'goodbyes' seem to get harder with time, not easier. At its core, a Transitions Team can help an international school community create rituals and processes which 'mark time' and at least ameliorate the more difficult consequences of a life on the road.

That is the very purpose of rituals, traditions, and ceremonies in our day-to-day lives: to mark important changes and transitions in our lives, and to provide people with structure and something to hold onto at times that can feel challenging or overwhelming. Our modern, technological, scientific

> *A Transitions Team will thrive best if it becomes the guardian of what I call the school's 'emotional calendar.' The Transition Team will only become such a guardian if it takes time, and timing, seriously.*

and especially secular lives have stripped us of much of the ritual and ceremony that used to shape our existence. Whatever the advantages of this modern sense of freedom might be, it has left us with one disadvantage: as human beings,we may be starved for ritual and tradition.

What does any of this have to do with how to start a Transitions Team at your school?

Why Making Your Start 'Clear' Is Important

I believe a Transitions Team will thrive best if it becomes the guardian of what I call the school's 'emotional calendar.' The Transition Team will only become such a guardian if it takes time, and timing, seriously. *In keeping with the First Law of Transitions, the emotional calendar logically begins in March or April, as people are gearing up for goodbye.*

If it is true that the Transitions Team should attend to first things first in terms of the kinds of programs it develops for the school community (meaning one of its first programs should be devoted to assisting people with leave-taking), then doesn't it make sense the Transitions Program should be attending to first things first in terms of the kinds of things it does for the Team itself (meaning it should be focusing energies on the start of the Team's emotional calendar)?

And is there a more fundamental start to the Team's emotional calendar than the birth of the Team itself?

Getting the birth of the Transition Team right is one key to healthy subsequent Team development, and therefore to Transition Program success. It's not a guarantee for subsequent Team success, but it certainly is a prerequisite.

So what are the key ingredients to getting your Team off to a 'clear start'? It should come as no surprise to hear they all have to do with ceremony and ritual:

- Gathering the nascent Team all together for a first 'launch meeting'.

- Having that meeting in a special location.

- Positioning chairs in a circle, to emphasize equality.

- Having refreshments and snacks.

- Creating ample opportunities for Team members to bond.

- Ideally using the first meeting as a step-up to the upcoming training sessions.

- Giving all participants a symbolic welcome gift.

- Giving all participants a reader full of information and pre-reading articles.

You know the core Team has created a successful meeting when it leaves people energized, hungry for more, feeling a sense of belonging and feeling valued, and looking forward to upcoming training sessions.

Tip #8: Foster Team identity

While it exceeds the scope of this 'Tip' to go deeply into ways to build a Team's identity, a few ideas, some of which have already been mentioned, are so central they deserve further explanation.

Ritual And Symbolism: Sacred Time And Sacred Space

In 1959, Mircea Eliade published his now classic account of myth, ritual, and symbolism entitled *The Sacred and the Profane* [48]. He introduced two central ideas to differentiate that which is important, special, or 'sacred' from that which is normal, regular, or 'profane.' Those two ideas were *sacred space* and *sacred time*.

In a nutshell, and without launching into the metaphysical, if you can infuse space and time with something which makes them special, then you leave the normal or regular world, and you enter a world which is different and extraordinary. For our purposes – and arguably for the purposes of any group activity or learning exercise in any setting – if you can get people to feel they've left their normal routine behind, the exercises and activities you have them do thereafter acquire special meaning.

In terms of time, this means marking off enough sacred time from people's calendars to get them into a 'Team zone' in a way that gives them the greatest chance of fully occupying that space, and not being distracted. Mornings work best, and full days for training and Team-launching purposes are even better. Having a ritual sound or activity to mark the beginning and end of Team activities can also lend an air of sacred time. Some Teams ring a chime. Others ring a gong or sing a song. Other Teams form a circle and hold the shoulders of the teammates to both sides, as if to symbolically say "we take care of each other here." *What* a Team does to mark its sacred time is less important than *whether* that time gets marked, because time collectively marked as 'sacred' boosts the Team's sense of identity.

A Team can also demarcate its space. Having a consistent Team space separate from all other spaces Team members normally frequent helps to mark that space as 'special.' For example, using a room at school that nobody generally uses for any other purpose gets people into a space they only associate with the Team. Better yet, as schools are full of interruptions and distractions (especially for staff members!), having a space off-campus forces people to go through the ritual of leaving 'work' space to get to the 'Team' space. A Team member's home nearby school, if possible, can serve that purpose, if anyone is willing to volunteer. While not too far away, it still forces Team members to symbolically leave school space and to enter somewhere designated as the space of the Team.

Mission Statement

Can a Team fully achieve its goals if those goals are not clearly articulated? Can a Team fully know what it stands for without proclaiming what it stands for? Can a Team *fully* feel like a Team unless these questions can be answered affirmatively?

These questions are rhetorical in nature. I would argue that the answer is 'no' to all three. A mission statement forces a Team to articulate clearly and concisely what it is trying to achieve. As such, it forces the Team to express the main motivational factors driving its work. And as a factor in Team identity, its formulation and completion allow Team members to step back and point to a shared statement, essentially saying collectively, "This is what we stand for!" The sense of shared purpose such a process engenders in its members contributes to the sense of unity of the Team. If members hear their words and sense their 'stamp' in the statement of the Team's purpose, they feel that the Team is theirs.

And unified Teams are potentially effective Teams. Non-unified Teams will invariably be less effective Teams.

A Well-Crafted Slogan Or 'Brand', And A Logo

When the mission statement and initial activities of the Team have become clear, it is time to turn towards the development of a well-crafted Team name, slogan, and logo to capture and convey the essence of what your Team stands for. Borrowing a term from the old USAmerican West, where cattle were seared with a certain mark to distinguish their owner or ranch, 'branding' is the process marketing people use for positioning a product or service in the market in a way customers quickly understand and recognize, and in a way that differentiates it from other products or services.

If the logo is the image, then the 'tag line' is the phrase that goes with the image. If you scan your visual memory, you can certainly conjure up dozens of brands – from Nike's 'Swoosh' logo and their 'Just Do It' tagline, to Federal Express' 'FedEx' mark and the matching mantra of 'The World on Time.'

For starters, your Transitions Program needs a name, of course. What do you want to collectively call the programs and activities your Team stands for?

A good name for the Team is:

- short (one or two words)

- sticky (people will remember it)

- straightforward (it tells what the program does)

A good logo complements a good title by conveying a vast amount of information to the viewer, consciously and unconsciously, in a split second.

"A picture says a thousand words," and that's true for an effective logo. With regards to a Transitions Program, I would argue an effective logo infuses the viewer with the feelings the Transitions Team is seeking to establish and foster throughout the school community. What these feelings might be should be no surprise by now. Sentiments like belonging, included, and safe all come to mind.

Questions that can help the Team devise an effective logo might be:

- what images or metaphors do you associate with the Transitions Program?

- how do you want people to feel as a result of participating in programs that the Transitions Program sponsors?

- how do you want people to feel when they look at the logo?

Questions that can help you devise a tagline might be:

- how would you boil your mission statement down to five to seven words?

- what would a witty aunt or grandmother say about the program if you tried to explain to her what the program tried to do?

- what do you hope people in the future will literally *say* about their time at your school, thanks to the school's comprehensive Transitions Program?

In Summary

While there are many ways to build team identity, this collection of a few examples hopefully provides you with the basis and inspiration to create your own. With the right sacred space, time, titles, taglines, and logos, your Team will have all the trappings for durability.

International school communities often harbor freelance or non-working spouses in their midst with all of the experience you need in areas such as marketing, design, and art. These types of people may be eager to put their expertise to good use for the community. Network your way towards finding them. They're probably there, and they could guide you on this road towards title, logo, and tagline development far better than a few brief paragraphs in this Tip ever could.

Tip #9: Establish evaluation measures and procedures

"If you don't know where you want to get," I once heard a High School Principal say, "any road will get you there."

Inversely, with Transitions Programs, we arguably know exactly where we want to get. We want people to feel safe, seen, included, and cared for, so parents can parent well, teachers can teach well, and all in the ultimate service of achieving a goal common to all schools, namely that students can learn well. The inverse of 'any road will get you there' does not mean only one road will lead to the outcome of people feeling safe, seen, included, and cared for. Many roads lead to Rome – both symbolically *and* literally. Sticking with the analogy, what's important is not necessarily which road the Team chooses, *but identifying how you will know when you have arrived in Rome.*

Do you see a huge arena missing a part of its upper echelons, like some monster took a bite out of a portion of an ancient stadium? And across the street, do you see lots of ruins moving slowly uphill, filled with pillar after pillar? And is there a massive arch linking the arena with the ruins?

If you answered 'yes' to these questions, then you were probably looking at the Colosseum, the Forum, and the Arch of Constantine, respectively, meaning you've probably made it to Rome. Wouldn't it be good to have those kinds of questions to help your Transitions Team know when it had reached, or was close to reaching, its destination?

Developing Evaluation Measures

As of the writing of this book, evaluation measures for the success of a transitions program do not yet exist. Arguably they belong in quality assurance measures used by school inspection or accrediting bodies. *Part III: Ensuring Safe Passage: Navigating Mobile Lives Through the Hearts of Schools* of this book, particularly *Chapter 10: Assessing Networks of Schools* moves the discussion in exactly that direction.

Each school is unique and the types of areas each school decides to focus on in developing its transitions program are likely to differ from school to school. The point is, with appropriate advanced planning, the ways to measure whether programs have been successful can be devised during the planning process, before programs get invested in and launched.

The time to do this is during strategic planning, which I have housed as a portion of Tip #6, above, entitled 'Training.' Strategic planning means devising goals that are **'SMART'– specific, measureable, attainable, relevant, and time-bound.** The 'M' for measurable means exactly what we've been talking about – you should be able to know when you've gotten there.

For example, let's say the Transitions Program decides to focus in its maiden year on an effective 'Parent Welcomer' program. The goals of this program include things such as:

- Having 100% of new parents welcomed to the community in an email from a Parent Welcomer with a cultural background similar to that of (one of) the new parents.

- Ensuring this email is sent quickly, within one week of these parents' receiving notification of acceptance to the school for their child.

Easy as this sounds, a number of systems will have to be developed to achieve these ambitions at the 100% level stated in the actual goal. The following factors will need to be arranged:

- Admissions will have to collect and maintain accurate contact information.

- Admissions will have to share that info in a timely and reliable fashion with the leadership of the Parent Welcomers.

- Parent Welcomers will need an internal and reliable system for getting the right target parent matched to the right Parent Welcomer.

- Parent Welcomers will need a system for how to handle new parents who don't respond to welcome emails – has their email changed, should the Parent Welcomers then reach out via another avenue, and does Admissions have that information?

Achieving challenging goals is never simple. But articulating exactly what the goals are, and the steps that will be necessary to achieving them, at least make their achievement more likely.

Parent Satisfaction Survey

The point of this Tip #9 is not to delve into the details of how to achieve this or any other goal the early Transitions Program might have. The goal here is to discuss some general concepts surrounding how a Program can best measure its progress on any of its goals.

A logical place to locate measures for parent satisfaction is on the annual parent surveys most schools use to partially evaluate how their programs are doing. An evaluation of the Transitions Program belongs in that survey too. For example, the way to evaluate the bulleted goal above could be via questions such as:

- "Were you welcomed to our community by a Parent Welcomer by email prior to your arrival at our school?" (Yes/ No).

- "If so, when were you contacted?" (Possible answers: a few days after my son or daughter was accepted; a few weeks after my son or daughter was accepted; a few months after my son or daughter was accepted; I was only welcomed when I arrived on campus.)

- "Could you express in a brief sentence or statement how you felt about this initial contact from the Parent Welcomers? And if you didn't get contacted, could you express in a brief sentence or statement how that made you feel?" (Space for an anecdotal response.)

Similarly, the evaluation of the work of other programs can be added to the parent survey, where appropriate. *The important thing is to identify the measures of success at the same time the program is being designed.* This means reserving some time for 'measurement' in the earlier Strategic Planning processes described in Tip #6.

Student, Staff, And Stayers' Satisfaction

Many principals and heads of schools ask their staff to evaluate them. Many HR departments ask new staff to evaluate the orientation process for new staff. Ironically, students are often not consulted about their feelings about processes which affect them. And also ironically, the stayers – those people on the shoulders of which the entire school rests, for students and for staff and for parents – are also rarely consulted about their experience of transitions-related services.

You can't claim your program is doing something unless you know what the situation was before your program existed. So consider taking measurements with your outcome measurements before you try changing anything.

A comprehensive evaluation of transitions services at any international school community would need to evaluate the experience of members of all nine domains of the 3x3 grid that was part of the umbrella graphic presented in Figure 3.3 of *Chapter 3: Land Ho!* (see page 81). Nascent Transitions Teams are unlikely to be well developed enough to undertake a regular comprehensive evaluation of the transition experience of all members of the school population,but they can begin by designing outcome measures for the new programs they do decide to invest in. Doing so also fosters credibility for the program with skeptics, or with those who appreciate seeing the data to back up the Program's claims or requests.

A Brief Note On Validity

It is obviously beyond the scope of this Tip #9 to venture deeply into a discussion of how to do evaluations and statistics correctly. I won't even try. But I do have a few general recommendations that will make any measure more 'valid' – which in statistical terms means that you're measuring what you think you're measuring (and not something else!).

- *Establish baseline measures:* You can't claim your program is doing something unless you know what the situation was before your program existed.[29] So consider taking measurements with your outcome measurements before you try changing anything.

In the case above, for example, new parents who couldn't have participated in the new Parent Welcomer program's services (because those services didn't yet exist at the time they moved) could still be asked the questions listed above, reworded appropriately. For example, the first question would read, "Were you welcomed to our community by a parent via email prior to your arrival at our school?" Similar questions to these give the program measures of what the situation was like *before* the new Transitions Team tried to do anything about it.

- *Avoid self-selection bias:* Self-selection bias means people could tend to answer a question if they have something to complain about. Alternatively, they might avoid the question if they had a bad experience, perhaps because they don't want to be perceived as negative or 'a complainer.'

The way to avoid this kind of biasing of results is not to 'wait and see' who returns a questionnaire. Doing so may lead to results skewed in the direction of overly-negative or overly-positive.

----

29 *Even if you do have baseline measures, you still cannot claim your program is responsible for a positive change that you will hopefully see in the future between baseline measures and measures thereafter. Why not? Because unless you kept people in a bubble and eliminated every other variable, a perceived change could have been coming from any number of other sources. Having said that, most people aren't statistically schooled, even those who frequently continue to make this 'causality' mistake. If you have baseline measures and a positive change in your target variables since the collection of these baseline measures, then the most you can say is that it seems 'reasonable and possible' that your Transitions Program played a role in effecting the positive change.*

You have two alternatives. The trick is to stick to one or the other, and not to mix the two.

The first alternative is to aim for a 100% return rate, and to pursue respondents to your questionnaire until they have turned their evaluations in. This is often unattainable and undesirable – you might eventually approach 100%, but you may also irritate and annoy a large swathe of the school population in the process – not the kind of PR you want for your program.

The second alternative is to take a random sample of about 10% of your population. The selection process for generating who to approach must be truly random. You then need to explain to the people who are selected for questioning exactly how you arrived at their name, and the kind of statistical choice the Team has made by going this route. You can explain it's very important for the accuracy and validity of the data that *each and every one of the randomly selected community members completes the survey.*

If you stick to the 10% rule, you can tell the subjects they will be doing the other 90% in the community a service, because they will not have to (or be allowed to) complete the survey. In short, you ask for compliance, and gently warn that you need to seek 100% completion of those who were 'chosen,' so the Team will be able to make reasonable claims about the results being 'representative.' You want to be able to state that your results are based on a 'randomly selected and representative sample' from the community.

By doing so, you'll be doing research that closely imitates the standards by which professional social scientists do their work. That, too, is a feather in the Transitions Team's cap of credibility. Again, as I said about non-working spouses in the community with PR or marketing expertise, it is equally likely that non-working partners with statistical expertise are in your midst. The trick is to find them, so they can help you develop effective outcome measures.

Tip #10: Plan follow-up

Lastly, the start-up Team needs to have its schedule of meetings set for the remainder of the year, and to set all the meetings for the upcoming year in advance. These early meetings need to include the whole Team, preferably take the whole day or even two days, and to be at broadly spaced intervals such as once per quarter. It is helpful to bring back the trainer(s) you originally employed for the training portion for one or more of these meetings, to give the Team an external sounding board and to hold the fledgling Team accountable to itself for its progress.

Having said that, the relationship with the trainer(s) needs to be weaned, as the fledgling program prepares to sustain and guide itself more and more on its own in future years.

WHEN YOU GET THIS FAR

Congratulations. The harbor has been built, sandbagged, and diked. Roads are appearing, and cranes are arriving to help load and offload arriving and departing ships. A Team has been born.

Chapter 5

SUSTAINING THE HARBOR – ENSURING THE TEAM SURVIVES

"But if you want to know the truth, I feel understood there.
I sit down to lunch with Bill or Bob or my sister and brother
whom I've known almost forever, and it's a conversation
you can't have with people you met yesterday…
I come home and feel so well understood.
I almost don't have to say a word."

> – Garrison Keillor, 'There's No Place Like Home',
>   *National Geographic,* February, 2014

After the Team has navigated its first year or two, it is time to turn to questions of sustainability and long-term implementation and maintenance. The purpose of this chapter is to highlight some of the considerations worth bearing in mind as your Team moves into this phase of what might be dubbed 'advanced harbor building.'

The previous chapter dealt with the first three phases of the process of developing a Team, which I called the preparatory, pre-launch, and launch phase. This chapter deals with the fourth and final portion of the process, the 'sustaining phase.' In keeping with the last chapter, I have again organized this material into a 'Top Ten Things To Tackle' list.

THE TOP TEN TIPS TO TACKLE: DURING THE SUSTAINING PHASE

1. Beware of the honeymoon

2. The Transitions Team is the Transitions Team for the Transitions Team

3. Keep it simple and sustainable (KISS)

4. Evolve towards management by steering committee

5. Start celebrating

6. Tend to the stool's balance: 'gender drift' and 'staff leg atrophy'

7. Recruit through education about the fountain

8. Recruit a PR specialist

9. Develop an annual calendar

10. Reevaluate program design using calendar

Tip #1: Beware of the honeymoon

"You can't beat a boat that's being rowed perfectly," my father once said. I had no idea what he was talking about, so I asked him to explain.

When he was a part of the heavyweight crew team at Harvard, my father was the coxswain for the men's varsity 'eight'. At one large regatta, which has since become the near-mythical setting for this particular story, his Harvard boat was dragging in last place by several lengths. My father, being the coxswain, was the only crewmember to be able to see how poorly they were doing, despite every rower's best efforts.

"Power twenty!" my dad called, signaling rowers to increase their stroke rate and give twenty strokes at full pressure. The cadence increased and the boat launched forward.

"Settle!" he called, and the stroke rate dropped, while oarsmen maintained steady pressure.

It was then, my dad explains, that the magic happened. The timing of all eight oarsmen aligned perfectly. The boat went silent. Oars ceased splashing. Seats and oarlocks stopped creaking. Filled with nine men, the boat felt and sounded as if it was being propelled by a single, cosmic oar. Without adjusting their stroke rate or pressure, the eight rapidly gained ground on the other boats, and proceeded to pass every one of them, winning a race they'd been losing badly only minutes earlier.

I heard the story forty years later – augmented, no doubt, by a tablespoon of hyperbole and a dash of nostalgia. His story ended with the punch line that a magical moment like that never occurred again in the rest of his collegiate rowing career. But the phrase that stuck with me more through the years was the explanation he gave to my fourteen-year-old self when I asked how in the world this could be possible.

"You can't beat a boat that's being rowed perfectly."

'Real Life' After The Launch

If you have been successful in gathering the critical mass of inspired individuals required to successfully launch a Transitions Team, the first part of the Team's journey can be exhilarating. Ideas synergize and cross-pollinate in rampant fashion, as Team members – many of whom have likely been pursuing transitions-related efforts in relative isolation for many years – discover they are not alone, and that the power in a Team far exceeds the sum of the individuals. As with my father's proverbial boat, the initial Team may launch forward, as energies align and unify. If and when this occurs, welcome yourself to the 'honeymoon phase.' I hope you get to experience this at least once in your career, and at least once with your Transitions Team.

Unfortunately honeymoons don't last forever, anymore than my father's heavyweight eight managed to row perfectly throughout the rest of their time together. Honeymoons are exactly that – a time to bond and enjoy, a period symbolically and intentionally set apart from the rest of 'normal' life, just as Eliade set 'sacred time' apart from the rest of time. As long as we don't mistake 'sacred time' for 'normal time' there's no problem.

We can only get ourselves into trouble if we're not adequately prepared for normal time, that phase in the Team after the honeymoon.

Tip #2: The Transitions Team is the Transitions Team for the Transitions Team

This Tip is so important it deserves its own chapter. It's so important it deserves to be mentioned in every chapter of this book. In some ways, it is so important it could deserve to be the title of this book.

Let me repeat it, and coin it the Third Law of Transitions:

LAW III

The Transitions Team is the Transitions Team for the Transitions Team.

What does this mean?

A Transitions Team attempts to develop programs to assist students, parents, and staff with the challenges associated with mobility. This is rewarding work, but also heart-wrenching work. The only way an Orientation program at the beginning of the year can go well is if the community has done a good job grieving for and with those who have to leave, bringing closure to yet another chapter of 'being together.' Assisting people in navigating intense emotions is intense work, exposing the helper not only to his or her own strong affect and grief, but also to that of wide portions of the community too.

Who helps the helper? If you don't watch out, the answer can be terrifying. *Nobody.*

As is true for many of the tips in this book, I learned this lesson the hard way. After the initial honeymoon phase of the American School of The Hague's Transitions Team, when numerous successful programs had been launched and our first presentations at conferences such as the European Council of International Schools (ECIS) Annual Conference had been positively received, I began to get a vague and uncomfortable feeling that the ground was shifting under our feet.

Our first founding Team members announced they were going to step down, due to other commitments. Then later in that second year of our Team's existence, other Team members announced they were going to be leaving the school.

In retrospect, the Team found itself in a position of having created programs for every constituency other than itself. We had ways of welcoming and saying goodbye to students, parents, and staff, but we had no program or process for parting with our own cherished Team members. Worse still, we didn't even know it. Valued Team members stepped down and disappeared – from the Team, at least.

The Dangers Of Unresolved Grief – On The Transitions Team Itself

To make matters worse, there was no text like this to explain the First Law of Transitions to us, namely:

- -

 You have to say a clear 'goodbye' in order to say a clear 'hello' *or* **You have to grieve well to leave well.**

- -

We never had the opportunity to consider this law logically extended to us too, as a Team. Based on some vaguely felt notion, perhaps, that we, as Transitions Team members, had somehow managed to elevate ourselves above the normal wear and tear inflicted on the psyche by the challenges of mobility, we failed to attend sufficiently to our own needs. (There are many sayings in many languages to highlight this danger. Most aptly in English we say "the cobbler's sons have no shoes.") We did not say sufficiently clear *goodbyes* to our own, making it impossible to say entirely clear *hellos* to new members who would join our ranks.

Without realizing it, remaining Team members were gradually accruing a psychological debt of 'unresolved grief.' This unresolved grief presented itself in various forms, including:

- doing a poor job of recruiting new members to the Team

- doing a poor job of training new members who wished to volunteer

- veteran Team members' beginning to show signs of becoming tired and burned out

- veteran Team members' beginning to harbor resentments towards the administration when sufficient support for key initiatives was not forthcoming

Psychologically speaking, all of the above manifestations are signs of a person's *own* needs not being met. A successful Transitions Team – like any successful and healthily integrated human being – must learn to monitor and take care of its own needs.

How A Transitions Team Becomes A Transitions Team For The Transitions Team

The million-dollar question is how to do this? How do you make sure the Transitions Team practices what it preaches by creating transitions programs for the Transitions Program?

Just asking that question puts a Team on the road to the answer. It is not asking the question that leads to problems. Once posed, the question logically produces many of its own answers – by creating programs for the Transitions Team itself, which achieve many of the same benefits as those created for students, parents, and staff members.

In a nutshell, a Transitions Team wanting to take good care of itself, so as to survive and thrive long beyond the 'honeymoon phase,' is going to need the following:

- closure rituals at the end of each year, to honor departing Team members

- orientation processes at the start of each year, to welcome and position new Team members in the Team's history, accomplishments, traditions, and goals

- recruitment processes that build publicity for the Team and ensure an annual flow of new volunteers onto the Team

- professional development opportunities to 'feed' the members and the Team with new ideas and inspiration

One way to develop these kinds of activities is for the Transitions Team to make 'The Team Itself' one of the early projects the Team sets to work on, during the strategic planning described in *Chapter 4: Building the Harbor*. Developing, implementing, and monitoring the kinds of activities necessary to take good care of the Team is no insignificant task, and I would strongly recommend having a group of people make it (one of) their primary foci as the early Team is getting underway.

Tip #3: Keep it simple and sustainable (KISS)

How many of you have heard the recommendation during a workshop of any kind to "keep it simple, stupid!" often abbreviated as 'KISS'? While I like the catchy acronym, I wouldn't want to offend anybody less familiar with USAmerican humor, so I've changed the corresponding words to something that works, in my mind, even better for our purposes – 'Keep It Simple and Sustainable.'

A successful early-phase Transitions Team is likely to have a tremendous amount of energy (thanks to the 'honeymoon' described in Tip #1 above) and a few key

Once born, a Transitions Team's programs must be maintained. That, too, takes time and energy.

initiatives they're focused upon doing well (thanks to good strategic planning, called for in Tip #6 of *Chapter 4: Building the Harbor*). The temptation for any Team as it moves beyond its first years is to try to repeat its successes in subsequent years.

Remembering that a boat, once perfectly rowed, cannot be rowed perfectly forever, it is important to bear in mind that the synergy of a new Team, however infectious and exciting, cannot and will not be maintained indefinitely. That synergy is needed to 'birth' the kinds of programs only a Transitions Team can create, but that same synergy has limits. Once born, a Transitions Team's programs must be maintained. That, too, takes time and energy.

It is easy and perhaps appropriate to draw analogies between human development and the development of a Transitions Team. Just as children and teenagers generally have more energy and exuberance than adults, so too does the nascent Team have more energy in the beginning than it will have once it becomes 'mature.' As many teenagers often haven't had too many large setbacks or failures, they often consider themselves omnipotent and immune to harm. In an analogous fashion, the early Team must be cautious not to wish to 'conquer the world' – or, more to the point, the entire school community – as it hasn't yet had to grapple with too many setbacks. Early successes are generally relatively easy for the Team to accomplish, because few comprehensive programs exist at a school. Early improvements sponsored by the Team are therefore hailed as welcome improvements.

Perhaps most tellingly, just as young people are generally free of too many responsibilities or commitments, so too is the early Team. These accrue gradually. As adults generally (if they're wise!) add responsibilities such as loans, mortgages, and children to their shoulders gradually, in step with their growing ability to bear each new load, so too must the early Team add new programs to the overall program sparingly.

The reason is simple. A new house, however exciting, has mortgage payments to be paid long after the excitement has waned, month after month. A new baby, however thrilling, needs care long after the magic of the birth and the visits from family and friends. Like children, the early programs the Transitions Team creates all require care and maintenance in years two, three, four, and far beyond. If these programs are worth creating in the first place, they will need maintenance and refinement indefinitely. It is not possible for a Transitions Team to create, for example, five solid new programs in its first year at an international school – and then expect to create five new ones in its second year. (That would be analogous to enjoying your first five children so much that you decide to have five more. Do you know any parents who have had ten children, or at least based the decision upon such logic?)

Keep it simple and sustainable. The programs that emerge from the careful training and strategic planning described in Tip #6: of *Chapter 4: Building the Harbor,* are your Team's 'children.' Add to them sparingly. Remember the key to success is whether your Team can *sustain* all of its activities, not only for the current year, but for the indefinite future.

Tip #4: Evolve towards management by steering committee

Sticking with the analogy of human development, this text has already de-scribed two stages in the development of the Transitions Team. Until now, these stages have been left implicit. The purpose of Tip #4 is to make these stages explicit, so the Team can chart its way to the next logical stage of its development, which I'm referring to as 'Management by Steering Committee.' The first stage was referred to in Tip # 2 of *Chapter 4: Building the Harbor.* This core group was depicted as the critical mass needed to launch a full-fledged transitions program run by a fully functioning Transitions Team. No single individual could ever run a program of this scope by him or herself.

In the graphic below, I compare the early core group to the image at the far left of the four-celled early version of a human embryo, shortly after fertilization. In this image, there are four to eight clustered cells, consistent with the notion that all members of the starting core group are closely bound and essential to the Team's early success.

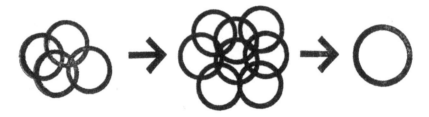

FIGURE 5.1 Early development of a comprehensive transitions program.

As Team development progresses in many of the ways described in Tip #5 of *Chapter 4: Building the Harbor,* the core group becomes complemented by additional, highly committed individuals who feel drawn to the 'cause' of the Team. This phase is depicted by the middle image in the above graphic. During the formation of the Team's early vision, the formulation of its mission, and the definition of its early programs and goals, it is natural and essential that the Team operate in an inclusive, empowering fashion, with all its members representing all the various constituencies. Students, staff, parents, and administrators from all cultural walks of life cluster together in a new, expanding organism, preparing to grow. Just as every cell in the human body harbors the same DNA, the early 'cells' in this analogy could be likened to stem cells, able to evolve into any kind of tissue or organ the body requires. Out of the sum of all of its contributing members will emerge the vision and course the later Team can build upon, just as the evolving embryo develops the basic structures and 'architecture' upon which its subsequent development forms.

After The Team Has Been Conceived: The Need For Differentiation

The third development in the Team likely comes in its second or third year, when the Team has created numerous programs, each being successfully run by small groups of people committed to each respective cause. For example, in its first year, a newly minted Transitions Team might have developed programs dedicated to:

- departure and orientation issues for students

- departure and orientation issues for parents

- departure and orientation issues for staff

- the Transitions Team's own needs

- program publicity

and in its second year, the still relatively new Transitions Team, committed to maintaining the solid programs described in the previous list, decided to sparingly add only two more new programs:

- community cross-cultural education

- community transitions education

As these programs develop, with about four to six people involved in the running of each program, the overall Team on which the total transitions program is being built becomes larger and more complex. In this sense, the term 'blastocyst' for the corresponding phase in embryonic development is fitting. The very term *blastocyst* seems to conjure a large aggregation of cells. Coordinating such a complex aggregation becomes increasingly difficult.

It is time for cells to begin specializing. Not every cell needs to maintain the stem cell's potential to 'be all things.' More for our purposes, not every Team member need be directly involved in the decision-making and steering of the larger Team. In fact, as the program takes off and adds second and third generation members to its ranks, it becomes likely that not everyone will be even interested in the broader process-management concerns. Many of these members support the work of the broader Transitions Team, but they become involved because of a particular area of interest where they prefer to focus their energies.

This third phase of the above graphic is intended to convey the notion that key parts of the evolving organism need to stay connected, but not every cell need be equally

Quite early in its development, a Transitions Team needs to consider creating a Steering Committee.

connected to the evolving whole. In other words, it is time for represen-tation. As arms specialize in things arms do – things which are different from that which legs and lungs and liver do – so too do the different work-groups formed by the early Transitions Team focus on different aspects of the whole. No one activity is more or less important than another, any more than we can say our legs are more essential than our arms. The important thing is that the Team's movements remain coordinated.

Purpose Of A Steering Committee

Quite early in its development, a Transitions Team needs to consider creating a Steering Committee. The purpose of a Steering Committee can be to create a smaller, more focused forum for representation and coordination of the wider whole. If each workgroup contributes its chair to the Steering Committee, then monthly meetings of this committee will be more than adequate to monitor and maintain the coherent development of the wider Program. Individual workgroups meet on a schedule to suit the needs of each group's particular members. The progress of each group can be monitored and integrated by the Steering Committee, enabling the Steering Committee to keep the wider Team on course.

Ongoing Identity Needs Of The Team As A Whole

The creation of a Steering Committee as the third, and final, phase in Team management for the long term should not be confused with other needs relating to the identity of the wider Transitions Team. Group identity stems from sharing things which involve the entire group. If all of the members of the Transitions Program do not occasionally come together to discuss and celebrate the work of this wider Program, then the identity of the program will suffer.

It is for this reason I would recommend holding at least one Team-wide meeting per year – and perhaps two – and building these events into the Program's master annual calendar (see Tip #9 in this chapter). These meetings could be:

- Late spring: to bring all key members of the Transitions Program together for a celebratory end-of-year lunch. Each committee can share its progress during that year, say a public farewell to its departing members, and welcome and introduce new recruits. This is also an opportunity to invite administrators and board members, to thank them for their support and let them listen in on the work being done by the Program.

- Late fall: to bring all key members of the Program together for a professional development event to 'feed' the program. This could entail a workshop from a visiting professional; a Team-wide strategic planning meeting, where each group reports on its vision for its group for the year; or a 'recruitment fair' for parents and/ or staff and/ or students interested in becoming involved in the Program.

Tip #5: Start celebrating

I always tell parents a child's behavior is like a plant, and our attention is like water and sunlight. What we pay attention to tends to grow.

Teams are no different. New Teams have an opportunity to still establish their norms, the norms by which the Team will operate over the long term. This is a great opportunity to 'start celebrating.'

By this I mean starting every Steering Committee meeting with celebrations of what's working or what's been successful. This can happen in a rather spontaneous fashion, by inviting each workgroup or committee to share its good news from the last month.

Is this just a feel-good exercise? It certainly is! When we feel good, we tend to do good. Unfortunately, the inverse is also true.

To prove my point, imagine a team that didn't start with celebrations, but with 'Disasters and Bad News.' Think about how you would feel if everybody at the table went in a circle sharing things that weren't working, things that had failed, and things they felt profoundly discouraged with.

Now think about which would be more effective.

Now think about which team you'd rather join.

This is more than just a feel-good exercise. If you chose to join the more positive team (and I hope you did, otherwise please write me an email so I can find out why!), then please know that research also bears out your choice. The Brazilian psychologist Marcial Losada coined what has come to be known as 'the Losada ratio.' In his studies of teams in organizations,

Losada discovered that highly effective teams tended to make, on average, five positive or complimentary statements to fellow team members for every one negative or corrective statement [49]. Moderately effective teams were in the range of 1.9 positive statements for every corrective statement. Ineffective teams hovered around three negative or corrective statements for every one positive statement![30]

So start celebrating. It's good for you, and it spawns more celebrations in the process.

Tip #6: Tend to the stool's balance: 'gender drift' and 'staff leg atrophy'

If you are not careful, several demographic realities will conspire over time to turn the most carefully balanced Transitions Team into a team of volunteer parents who are primarily female. These demographic factors are:

- most staff at the primary and secondary levels are female

- staff have less flexibility in their schedules than non-working partners

- more non-working partners are female

Extrapolated over time, it will likely be easier to find female replacements for departing Team members as opposed to male replacements, while it will also likely be easier to find replacement parent volunteers for the Team compared to replacement staff volunteers.

And what will these forces do to your Team over time? If you're not careful, Team composition will gradually 'drift' towards the female. Losses to the staff leg will be consistently easier to compensate for via the addition of a non-working spouse or partner. And the result will be a Team imperceptibly drifting towards female parents.

Now please don't get me wrong – this population of non-working parents is rich with volunteer energies and professional expertise. Numerous tips in *Chapter 4: Building the Harbor* highlighted the skill sets hidden right under the surface amongst the non-working parents. My statements here have nothing to do with the talents these parents bring to the table. My statements here pertain only to the value of proportional representation. The Team needs to accurately represent the community it's trying to assist.

----

30 *The Losada ratio also pertains to marriages. But that's a different discussion. If you're interested in further reading, see [49].*

How do you address these 'drift' and 'atrophy' processes? First of all, by being forewarned. Knowing that the inertia of dominant demographics is pulling your Team away from a 'balanced stool' – towards one with an atrophied 'staff leg' which tends to be female across the board – will help you take steps to correct this as it occurs.

I believe the key lies in recruitment, and the key to recruitment lies in educating your community about how the 'fountain' of transitions works. And that takes us to Tip #7.

Tip #7: Recruit through education about the fountain

Comprehensive transitions programs provide considerable benefits to all members of an international school community at minimal cost. If the return on an investment in a Transitions Team is so great, why do such programs risk the 'gender drift' and 'staff atrophy' described in Tip #6? In other words, why would a Transitions Program be at risk for survival over the long term? The answer resides in the only equation[31] you will find in this book:

Risk to Transitions Program = Transitions + Insufficient Community Education

You know the first part already – the biggest risk to a Transitions Program comes from transitions itself, as mobility whittles and nibbles away at the people who have given of their time, energy, and creativity to build the Program's services.

The second part is trickier because it entails a process that is less visible.

When I was a little kid in California, I thought it was strange I would walk out of the ocean at a place on the beach different from where I'd gotten in. Looking up at the boardwalk, I would mark my place as 'left of the bungalow,' and be amazed I would be getting out of the ocean a hundred yards to the right of it. My mom would say something about 'a current' and 'not to worry,' but I thought it was perfectly strange (and unacceptable to my eight-year-old brain) that I couldn't *perceive* this current. If I tried to resist this current by really paying attention to the way I was swimming, or by really trying to stay 'left of the bungalow,' I would unfailingly end up, before I knew it, to the right of the bungalow.

---

31 *The wisdom of including a maximum of one equation in a popular book is attributed to the great physicist Stephen Hawkins. In his* A Brief History of Time, *he promises that the only equation he'll use is* $E=mc^2$. *If he kept his promise in a book about physics, I can certainly do the same in a book about feelings.*

A similar process happens to people in transitions. If they are lucky, they 'get into' a school's waters during a warm orientation process, where the school community lavishes considerable welcoming ener-

Living in the international school world accelerates the psychological experience of the normal human life cycle.

gies and resources upon them, hoping – correctly – to help them get off to a good start, since the way somebody starts has a considerable influence on their subsequent trajectory.

However, students, parents, and staff who might have been new in September are no longer entirely new the following April. By then, these 'newcomers' have drifted towards the status of being 'stayers.' Just as I did in the Pacific as a kid, they have drifted imperceptibly to a new place. Their identities have gradually morphed towards becoming veterans.

The problem is, many of them will not have realized this change has occurred. They're either new to the dynamic, or else nobody has ever told them. Or both.

Eventually, their identities will shift further, towards being near-departees. By then, for Team purposes at least, it is too late, because these people will soon be leaving the community entirely.

Parallels with the human life cycle are unmistakable. When David Pollock used to say, "Many TCKs have experienced more loss in their developmental years than most adults experience in a lifetime," he wasn't using hyperbole. The reality is that *living in the international school world accelerates the psychological experience of the normal human life cycle.* People are 'born into' and 'depart from' the community at a rate that would have made our village-bound forefathers dizzy. Cycles of proximity-seeking, bonding, friendship, and farewell span not thirty to fifty years, as they used to, but one to five – or less.

And here's the clinch for Transitions Teams to recognize – people *feel* this reality to be true, but most don't *know* it at a conscious level. It happens quietly, imperceptibly, like the drift of a Pacific current.

Putting The Idea Of 'Identity Drift' To Work For Your Transitions Program

Returning to the equation that started this section, the trick is to provide all portions of the community with education at the front door about how 'identity drift' works. Furthermore, I would argue that such community education represents an aspect of 'citizenship education' particular to international schools.

We educate our children to appreciate the benefits of democracy. With those benefits come certain responsibilities, such as voting. We educate our children that taxes are a necessary evil. We may have to forfeit a percentage of our income, but we know, deep down, that those taxes pay for the roads we drive on to take our children to the schools those same taxes help finance. We may differ on the end goals of democracy or the politics of tax laws, but few would dare to genuinely argue they would prefer a dictator over democracy, or that all taxes should be abolished in favor of an anarchical free-for-all.

We 'know' these things because society teaches us about them little by little. Shouldn't we be doing the same with regards to the citizenship demands created by mobility at any school with a substantial degree of turnover?

While people are being welcomed at the front door, they need to know they're going to be drifting, little by little, to the center and heart of their new institution over time. They need to know the same people who welcomed them are going to need replacement over time. While we can share our understanding and recognition that people lead busy lives, we can also politely remind them that 'being busy' has never been an acceptable excuse for failing to vote or to pay their taxes. *You have to find the time to fulfill the duties that come with responsible citizenship.* We might all convince ourselves that traffic lights turn red at the moment we're most in a hurry, but nobody would reasonably dare offer that as a compelling excuse to the police officer after being pulled over for running a red light. *We all benefit the most when we recognize we're in the same boat, and when we accept the responsibilities that accompany membership.*

This kind of thinking need not be given in the admittedly moralistic tone in which I've laid out the argument in the preceding paragraphs. The message can, and should, be conveyed in a way which emphasizes the joy and fulfillment gained from doing something so intrinsically meaningful for other people. The message can be tied to the fun and positivity with which the early Team has hopefully infused its norms. But at the end of the day, there's nothing wrong with putting a stop towards the excuses that can, and will, cause the best of Transitions Teams to wither over time.

Too much is at stake. We're talking about human feelings here. The 'Golden Rule' to "do unto others as you would have done to you" is operative in one fashion or another in every culture around the world. Tip #7 constitutes a gentle nudge to Transitions Teams around the globe not to be afraid to politely remind students, parents, staff, and administrators of this rule. In fact, it is so essential I would deem it the Fourth Law of Transitions, which we might dub the 'Rule of the Fountain':

A person's role at a school with a high degree of turnover is subject to drift. Arrivers become stayers, and stayers become leavers. People are not consciously aware of this drift. Arrivers need to be helped to consider accepting the roles and responsibilities of the stayers when the time comes.

This message can be politely delivered:

- towards the end of new student orientation

- as a part of the orientation for new parents

- as a part of the orientation for new staff

- during the first 'open house' events for parents

This message, once delivered, is likely to act as a seed in the minds of audiences. When the time comes later in that or subsequent years for active recruiting of new members of any of the Transitions Program services, reference can be made to these seeds that were sewn.

And statistically speaking, a certain percentage of seeds always germinate, take root, and grow.

Tip #8: Recruit a PR team

A consistent finding regarding the personalities of people who are attracted to the helping professions is that they tend to think of others before thinking about themselves. They lean towards attending to the needs of others before attending to their own. This generalization pertains to nurses, counselors, aid workers, psychologists, educators, and many parents.[32] By focusing their energies primarily on the needs of others, these professionals accomplish important shifts in the lives of real people, but risk overlooking their own needs and burning themselves out in the process.

----

32 *Please note I intentionally include 'parents' in this list of professionals. There is no job on earth more important, more demanding, or more rewarding.*

This reality is generally no different for the members of a Transitions Team. The types of volunteers drawn to such a team, be they students, parents, or staff members, are likely to be 'helper types' with personality profiles similar to those entering the helping professions described above. They will be good at attending to the needs of others, and less good at attending to their own. Many of the tips in this chapter and in *Chapter 4: Building the Harbor,* are ways of coping with this reality, such that the Team can sustain its important work without allowing its members to burn themselves out.

The advantage of any team is that the mixture of members is likely to produce a portfolio of personalities, where the weaknesses of certain members are compensated for by the strengths of others. On a Transitions Team, the natural variation in personality type is likely to bring in a broad variety of volunteers. In my experience, the 'helper type' profile is likely to predominate, meaning the entire Team will focus more on what it can do for others than what it can do for itself.

As noble as this might sound, the Team does need to attend to its own needs if it is going to achieve anything meaningful for anyone else over the long term. A nurse, counselor, aid worker, psychologist, educator, or parent who gives and gives relentlessly, with no view to his or her own hunger or fatigue signals, will not be able to sustain the work for long. And one of the things all members of this new Team need is effective public relations or 'PR.'

'Natural helper' types are often bad at PR. Things such as advertising, fund-raising, and publicity stunts smack of 'tooting one's own horn,' which people in the helping professions are generally less inclined to do than people in many other professions. I am aware these are sweeping generalizations, but I believe they contain at least a grain of truth.

"The point is not to aim to have no blind spots," a wise colleague once said, "but rather to know where they are." The point here is not to turn natural helper types into something they're not, namely PR experts who thrive by 'tooting their own horns,' but rather to mobilize the Team to recruit people who compensate for their natural weaknesses. As has been stated repeatedly in this book, school communities are rich with non-working professionals who have taken breaks from their careers to raise families or to allow an international relocation. Professionals with latent marketing, fund-raising, and PR-expertise are in your midst. The question you have for them is, "Can you help us build systems and programs for informing the community about our work and promoting it in the future?"

If these individuals can be recruited onto your Team and asked to help, all of the tips in this chapter and *Chapter 4: Building the Harbor* are likely to flow more effectively. And that will make the Team's work more effective.

And that will make all the difference to all the lives of all the people your Transitions Program touches.

Tip #9: Develop an annual calendar

After the Transitions Program has been operative for a year or two, it can be extremely helpful to create a master calendar of all the events the Program believes in sponsoring, when these programs occur, when the preparation and publicity for these programs must occur, etc. Again, as emphasized in Tip #1 in this chapter, initial Team enthusiasm can make the initial offerings of a particular program fly, but over time, it is helpful to have key points plotted on an annual calendar for the whole Team. This helps 'the right hand to know what the left is doing,' while also building in an additional safeguard for when Team members have to step down or leave the school community for good.

The most logical way to do this is to have each workgroup or committee make an annual calendar of key events and when they need to happen. The most essential of these events can be extracted from the workgroup calendars and posted on the annual calendar for the entire Team.

If your Team has chosen not to have a workgroup or committee charged specifically with taking care of the Team (Tip #2 of this chapter), then it is important for the Steering Committee to take ownership of a process for identifying what the 'taking-care-of-the-Team' events need to be on an annual basis. In addition to the suggestions listed under Tip #2 in this chapter, the Steering Committee could consider welding the following points into the Team's master calendar:

- Monthly Steering Committee meetings, including a time, reliable day of the month (for example, the first Wednesday of the month), and location. These meetings are only adjusted when the school calendar necessitates a deviation. This boost to predictability will also boost attendance.

- Annual full-Team kick-off meeting or professional development training, preferably in the late fall (see Tip #4, above).

- Recruitment event for the Transitions Program.

- Annual end-of-year full-Team closing celebration, also for new recruits.

- Publicity events, such as when to publish articles in school publications, who to author such articles, etc.

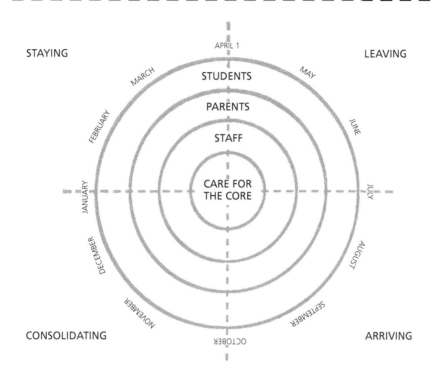

STAYING   LEAVING

MARCH   STUDENTS   MAY

FEBRUARY   PARENTS   JUNE

STAFF

JANUARY   CARE FOR
THE CORE   JULY

DECEMBER   AUGUST

NOVEMBER   SEPTEMBER

CONSOLIDATING   OCTOBER   ARRIVING

APRIL 1

FIGURE 5.2: Comprehensive transitions program annual calendar.

Tip #10: Reevaluate program design using a calendar

At the end of each school year for the early Transitions Team, it can be invaluable to evaluate the current status of the program using Figure 5.2.

During an extended Steering Committee meeting, workgroup – or committee chairs, along with other participants, can write the up and running programs on sticky notes, and place those sticky notes in the corresponding area by asking two questions: Who is this program for? And when does this program occur across time?

I would recommend projecting the above graphic on a large screen, so you have enough surface area to plot all the sticky notes likely to result from such a conversation.

A number of questions will readily avail themselves, including:

- how is the balance of services between the four populations depicted in this graphic – Transitions Team, staff, parents, and students?

- how is the distribution across time?

- are we paying more attention to arrivers, or to stayers, or to leavers?

- are there populations being neglected, or are there populations at particular times of the year that are being neglected?

I would also like to call the reader's attention to the flow of this particular fountain, which is anything but arbitrary. The Transitions Team's needs go in the center, followed by the staff, followed by the parents, and only then the students. "Why," I can hear many readers ask, "aren't the students' needs placed in the center? Aren't schools supposed to be for students? What is a Transitions Team doing putting its needs in the central zone?"

An answer to that question can again be found in the statement made at the beginning of any flight on any airline around the world:

"Should the cabin lose pressure, oxygen masks will drop from the overhead area. Please place the mask over your own mouth and nose before assisting others."

If we don't have enough oxygen in our own brains, we can't attend well to our own needs or those of anybody else. Taking care of transitions for an entire educational institution requires that the Transitions Team remain vigilant regarding one unflinching reality: it, too, is a target for the very issues it seeks to redress. If the Transitions Team gets dizzied by mobility, the entire vessel suffers, and the Program falls from the sky.

You will know you have a mature Transitions Program when Figure 5.2 gets projected onto a large screen and you see it proportionally covered by sticky notes that span both populations and time.

IN CLOSING

Over the span of *Chapter 4: Building the Harbor,* and *Chapter 5: Sustaining the Harbor,* we have a comprehensive list of developmental tips and suggestions that can be attended to over time, as the nascent Team moves through various stages of its growth. For a new Team, these suggestions could seem overwhelming. While they cannot possibly be addressed all at once, it would be folly not to at least expose the interested reader to issues it will encounter further down the road. After all, if you happen upon an idea that seems far too advanced the first time you read it, you'll at least have a sense you bumped into that idea later, when the time might be more ripe for its implementation.

It is my hope that *Chapter 4: Building the Harbor,* and *Chapter 5: Sustaining the Harbor,* provide the reader with a smorgasbord of options, from which they can pick when their appetites tell them they're ready.

In the meantime, after so much theoretical discussion, it's probably most helpful to see real programs in action. What does this look like in reality? Let's turn to real Transitions Programs in real schools, affecting the lives of real people in real ways.

Chapter 6

AN EXEMPLAR HARBOR –
AMERICAN SCHOOL OF THE HAGUE'S
'SAFE HARBOUR'

"Gandalf: *Well, why does it matter? He's back!*

Thorin Oakenshield: *It matters. I want to know – why did you come back?*

Bilbo Baggins: *Look, I know you doubt me, I know you always have. And you're right... I often think of Bag End. I miss my books, and my armchair, and my garden. See, that's where I belong. That's home. That's why I came back... 'Cause you don't have one, a home. It was taken from you. But I will help you take it back if I can.*"

– From the film, *The Hobbit: An Unexpected Journey*,
Warner Brothers Pictures, 2012

As we come to the end of *Part II* of this book, it seems fitting to turn to the question, "So who is doing all of these things? Who is successfully addressing transitions across cultures in a comprehensive fashion? Are there any exemplars we can turn to for inspiration?"

The answer is both 'yes' and 'no.'

On the 'yes' side of the equation is the American School of The Hague's 'Safe Harbour' program, which got started in the late 1990s and went on to become lauded as the best of its kind. This chapter focuses on Safe Harbour's strategy, membership, and programs, to provide the reader with one model of how transitions work has been implemented at one international school. Other schools with effective programs for addressing mobility include the International School of Düsseldorf and Jakarta International School. The interested reader is referred to page 295 for additional information.

On the 'no' side of the equation is the reality, addressed at the end of this chapter and explored more fully in *Part III, Ensuring Safe Passage: Navigating Mobile Lives Through the Hearts of Schools,* that no single school can success-fully address the challenges of mobility on its own, regardless of how fine a transitions program that school might have. Why is that? The emotional swells generated by mobility operate according to a different calendar than schools use to organize the academic year. While not visible to the naked eye, individuals and families are riding these emotional swells all the time. These emotional swells ignore school walls. They circle the globe and span multiple schools. It would be no exaggeration to say that these processes span all of the schools involved in educating a family's children. Mobility is only being addressed comprehensively when:

- all of the schools involved realize this fundamental truth

- all of the schools take action to address it in a concerted fashion

Gauged against this standard, no school – or, better said, no network of schools – is yet achieving this level of services.

But I am getting ahead of myself. We have to start somewhere, and the most logical unit for our initial attention is the individual international school's comprehensive transitions program.

Getting Our Bearings

We will begin by tacking outside of the harbor, getting a general feel for its layout and blueprint. What is Safe Harbour's general shape? Thereafter, we will narrow our angle of approach and take a tour inside the harbor, sailing in a broad circle around the harbor's inner perimeter. What are the different channels and docks? How are they organized?

We will not be pulling up to any one dock and disembarking. In other words, we will not be doing a detailed 'how to' analysis of any one of Safe Harbour's programs. Our tour will be general, designed to give the reader an overall view of how the entire transitions program works together in an integrated fashion.

Our tour will be timeless, too. To get into the harbor, we have to sail through a low-lying mist at the harbor entrance, one that seems to loosen our temporal senses. As we emerge from the mist into the heart of the harbor, we won't be sure if the people and structures we'll be seeing come from 2000, 2010, or 2020. If that feels a bit bewildering, checking the date on the stub of your harbor tour ticket won't help. All you'll see is 'Valid Today,' with no mention of a date or year.

Why Our Tour Of ASH's Safe Harbour Occurs 'Outside Time'

This chapter does not attempt to provide the reader with an accurate blueprint of the current structure of ASH's Safe Harbour. The reason is simple: programs constantly evolve, while texts like this do not.

While I could have attempted a faithful rendition of the Safe Harbour program in 2014, the year of this book's first publication, I thought it more important to provide the reader with an analysis of the best components of this program, regardless of when those components were implemented, and regardless of whether they have been reorganized into a different shape or structure since. *This chapter is written in the present tense, but some of these programs may have already evolved slightly or dramatically from the shape I'm depicting.* I make this choice for the following reasons:

- This chapter is primarily about inspiration. It is about *how* Safe Harbour does what it does, and not about when exactly it did this or that.

- Even an exemplar program like Safe Harbour has exemplar programs within it. In particular, my choice of a 'timeless approach' for reviewing Safe Harbour allows me to zoom in on the time when these exceptional programs were being developed, including what led them to be developed.

- Similarly, the success of the Safe Harbour program is largely due to the sustained contributions of many dozens and even hundreds of committed, inspired individuals. Where these individuals passed through the Harbour's ranks, it is particularly worthwhile to zoom in on the projects they spearheaded while a part of the school community.

- A description of Safe Harbour in any one particular year might be more likely to inadvertently encourage imitation. Such imitation would be unlikely to lead to real success, as each school's solutions to the issues discussed have to be an accurate response to the contextual factors at work in that school's particular community.

- The 'timeless' approach used here hopefully helps readers think in broad concepts, allowing them to grasp the key general principles that need translation to their own school settings.

STRUCTURE

At one point in its evolution, the Safe Harbour program had twelve different programs, which could be situated much like the hour markings on a clock face:

Figure 6.1: The blueprint for Safe Harbour

Steering Committee

The Steering Committee provides the central axis of the clock, ensuring that the twelve groups pool their energies in a coherent fashion across the passage of time. The Chair of each committee sits on the Steering Committee, which meets once a month. Steering Committee meetings tend to last one hour, enjoy a consistent location, and have a predictable flow:

- opening, including welcome to visitors or new (potential) members

- sharing of 'Celebrations' (update on successes from any committee)

- updates on current or upcoming work from each committee

- sticky-note writing during these updates, such that chairs who are not speaking can still share ideas without necessarily using group time

- work/ discussion on the key topic(s) that month

- closing query, where each chair has the opportunity to share final questions or issues at the meeting's end

Representation by each committee's (co)chair allows for the maintenance of the coherence of the organization, so that the various 'limbs' of the Program are aware of what the other limbs are doing.

What follows is a brief description of the work of each of the twelve committees, as their efforts get coordinated by the Steering Committee.

#1, #2, #3: Student Ambassadors

The purpose of the Student Ambassadors program is to guide the student population through the challenges of mobility. The reason the header above is numbered "#1, #2, #3" is because the mission of the Student Ambassadors actually gets addressed by three entirely different teams, one for each of the school's three divisions: Elementary School, Middle School, High School.

The following description focuses primarily on elements in the High School's program. There is a simple reason for this: I founded this program when our Team got started in 1998, and I know this division's program best. Some of the elements from this description will apply to all age groups, while others are specific to high school-age youngsters because of their relative level of maturity and independence when compared to their younger peers.

In a nutshell, the High School program strives to assist all students with the experience of mobility. Heeding the First Law of Transitions, the program starts by ensuring every departing student leaves the school well, and the school community takes leave of that particular student well.

Only after students have been assisted to "grieve well in order to leave well" does the program turn to new arrivals. Every new student is personally welcomed by a well-matched Ambassador in a timely fashion. And in the middle of the year, when few tend to be leaving or arriving, the program attends to some 'self care' by recognizing the stayers who make it all possible.

Divided across the phases of the year, the program includes:

PHASE OF YEAR	PROGRAMS THIS COMMITTEE SPONSORS TO ADDRESS THAT PHASE:
LEAVING	Planning and execution of annual goodbye ceremonies, including presentation of wooden clogs signed by classmates, boxes stuffed with goodbye messages, speeches for departees.
ARRIVING	Participation in and (in the High School) responsibility for planning and execution of week-long Orientation Program for new students.
STAYING	Recognition at assemblies for 'students who've stayed,' including presentation at awards assembly of the 'Endurance Award' for long-term stayers.

Besides the obvious benefits this program creates for arriving and departing students, it is worth noting that many of the program's greatest benefits fall to the students who provide the services, the Ambassadors themselves. In fact, the more responsibilities they have in this program, ranging from regular 'Student Ambassador,' up to 'Captain,' and all the way up to 'Coordinator,' the more these benefits seem to accrue. The key program in the High School's Student Ambassador program is arguably the 'Student Ambassador Leadership' group, which runs all aspects of the program, under the supervision of a member of staff.

COLLEGE APPLICATION ESSAY

"It is funny how certain experiences can change you. One that lasted more than three years and changed me in various ways was participating in the Student Ambassador program (SA) at my school. It made me a more competent leader, more positive and tolerant, better at dealing with stressful situations, and an even better team player. I am not the same 14-year-old boy who walked into my first student ambassador meeting that warm spring of my 8th grade year.

Moving is extremely hard; families must get used to a completely new life, leaving their friends, and sometimes other family behind. They must adapt to a new culture, a new language and a different lifestyle. The SA's mission is to ease these transitions. This is a noble mission, which was why I joined. I knew how hard moving was; I still remember my taxi ride as my family and I left Sao Paulo on our way to Barcelona. The tears I shed during that ride lived with me throughout my time with Student Ambassadors, and I vowed to help others with that pain, having known it so well in myself.

I was a grade level captain for two years, and this past year was one of the two coordinators. Being a co-coordinator meant weekly meetings with our advisor, weekly meetings with our leadership team, and five training sessions with the whole group of Student Ambassadors, all of it geared towards 'Orientation Week.' During that time I always felt at ease with my team. My leadership style mixed lighthearted jokes with hard work, making way for a cohesive and productive team; a style that I carry everywhere from the school hallways to the soccer pitch.

We welcomed more than 170 students to the school, and said goodbye to more than 50. As I had two firsthand experiences moving, I had a special bond with SA's mission. However as the years passed and my involvement increased I realized that there was something else which created such a powerful bond between Student Ambassadors and myself. It was the message that it gave, that regardless of what happens we should stay positive. No matter how difficult the situation, you must think of the opportunities it opens up, and look on the bright side of things. Increasingly that is how I began to tackle adversities in my life. When my grandfather was passing away, it was a very hard time for me. Nevertheless I remained strong and realized that it would ease his suffering, and help my family. Although that is an extreme case, even in less intense situations, such as unexpected test grades, or bad soccer games, I transform them into a motivation to do better. That is perhaps the greatest realization that this experience has brought me: that positivity is an integral part of my life now and something I intend to hold on to.

Helping hundreds of students and their families with SA was extremely gratifying, but I must say thank you to the program itself. It developed me in so many ways, and my time in it, particularly this last year, made me a better person. As I prepare myself to undergo the biggest transition of my life, I will take the lessons the program has taught me, and keep an open mind to the many lessons life still has waiting."

Daniel Arvidsson, Student Ambassador Co-Coordinator 2012-2013

The two Student Ambassador Coordinators, elected annually by their peers, arguably have the most demanding student leadership role in the school. They are responsible for running a weekly Student Ambassador Leadership team meeting at lunchtime, with their two captains from each grade. In a separate meeting the day before, the advisor helps the coordinators plan each weekly meeting, so they can execute it themselves. (These weekly meetings are also popular because members of the team – including the advisor – take turns providing lunch.)

At the weekly meetings, the following issues are addressed throughout the year:

- Coordinating the application and 'hiring' process to fill sixty Student Ambassador slots.

- Interviewing and selecting two captains per grade for the Student Ambassador Leadership group.

- Learning the art of denying applications and 'bad news' conversations for captain applications.

- Planning and executing roughly half of the training for these students, spread out over five to ten afternoon training sessions in the spring (the advisor takes the other half, focusing on affective and/ or psychological issues).

- Leading the entire Student Ambassador program in the planning and execution of the annual goodbye ceremonies for departing students in June in all four grades in the High School.

- Leading the entire organization in the planning of the week-long Orientation Program for new students and families in August. Executing the week-long Orientation program for new students and families.

- Planning and executing the 'hiring' process for the next year of Student Ambassador leaders, including the administration of an election process (with speeches) to allow their peers to choose the next generation of Coordinators and Captains.

It is beyond the scope of this brief description in this book to explain all of the programs the High School Student Ambassadors developed and sponsored. In a High School of four hundred students, however, 20% of students participate directly in the program, assisting their peers in saying goodbye to more than 100 friends per year, and welcoming more than 100 new ones in their stead. Even in the face of this high rate of transition, one that places a massive load on the attachment system of the entire student body, the Student Ambassadors can be credited with helping to create and maintain a school climate that can only be characterized as nurturing and caring.

#4: Parent Welcomers

The Parent Welcomers assist parents primarily in the arrival phase. Chaired by a parent veteran of transitions assisted by divisional representatives well-integrated into the Elementary, Middle, or High School parent populations, this committee recruits and trains several dozen parents who will be physically available during the summer to assist new families when they arrive in the Netherlands. With the advent of the Internet, this assistance process has become virtual, allowing for early contact by email from an appropriately matched parent long before the family arrives in the country.

Making such contact happen in a timely fashion requires close coordination with the Admissions Office, so that a family can be welcomed by an appropriate Parent Welcomer shortly after their child or children have been accepted to the school. The Director of Admissions therefore usually sits on the Parent Welcomer committee.

#5: Monday Morning Networking

Monday Morning Networking (MMN) provides new parents with a reliable and regular forum to meet one another and learn about practicalities of life in the Netherlands. MMN works like clockwork – it meets every Monday morning from 9-11am, with a weekly curriculum spanning everything from banking to the butcher, from biking to public transportation, from local laws to a visit from the local police officer to clarify those laws.

MMN strikes an even balance between essential practical and emotional needs, while getting pressing practical problems resolved. Parents have an opportunity to meet and get absorbed into their new communities. MMN's leadership knows this need to attach to one's new community is not resolved as soon as the boxes are unpacked and the suitcases

"In the end, I know I did the right thing helping so many along the way. It was more than strange to help them move in and out, while our life just continued on. Now, I only wish I could find that same support here. I just have to take things step by step."
    – Lora Lyn Frederick, chair of MMN, after having to move away herself

stowed. David Pollock rightfully said, "It takes six months to pack up your heart and six months to unpack it." For this very reason, MMN spans the entire year – excluding holidays.

Monday Morning Networking is run by parents and chaired by a veteran parent who knows from first hand experience how important services like MMN are.

#6: International Committee

The International Committee maintains a list of contact persons by country so an incoming family can be matched with a representative from their home culture who is familiar both with the school and with life in the Netherlands. The number of countries the school encompasses has hovered around sixty in recent history. While not every country always has a representative at the school, it is generally possible to assign a family to a parent representative from the same region, as this parent would likely have some affinity with the arriving family's home culture.

The International Committee is a collection of cultural subcommunities, some of them quite large and well-organized (for example the Korean or Swedish parents), others quite small (for example Kazakhstan or Trinidad and Tobago). These subcommittees form the nuclei for the International Committee's main annual event – International Day. While most international schools have a day like International Day, ASH's celebration (historically in February, but now in October) is particularly well-coordinated and successful.

Coordination of the International Committee is carried out by a cluster of committed parents from various cultural walks of life, one of whom chairs the committee. International Day is so large and all-encompassing it has its own Chair.

To return to the narrative metaphor underpinning this entire text, it is worth noting that International Day is a textbook example of life stories being validated. Throughout the school, cultural heritages and ways of being that are largely hidden for the majority of the year are placed proudly on display during International Day, for all to see, for all to 'read.' Important parts of who a person is – be it student, parent, or staff – are 'taken out of storage' and put on public view, via dance, art, song, food, or dress. Combined with a spirit of open curiosity infusing the whole school, International Day creates a safe platform to explore the reality that, with all our human similarities, we shape life very differently.

Two Committees Welcoming Most New Parents?

The astute reader will note that the existence of the Parent Welcomers and the International Committee would lead to a new family being welcomed by two different welcomers, one from their 'cultural home' and the other from the Parent Welcomers. This is true, with one exception – USAmerican families only get welcomed by the contact person from the Parent Welcomers.

Why? The answer is cultural-historical and particular to the American School of The Hague. The Parent Welcomer committee at ASH logically grew from the commitment and initiative of parents from the dominant culture, namely the USAmerican parents. While the proportion of USAmerican families hovers slightly around one quarter of the school, down from closer to 100% when the school was founded in 1953, students from these families logically feel most 'at home' in the school's structures and values, because these structures and values evolved from a USAmerican educational model. As explained earlier in Tip #5 of *Chapter 4: Building the Harbor,* the early Transition Team reflected the dominant culture more than it does today, meaning early parent-welcoming efforts also reflected this dominant cultural heritage.

At first, that is. The efforts and initiatives of the International Committee grew in parallel to those of the Parent Welcomers over the years, and both avenues for welcoming parents now function fully. If it's nice to be welcomed well, it's even nicer to be welcomed well twice!

#7: Expat Life Issues

The Expat Life Issues group was founded to address something all of us on the Team knew but hadn't yet found a way to adequately address: the issues associated with an internationally mobile lifestyle repeatedly confront a person with challenging questions about identity and grief. These questions come back on an annual, predictable basis. While there were curricular avenues for teaching children about these challenges, no such curriculum or forum existed for parents. More poignantly, since schools are set up primarily to teach children, it was obvious no such curriculum would ever exist unless parents created it themselves.

Expat Life Issues therefore set out to create and offer an annual curriculum to educate parents about the challenges associated with mobility across cultures and what could be done about it. The first presentation entitled

'Culture Shock' and offered shortly after the settling-in period (October), looked at the predictable cycle of arrival excitement and post-arrival depression that generally occurs when people move.

A second presentation during the middle 'quiet' part of the year (February) looked at the identity and 'third culture kid' issues that can only reasonably be examined when people feel a modicum of stability, i.e. when masses of people aren't arriving or leaving.

And a third and final presentation readied the soil for the most difficult, but also most important phase in the annual calendar. This 'Leave-taking' presentation in late April helped people prepare to say goodbye to those they cared for. Armed with the knowledge from the 'Leave-taking' presentation and the tools to act on the First Law of Transitions, parents were better prepared to navigate the difficult 'departee months' of April, May, and June – and to help their children do the same.

#8: On-Going Staff Support

The On-going Staff Support Committee (OSSC) focuses on the transitions-related needs of staff across the entire calendar. They run both a 'social buddy' and an 'academic mentor' program. The social buddy is a volunteer member of staff with a compatible social profile (i.e. similar age, marital status, interests) who makes contact with the new staff member after he or she is hired and who will also be available to assist in a practical fashion (i.e. moving, settling in) during the summer. The academic mentor is a veteran member of staff with a similar job (i.e. in the same department or grade-level team) who can assist and explain the practicalities of how the new job and school works throughout the first year of employment.

Social buddies are needed primarily during the settling-in phase – once a staff member has found his or her way socially, the social buddy program naturally fades into the background. (As with the Student Ambassador program, the primary purpose of the matching process for social buddies is a smooth transition for the arriver, not friendship. If friendships evolve out of the matching process, then that's an added bonus.)

Academic mentors, in contrast, are explicitly guided by the committee in helping new staff members *throughout the first year*. The OSSC develops and maintains an annual calendar-based job description for mentors. Divisional OSSC committee members at the Elementary, Middle, and High School levels periodically update mentors on things they should be remembering to help their new staff members with at important junctures throughout the first calendar year.

In addition to divisional representatives on the OSSC, the school's HR Manager also plays an active role on the committee. He or she liaises closely with the Superintendent so newly hired members of staff can be matched with appropriate buddies or mentors in a timely fashion. In my message to HR Managers (see Message #7 of the 'Messages in Bottles' in Appendix A on page 249), I promised that a comprehensive transitions program would make an HR Manager's job more efficient, effective, and enjoyable. The OSSC helps make that promise a reality.

#9: Orientation Committee

In the beginning, there was chaos.

Actually, it wasn't that bad, but prior to the advent of a comprehensive transitions program at ASH, there was little coordination or coherence in the whole-school approach to welcoming new students, parents, or staff. The Orientation Committee was the birthplace of the original transitions program at the American School of The Hague. It offered a forum and synergy for many of the best ideas to spring forth that would become the trademark traditions of the Team. After all, coordinating a successful orientation for a school of one thousand students – when fully one-third of those students and families are new every year – is a massive undertaking.

Over the years, the early work of the Orientation Committee naturally evolved and matured into the programs that carry its work forward – the Student Ambassadors for students, the Parent Welcomers and International Committee for parents, and the On-going Staff Support Committee for staff. The Orientation Committee now comes together when needed, usually only in the late spring, to discuss final logistical and practical preparations for the Orientation Week that occurs in the first week after the summer holiday. Because of his or her coordinating role liaising between so many of the Team's committees, this committee is chaired by the Director of Admissions.

#10: Leave-taking

The First Law of Transitions[33] would logically imply that the Leave-taking Committee is the most important committee on the entire Team. The First and Second[34] Laws would indicate that leave-taking issues need to be adequately addressed in order for a transitions program as a whole to be

---

33 You have to say a clear 'goodbye' in order to say a clear 'hello'
34 For a person to connect to somebody else, that other person must be willing and able to make the connection.

successful.

Leave-taking is where the foundations for a successful Transitions Team and Program get laid – or fail. A poorly managed leave-taking process erodes a community by wearing down the attachment systems of its members, as discussed in *Chapter 1: Attachment.*

Conversely, a successfully managed Leave-taking Committee positions members of the community to keep their attachment systems clean and strong enough to cope with another round of mobility, year after year. Participating in a mobile community never gets easier (that would be a sign of becoming calloused, which would entail the opposite of a healthy engagement with one's feelings). But it is possible to keep our participation in such a community unnecessarily cluttered with issues of unresolved grief.

The Leave-taking Committee, therefore, was appropriately one of the first initiatives tackled by ASH's early transitions program. Largely because of the unpopularity of its initiatives (consider the repulsion factor discussed in *Chapter 1: Attachment,* page 3), it was difficult to find sufficient manpower for the committee or adequate instrumental support from the Administration for its proposed initiatives. Many of the Team's early ideas never received sufficient support to get launched, but they continue to be brilliant ideas worth revisiting – memory books in the Elementary school, hand-painted tiles for departing students to decorate pillars throughout the school, and so forth.

These unlaunched initiatives nonetheless laid the groundwork for subsequent initiatives that did succeed. Every departing student and member of staff signs the permanent signature boards which decorate the walls of the cafeteria, and every departing student receives a wooden clog hand-signed by his or her classmates. These kinds of leave-taking initiatives have achieved maturity, by which I mean they have been largely incorporated into the work of other committees. For example, the presentation of clogs, signing of signature boards, and delivering of farewell speeches are now fully incorporated into the work of the Student Ambassadors and the On-Going Staff Support Committee for students and staff, respectively. What the Leave-taking Committee does now is largely to coordinate the practical needs of the program, such as the purchase and distribution of hundreds of Dutch wooden clogs every year, or the opening and readying of the signature boards so departing students can 'leave their mark.'

#11: Communications

A description of the work of the Communications committee is simple –

it facilitates anything to do with publicizing the work of the Safe Harbour program. This might include updates to the website, or the writing of columns about transitions-related issues in school publications, or the PR for an upcoming speaker or Safe Harbour-sponsored event.

The Director of Public Relations chairs this committee, and is joined by the school's webmaster as well as other parents with a marketing or communications background.

#12: Cultural Awareness

The Cultural Awareness committee evolved to correct a conclusion the early Transitions Team at ASH reluctantly drew after its first several years in business, namely that the Team's efforts reflected the dominant USAmerican culture at the school – and not the full spectrum of cultures present at the school.

The Cultural Awareness committee called the Team's attention to the USAmerican cultural slant in its early work. It shifted the Team's attention towards dormant opportunities for cross-cultural learning and understanding by creating venues for various cultural heritages to share their identities and traditions.

The trademark program of the Cultural Awareness committee is 'Food for Thought.' In Food for Thought presentations, groups of parents from a particular country or region of the world present about their country to the Elementary, Middle, or High School faculties. These presentations take a portion of one of these faculties' regular staff meetings. The emphasis in these workshops is on the educational values instilled in the children from these cultures, so staff build a real appreciation for what it means to be, for example, a Norwegian child in a Norwegian school, or a Korean child in a Korean school. What is 'a good student' in that culture? What is an appropriate relationship between a student and a teacher? How much distance should a parent maintain – or not maintain – towards the school?

'Food for Thought' presentations scramble the roles that generally prevail at schools. Instead of teachers doing the teaching, students doing the learning, and parents looking on, 'Food for Thought' leads to parents doing the teaching, teachers doing the learning, and students looking on. This shuffling of expected roles is a classic example of the notion of 'crosshatching' referred to in *Chapter 3: Land Ho!* Such novel arrangements of roles lead to an enthusiastic learning climate for all involved, with parents thrilled to have the opportunity to teach teachers about how life and education operate in their home cultures, and teachers thrilled to sit for a change on the receiving end of the desks. The work of the Cultural Awareness Committee is an exemplar of what I have called 'audience recreation,' discussed in *Chapter 2: Finding the Ship's Log.*

Presenting parents also bring snacks and treats typical of the cultures being shared, leading to the intentional pun in the 'Food for Thought' title. Staff tend to hurry to be on time to such presentations.

THE NEEDS OF PEOPLE MOVING ACROSS CULTURES

The central argument of this book is that people in transition need to reestablish safety in their attachments and coherence in their stories. These two needs are linked in that receiving the opportunity from another person to share one's story fosters the growth of an attachment to that person. We share our stories with those with whom we feel safe, and we are safe with those with whom we can share our stories. Stories build attachments.

How does Safe Harbour foster conditions for people to share their stories with others, so they can attach to others and build community, and therefore thrive in the face of mobility across cultures?

To answer that question, we break the process into the four phases described in *Chapter 3: Land Ho!*, namely:

- leaving

- arriving

- staying

- and doing any of these things 'out of sync' with one's surroundings

The following discussion will explore what occurs in each of these phases for the three populations involved, namely students, parents, and staff/administrators.

LEAVING

Students In The Leaving Phase

The Student Ambassadors at the High School level plan and host what are known as 'Goodbye Homerooms' for each grade level. They assign a classmate or group of classmates with the task of presenting a brief tribute to each departee. The departing classmate is then presented with a wooden clog (a typically Dutch article of traditional clothing), which has been signed in the preceding weeks by every classmate, and then stuffed with goodbye notes in the open space of the shoe. (Receiving a shoe is not a surprise. Departees participate in the preparation for the 'Goodbye Homerooms' too, since they are not the only ones leaving. They also have people they need to say clear 'goodbyes' to.) After these presentations, some technologically savvy Student Ambassadors often make video tributes for the departees, full of interviews with his or her friends, funny or memorable anecdotes, and quotes and music. Many an adult around the world could learn a thing or two from the integrity and professionalism with which the Ambassadors approach the daunting task of saying goodbye to their friends.

After the 'Goodbye Homerooms,' departing students move with their friends past a central location where the signature boards (the signing of which is coordinated by the Leave-taking committee) have been readied for them to leave their mark. Each departing student signs the boards, which return afterwards to their permanent displays along the walls of the cafeteria.

Parents In The Leaving Phase

A school community cannot provide parents with the same degree of structure or curriculum afforded to their sons and daughters. Nor would that be an appropriate goal – children are the students, and parents are the parents. Still, one of the central arguments of this book is that all parties can fulfill their roles more fully and successfully (that is to say students can be better students, parents can be better parents, and teachers can be better teachers) if they transition well compared to if they transition poorly.

So what is an appropriate level of servicing for parents to insure that they navigate the leave-taking process well? It must be emphasized that leave-taking services are as much for the parents who are staying as they are for those who are leaving. In keeping with the Second Law of Transitions[35], staying parents need to resolve their grief well in order to be genuinely open to new connections in the new school year. What's the right balance, then, for a school in terms of assisting parents with an important challenge, without stretching resources too far away from the school's main priority, namely the education of its students?

I believe the answer resides in periodic parental education, and ASH's Safe Harbour provides a healthy model of how such parental education can work. The Expat Life Issues group runs their annual 'Leave-taking' seminar in April, emphasizing the First Law of Transitions, namely that "you have to

---

35 *For a person to connect to somebody else, that other person must be willing and able to make the connection.*

grieve well to leave well." This First Law is also emphasized in the training workshops for Parent Welcomers and the International Committee, further building and reinforcing the community's understanding of the importance of priming one's attachment system by saying 'goodbye' well first in spring – rather than trying to skip right to saying 'hello' in the fall. The Safe Harbour program gently massages the First Law into the community at appropriate educational junctures during the year, be it a column in a newsletter, a midyear presentation, or even their own Student Ambassador son or daughter explaining at the family dinner table why it is important to say goodbye well.

Staff In The Leaving Phase

Traditions abound at ASH to recognize staff who leave, be it for another school, a departure from education, or retirement. Many of these traditions predate the Safe Harbour program. After all, every cohesive human group will attend to the needs of the group if given the opportunity, and the staff of the American School is a generally cohesive group that does an excellent job of taking care of the leave-taking needs of both the departees, as well as those left behind.

It is perhaps this 'staff' variable that accounts for a program like Safe Harbour taking root and taking off at a school like the American School of The Hague in the first place. Staff turnover is moderate, neither too quick nor too slow, such that a core of long-term staff get refreshed with the new ideas and energies of new arrivals. One of the long-term values that seems to be shared by the long-term staff, and by the school in its very ethos, is a considerable degree of care for the feelings of the individual – especially one's colleagues. Could an effective Transitions Team be built upon a staff who did not hold fellow colleagues in high regard? I think not.

This regard continues to be reflected by heartfelt departure speeches and ceremonies for departing colleagues, given by fellow colleagues, principals, and directors. Staff, too, sign a permanent board with the signatures of 'departees.' ASH continues to be a school that 'takes goodbye seriously' – which I would argue is the foundational explanation as to why they can do such an outstanding job greeting newcomers.

ARRIVING

Students In The Arriving Phase

With the assistance and guidance of the counselors, the High School Student Ambassadors coordinate a week-long orientation program for new students that attempts to comprehensively deal with all of the new students' needs. Ambassadors in the Middle and Elementary divisions of the school are also closely involved in the orientation programs in their respective divisions, but their degree of responsibility and autonomy is naturally proportional to what those age groups can handle.

Seventy new students (the rest of the new students trickle in throughout the rest of the year, at times I've described as 'out of sync'– see later in this chapter) interact with seventy Student Ambassadors in groups that shift in composition over the course of the week, having an opportunity to:

- truly get to know other students, both those who are new and the Student Ambassadors

- find out about life at school and opportunities for involvement

- find out about life outside school (transportation, safety, tours)

- get versed academically about the appropriate course of study

- sign up for classes

- play getting-to-know-each-other-better icebreakers and games

- eat

By the end of the week, counselors can stand on the 2nd floor mezzanine and look down upon the cafeteria, observing seventy well-fed, well-versed new students mingling with each other and with seventy Student Ambassadors in colored shirts. When the whole group appears to move and fold as a new unit, with new and veteran students exchanging cell phone numbers and Facebook names prior to the upcoming weekend, counselors can feel like they've just baked bread.

When we would stand on the balcony and see the group gradually rise and head out the door together, we knew the baking had gone well.

Parents In The Arriving Phase

During that same week, the Parent Welcomers run an analogous program for new parents, operated in close conjunction with the Student Ambassador program. When the parents have 'time off' (i.e. when their sons and daughters were busy with a Student Ambassador activity), Parent Welcomers run their own curriculum that covers:

- An 'Academic Life at an American School' session, offered by the Cultural Awareness committee. This session seeks to unpack the implicit value structure for an American School like ASH, particularly for parents who come from other national education systems who might be new to a USAmerican educational philosophy. This session is generally recommended for anyone new to an American educational model, and it examines things such as the importance of extracurricular activities at ASH, the role of the parent in the school, parent-teacher and teacher-student relationships at an American school, etc.

- A tour of the school.

- A lunch for parents, while the students are having their own Student Ambassador-sponsored lunch.

- Extra assistance with navigating the curriculum and picking appropriate classes, where a veteran Parent Welcomer assists new parents with relatively simpler questions not requiring input from a specialist, such as a teacher or a counselor.

Staff In The Arriving Phase

Two programs sponsored by the On-Going Staff Support committee have already been mentioned earlier in this chapter, namely the 'social buddy' program, and the 'academic mentor' program. What hasn't yet been sufficiently emphasized is the relief these two programs bring to the HR department, the principals, and the head of school, all of whom are otherwise on overdrive dealing with the many questions and concerns that naturally arise from a new member of staff. Having the additional volume of volunteers reaching out to new staff (one 'social buddy' and one 'academic mentor' per new staff member) effectively spreads the load for dealing with the integration of new colleagues into the school.

Such 'spreading of the load' helps those new colleagues function better, which logically helps the school function better, which ultimately should help students learn better.

STAYING

An explanation of what Safe Harbour does to address the 'Staying' phase opens with a program that is not population specific, namely International Day.

This massive event in October involves students, parents, and staff and is a huge example of one of the core ideas in this book, namely the importance of validating life stories.

We all long for our identities to be seen and validated. Having our cultural identities seen and validated makes a massive contribution towards our sense that who we are counts here too – that a chunk of identity didn't get lost in our luggage or confiscated at the border.

Consider what life at the American School of The Hague looked like before International Day. Without any school-sanctioned celebration of all the various cultures represented at the school, entire ways of life remained hidden beneath the surface. What people ate, how they sang, how they spoke, how they dressed, how they thought, how they prayed, how they danced – most of these things remained invisible and largely unseen by the very people you taught with, you studied with, you spoke to in the parent parking lot.

Consider what happens when:

- The school dedicates an entire day to dressing up the majority of school classrooms in the decorations and design typical of one particular culture or another. As a Japanese mother, you're invited to dress up a classroom as though it were in Japan.

- Everyone arrives at school dressed in the clothes or national costume they associate with the word 'home.' As a teenager from Maharashtra, India, you're allowed to put on your grandmother's sari.

- There is an opportunity to gather in a group with students and parents and teachers under a flag of Singapore and march in a parade.

- You and your fellow New Zealanders are given five minutes at the school-wide performance to perform the Haka.

- You and your fellow USAmericans are given five minutes to demonstrate a square dance.

- You're allowed to occupy a booth with tourist information and food from Zimbabwe.

- As an 11th grader, you're allowed to miss an entire math class to visit a group of wide-eyed 1st graders to tell about your life growing up in a mud hut in Nigeria.

- You receive dozens of compliments on the delicious dish you made from your home town in Ukraine – seven parents ask for the recipe.

All of these things happen in a typical International Day at ASH, and all of these things are examples of one fundamental truth: we all long for our identities to be seen and validated. Having our cultural identities seen and validated makes a massive contribution towards our sense that *who we are counts here too* – that a chunk of identity didn't get lost in our luggage or confiscated at the border. In short, International Day creates legions of opportunities for people to write their identities and for their identities to get read. This leads to growing attachments amongst the members of a group, and the increasing stability and cohesion of the social group. And this basis of community resides at – or forms – the heart of a school.

OUT OF SYNC

Students Out Of Sync

One of the main challenges for the Student Ambassador program entails how to deal with students who do things out of phase with the rest of their peers. With the best of orientation programs for August, some students arrive in September, or even April. With the best of leave-taking programs in the spring, some students have to depart at an odd and unforeseen time, like November.

Because a number of students would always arrive in early January, a 'mini orientation' is planned for these five to ten students, much like a condensed, two-day version of what is done in a week in August.

For students who arrive at other times in the year, a separate referral process is required. Admissions now notifies the Student Ambassador Coordinators, who then notify one of their grade level Captains. Using a 'New Student Info Sheet,' the Student Ambassador Captains pick the Ambassador in their grade with the most compatible profile. On the new student's first day of school, he or she gets met by both the designated Ambassador and one of the grade-level Captains, the latter of which is present to make sure everything runs smoothly. The Student Ambassador then meets the new student at reception and at every break or lunchtime for at least the first two days of school.

Analogous alternate processes evolved for dealing with students who leave at odd times. Grade level captains initiate a clandestine clog-signing process for the student in question, the Leave-taking committee gets activated to open the signature board at a designated time, and friends and classmates get told to meet at the board at a specific time, bringing the departing student with them. Friends (or, failing that, the Student Ambassador grade-level captains) give a brief tribute, the departing student signs the signature board, and the clog with signatures gets presented.

These 'out of sync' processes only become well-oiled and efficient over time. However, it is worth noting that regardless of how finely tuned such alternate processes are, the students who arrive or leave 'out of sync' with their peers always seem at a slight or considerable disadvantage compared to students going through such processes at 'normal' times.

For example, of all the students who experience considerable adjustment problems after arrival, I would estimate that the vast majority of them are out-of-sync arrivals. I can only speculate on what happens to the students who leave midyear. However, if one can reasonably assume that the kinds of out-of-sync students Safe Harbour receives are not significantly different from the kinds of students who leave out of sync, then it is safe to assume that out-of-sync departures also experience a less-than-optimal adjustment in their new settings.

It would seem, then, that even transitions has its seasons. There is a time for leaving. There is a time for arriving. And there is what a given community considers to be a 'normal' amount of time to stay. To arrive or leave 'out of sync' with other arrivees or departees comes at a price. To stay longer than most others feels somehow wrong. That is why my advice to organizations and multinationals is: *don't make something that is already hard even harder by making people move out-of-sync.* If they still don't feel like listening, then I point out that an unhappy child or spouse creates drag for an employee, and enough drag can slow, stop, or even sink a boat. By now, employers *should* be paying attention to the adjustment of their employees' dependents.

Staff Members Out Of Sync

The transition for a staff member who moves out of sync is likely to feel easier if only for the reason everybody knows and expects it to be so hard. Inheriting a job or a classroom midyear is one of the most difficult challenges a teacher can face, as it has almost certainly been preceded by a turbulent period (the morning sickness associated with a pregnancy leave, or the underperformance of the preceding teacher who's job was terminated, or the illness or death of a beloved teacher). Because everybody generally expects such a transition to be difficult, the person who steps into this role usually knows to take proactive steps to address the challenge, and supporting personnel usually extend additional support to the teacher in question.

When resources match the challenge, a person will usually be alright.

Parents Out Of Sync

The aforementioned warnings logically extend to parents too, if only because an adult's emotions are analogues of a child's. Adults, too, have a season for opening their hearts and homes whether they consciously intend to or not, and families who arrive beyond this window usually have less access to those same hearts and homes. A school community at the beginning of the year is highly attuned to the experience of newness and fresh starts. People who arrive are looking for new friends. Those who have successfully said goodbye to old friends – however painful that might have been – are now ready to make new connections. All signals, in other words, say 'connect.'

What happens to the parents who arrive after these signals have waned, after people have (re)connected with new and old friends, after people have joined their new groups for the year and made their commitments? I would liken it to somebody who had pneumonia from mid-December through mid-January, and then wants to still celebrate Christmas and New Year's once he or she is better. A claim of "I missed it!" wouldn't be enough to motivate any but the most ardent of Christmas lovers.

And again, I have no reason to believe parents who arrive out of sync are any different from those who depart out of sync, meaning out-of-sync departees are likely to encounter circumstances in their new settings that are anything but optimal for somebody wanting to fit in.

It would seem there are not only seasons to the experience of transitions, but that these seasons – like the real seasons – do not distinguish between ages, roles, or intentions. Feeling as if you can't find real friends is likely to feel just as cold to a parent as it does to a child.

Empty Nesters

An exceptional initiative that emerged at ASH addressed a particular type of out-of-sync experience for parents. The purpose of the Empty Nesters group was two-fold. The main purpose was to assist parents with the transition from having children at home, to not. But as the group got started, other subtler needs emerged, such as those of parents who left older children behind at college and moved with their younger children to the Netherlands. These parents found themselves straddling two realities, needing to stay connected to their older children living 'back home' while helping the family build a new life in the Netherlands without excluding the older family members.

How does one approach these challenges? The birth of the Empty Nesters group was an attempt to help parents grapple with the task of feeling 'out of sync' with their fellow parents and even with their own family members.

In other words, the advent of the Empty Nesters group was a sign that Safe Harbour was broadening the meaning of 'transitions' to encompass other types of life transitions.

Parents whose children have already all moved off to college or university are logically older than their younger peers with children still in the 'nest.' The Empty Nesters group was infused from the outset with a wisdom conferred by maturity, a wisdom able to tackle the bigger, stickier questions of life. Who are you when your youngest child leaves the house? Who are you when you are no longer a day-to-day parent giving day-to-day feedback (or consequences) to your children?

Most parents anticipate this transition coming. Even with that anticipation, the change can jar a parent's sense of identity and orientation. The Empty Nesters group gives parents a forum to discuss what's happening and what comes next. Many of these parents have been long-standing contributors to the life of the school and the activities in the community. When their last child leaves home, many wake with a strange sensation they had not anticipated. Some unquestioned status as 'stakeholders' in the school had shifted. Are they now allowed to show up at school, to still be involved? An invisible diploma has been conferred upon them at their son or daughter's graduation in June, and suddenly they are not sure if they still 'belong' to the school, and if so, to what degree.

The Empty Nesters work is an elegant solution to the attachment needs described in *Chapter 1: Attachment*. We all have the need to attach and to feel secure with and in our families and communities. As these families and communities complete their functions, such that it becomes time to move on, we also need processes and rituals which allow us to let go. Students have graduation. Staff have retirement. What do parents have when the last of their children is no longer a 'child at home'? Nobody doubts that they are still 'parents.'

And yet, as anybody who has ever been through that transition can attest, something departs when a child leaves the home – particularly when the last child leaves.

Thanks to the Empty Nesters, parents in the ASH community have a forum in which to discuss these issues. Much as the school can serve as a transitional attachment object for new members to the community, the Empty Nesters group positions itself as a transitional attachment object for parents whose old identities have quietly departed. A room full of 'empty nesters' becomes something members can hold on to, en route to their next decisions about who they are to become in their lives after raising children.

ALIGNING ASH'S SAFE HARBOUR PROGRAM WITH OTHER SCHOOLS' HARBORS

As we sail out of ASH's Safe Harbour, we pass the boundaries of what any harbor can do, however safe. Every harbor ends with a wall. Beyond the walls roll the open seas. Harbors can only control that which happens within their walls. Yet what has happened on the seas prior to arrival is written all over the faces of those arriving. And the way people leave Safe Harbour gets stamped on their hearts as they embark, hopefully leaving signs of healthy grieving and positive leave-taking.

In other words, as of the writing of the first edition of this book, *no international school has any control over the starting condition in which their new arrivees reach their shores*. Each international school only has control over the degree to which they help departing members leave well.

This reality confronts schools with a conundrum:

Mobility across cultures can only be addressed comprehensively if schools collaborate.

Schools are mutually dependent upon one another in dealing with transitions, because the issues involved occur on a timeline that spans multiple schools.

By now it should come as no surprise that I perceive challenges as opportunities. The apparent limitation to what one harbor can do is an invitation in disguise to what an association of harbors could do.

A Future Course To Sail By

What we need is a network of harbors for children and families to sail between. What we need is a way for students and their families to know they are sailing from one safe harbor to another, and that the next harbor will take equally good care of their very real transitions-related needs. And once they've arrived there, they can climb out of their boats and man the docks themselves, contributing to the harbor on that end for as long as they can be contributing 'stayers' in that place.

What we need, in other words, are a set of standards schools should meet in order to be justifiably recognized as safe harbors. Because only then can a family, student, or staff member sailing from one safe harbor to another know that programs are truly in place to guarantee – to the degree that life can offer guarantees – safe passage.

We need appropriate accreditation criteria, or another form of effective quality assurance criteria wielded by an educational system, that safeguard these needs as the priorities they deserve to be.

Part III, Ensuring Safe Passage: Navigating Mobile Lives Through the Hearts of Schools, propels us towards the criteria required for safe passage.

ENSURING SAFE PASSAGE

*Navigating Mobile Lives Through
the Hearts of Schools*

Chapter 7

THREE-PART PARABLE OF A SEASICK SAILOR

"Seasickness, in layman's terms, is confusion within the brain, caused by contradictory signals between the inner ear and the eyes. The inner ear which controls our sense of physical balance recognizes motion which the eyes may not. The results of this confusion are fatigue, dizziness and nausea... During a severe bout of this illness very little else matters, not finances, not romance, not even life itself."

   – *Cruising Fundamentals,* American Sailing Association

Part III, Ensuring Safe Passage: Navigating Mobile Lives Through The Hearts Of Schools, explores three ways for assessing the effectiveness of comprehensive transitions programs. It is designed to help the reader evaluate his or her own school's transitions services, or those of another school – possibly one the reader is considering moving his or her family to, working at, or even attending.

   Like a lens zooming outwards, we will start with a close-up focus on the experience of the *individual,* and ways of assessing whether a comprehensive transitions program has met the needs of an individual person. Panning outwards, we then broaden our view and examine the functioning of a school's *Transitions Team,* its stage of development, and the degree to which it is truly embedded in and supported by the school. And lastly, based on the reality discussed at the conclusion of the previous chapter, namely that no one school can successfully address these issues entirely on its own, we zoom out to the widest angle possible. This view requires that we examine the functioning of any given school as a part of the broader *network of schools* within which that school operates. This view asks the question, "How well does the *network of schools* address the challenges and opportunities involved in mobility across cultures?"

I will argue that the effectiveness of a program for addressing mobility across cultures can only be realistically evaluated by considering all three levels of functioning simultaneously. What are the real experiences of real individuals, as these experiences are shaped by the services of real Transitions Programs, and how do these programs function in real networks of real schools worldwide?

We have a large theoretical journey ahead. To succeed on that journey, we're going to need maps and charts connected to this book's maritime metaphor.

A NAUTICAL PARABLE – IN THREE PARTS

The word 'nausea' comes from the Greek root *naus* for 'ship.' It is no wonder that the Greeks, as they moved amongst the six thousand or so islands peppering their horizons, had a need for the Greek word *nausia* to describe the effect being at sea could have on virtually anybody. The effects of seasickness were as pervasive then as they are now: nothing – literally nothing – matters to a nauseous person besides ceasing the sickness.

People struggling with mobility don't generally get physically nauseous.[36] But 'feeling sick' is an apt comparison. People in transition have lost their bearings. Something about their surroundings feels as if it is moving in unpredictable ways – even though the dining room table and chairs that were unpacked from the shipment look as fixed and stable as they did 'back home.' People in transition don't want the brief relief of a sip of water or the distraction of even the funniest of jokes. The only thing they want is to get the boat to calm water and to get their legs on land. They want relief that will **LAST**. Remember that word. It will become a handy acronym.

What can you do to assist a seasick soul? Three things come to mind:

1. You can relieve the seasickness. This is short-term relief.

2. You can get him to a safe harbor. This is medium-term relief.

3. You can teach him the skills to find safe passage to any port.
   This is long-term relief.

----

36   *Some people do.*

Short-Term Relief: Getting Rid Of Seasickness

To begin with, you can get the nauseous individual to the most stable point in the boat. Many people think this is below deck in the hull, the physical point in the vessel with the least amount of rocking and rotation. Yet anybody who has ever been seasick knows this is the last place you want to be. The closed, humid air, drenched in moldy fumes, odors, and exhaust, usually makes people feel worse. Before our fictitious seasick soul actually vomits (which, by the way, provides no relief whatsoever, as anybody who's been seasick can readily attest), let's get him to the point in the boat that truly is the most stable.

The stern.

Moving towards the rear of the boat is known in seafaring jargon as 'going aft.' As our fictitious passenger goes aft and grabs the wheel, he immediately starts feeling slightly better. He's not only out in the fresh air, he's also standing at the point that affords the best view of the horizon *in relation to* the ship, such that the vessel's up-and-down motion can be seen for what it is, namely *movement in relation to the stable horizon*. His brain can do what it has been trying to do all along – experience motion relative to fixed objects. The original discrepancy which led to his brain's confusion and nausea in the first place – the clash between the inner ear's certainty that 'we're moving!' versus the eye's equally convincing rejoiner 'no we're not!' – finally gets resolved. (This is why moving below deck was such a bad idea. Below deck, the eye loses any and all indicators that anything is moving, as the tables and benches are bolted to the floor. But the fluids in the balance mechanisms of the inner ear keep sloshing in every which way, screaming to the brain that movement most definitely is occurring!) As this sensory discrepancy gets resolved, the color in our fictitious passenger's face slowly returns.

It helps even more to put him behind the wheel. The wheel or helm of any sailing vessel is located *aft*. Just as the driver of an automobile also rarely feels ill him- or herself, even on the windiest of roads, so too is the helmsman of a ship less prone to seasickness. He can see when the next wave is coming, and his brain can anticipate the surging and plunging motion that follows. Standing at the helm affords both a perceptual and a very real sense of efficacy and control. This sense of efficacy, combined with the fresh air and the clear view of a stable horizon, are all boosted by heading *aft*.

Chapter 8: Assessing the Sailor explores the deeper significance behind the notion of going *aft,* and how **AFT** is actually a useful acronym for the actions, feelings, and thoughts an individual needs to master to thrive through transition.

Medium-Term Relief: Getting To A Safe Harbor

Our passenger might feel a bit better, but his coloring still looks pallid. The best thing for him now is to pull into a safe and well-provisioned harbor, with stable docks, inviting cafes, and plenty of delicious food and fresh water.

Provisioning a harbor well is no small task. As our fictitious passenger recovers with a pint of ale and a plate of fish and chips, he admires the well-oiled systems moving goods into the harbor and shipping goods out. He notices smiling crowds welcoming arriving passengers off one ship. Turning, he catches a few saddened faces watching another group of passengers ascending the gangplank with suitcases. He notices how hard the people on the dock work. But they also look well cared for. And, most striking, he notices how much they seem to watch out for one another. Everything is happening simultaneously in this harbor, but it seems coordinated, integrated, smooth. As he downs his last sip of ale, our fictitious passenger reflects on how fine it is to spend time in a well-run harbor.

Chapter 9: Assessing the Harbor examines how to evaluate the level of transitions services that any one school provides.

Long-Term Relief: The Skills For Safe Passage

His stomach full, our fictitious passenger is no longer seasick.

He's had a chance to recover in a well-run harbor.

And yet he knows that harbors are not places where many people stay or live long-term. Harbors are places where people off-load goods, restock on supplies, recover from journeys, and then sail on.

That's his fate too – the crew of the boat told him they would be sailing on after lunchtime. Back at sea, it's all well and good for him to be familiar with *Chapter 8: Assessing the Sailor*, so he knows to stay aft to avoid nausea. It's all well and good for him to be versed in *Chapter 9: Assessing a Harbor* so he can evaluate a harbor when he sees one. But what should he do when he's at sea, moving from one harbor to the next?

The helmsman grabs the wheel and orders our fictitious passenger to assist at the mainsheet. Another sailor yells something about slack in the halyard. Yet another growls something about the loosening of the winch. Our fictitious passenger looks left, then right. (Baffled, he wonders if the last sailor just insulted him.)

"Make ready to jibe!" the helmsman screams.

The rest of the crew hollers, "Ready!"

The helmsman howls, "Jibe-ho!"

As our fictitious passenger contemplates the irony of having traded his feeling of seasickness for a feeling of uselessness, the boom swings around and knocks him full force in the chest, carrying him clear over the cockpit and hurling him against the starboard lifeline.

The helmsman leans over the wheel to make sure our passenger is alright. Frightened, swallowing a frothy aftertaste of sole sloshing in ale, our passenger slowly rights himself and reassures the helmsman he's unharmed.

"You're a real landlubber," declares the helmsman. Our passenger isn't sure what that means, but thinks he's probably expected to agree.

"Yes, sir."

"Well, then, we best teach you to sail."

If the first step in our passenger's development was overcoming his seasickness, the second step is clearly learning how to sail. And once he learns how to sail, he's going to need to know where to go. How do you plot a course to your next harbor when you can't see a centimeter of land? How do you use charts and speeds to trace a course when you're not sure what the current is doing to your trajectory?

Over the next weeks and months, as our fearless passenger learns the complex arts of sailing and navigation, a more troubling question begins to settle upon him. Suppose he does master sailing? Suppose he does master navigation? He has no control over how things will work at their next harbor.

Will they have provisions there for food and water? Will the crew be able to communicate with the locals? How will the locals be? Will they know anything about where the ship's just come from? Will they even care?

Our passenger notices for the first time that the wind has slackened.

The doldrums.

How long have they been here? He realizes he's lost all track of time. He has no idea how long they've been sailing. As he sits on the deck in the bleaching sunshine, parched from scurvy and a lack of water, he falls into a feverish sleep.

"Land Ho!" belts a sailor atop the lookout. Our passenger sits up and, rubbing his eyes, spies a blanched lighthouse atop a scraggly bluff. It's the entrance to a harbor. Our passenger feels a strange sensation in the pit of his stomach, an uncomfortable cocktail of apprehension and relief.

If the people at this harbor have read *Chapter 10: Assessing Networks of Schools*, there's an increased chance this harbor will work as well as the last one he visited. After all, the needs of a mobile sailor don't change dramatically from one port to the next.

CONNECTING METAPHOR TO REALITY

This maritime tale in three parts provides the introduction to the next three chapters, which explore the three levels at which a school's transitions services can be considered and assessed.

The first level pertains to short-term relief. It focuses on the individual passenger's inner mental and psychological world, examining whether the school's transitions services help to relieve the 'seasickness' of each individual passenger. *Chapter 8: Assessing the Sailor,* investigates how to evaluate a program at this level, by examining how well a school helps the individual maintain his or her attachment system.

The second level considers medium-range relief. It assesses the functioning of the entire Transitions Team and Transitions Program as a whole. This level pertains to the harbor, that fictitious place where our fictitious passenger arrived for his brief respite – and a plate of fish and chips. How effective, comprehensive, and integrated are the services of the school community in addressing the challenges and maximizing the opportunities of moving across cultures? *Chapter 9: Assessing the Harbor* provides a discussion and several tools for assessing a Transitions Program at the school-wide level.

The third level of evaluation lifts the dialogue to a consideration of long-term relief. As discussed at the beginning and end of *Chapter 6: An Exemplar Harbor,* regardless of how well-run or well-provisioned a school's harbor may be, *no one school can successfully address the issues involved with mobility across cultures entirely on its own.* However dedicated the personnel of one harbor may be, they have no control over how other harbors prepare people to sail their way. And later in the process, regardless of how well these same dedicated harbor personnel have prepared people to sail onwards towards future harbors, they ultimately have no control over how those future harbors actually treat 'their' passengers when they arrive. *Chapter 10: Assessing Networks of Schools* considers the following paradox: all involved require safe passage, but no single school can provide it on its own. What are schools then to do?

People who leave need the skills to exit the harbor safely. But they also need destination harbors that are properly equipped to help them when they arrive. In mirror fashion – and equally important – the people left behind in the harbor of departure also require safe passage, at least in an emotional sense. Laboring to guarantee the safe passage of those departing while ignoring one's own emotional needs is comparable, in investment terms, to squandering one's capital. There are only a certain number of unresolved and painful goodbyes a human being can digest before beginning to shut down his or her attachment system out of an instinctual sense of self-protection. *Chapter 10: Assessing Networks of Schools* launches several concrete recommendations that pertain to the highest levels of quality assurance programs for any school with a substantial stake in mobility.

Our nautical tale provides the framework for comprehensively assessing comprehensive transitions programs, at the level of the individual person, for a single school, and for networks of schools worldwide. Let's start assessing.

Chapter 8

ASSESSING THE SAILOR – THE ATTACHMENT SYSTEM OF THE INDIVIDUAL

"Everyone has a flower inside,
and inside the flower is a word."

> – Saying of the Seri people of the western
>   Sonoran Desert

POLLOCK AND VAN REKEN'S RAFT

One of the groundbreaking ideas in *Third Culture Kids* was the notion of building a 'raft' to facilitate a positive leave-taking and arrival process. For those unfamiliar with David Pollock and Ruth Van Reken's ideas, building a successful 'RAFT' to get from your current place to your next place entailed four crucial, sequential steps:

'R' for **Reconciliation:** making up with people with whom you've had differences, or with whom you still feel friction.

'A' for **Affirmation:** letting people you care about know why you care about them and what you appreciate about them.

'F' for **Farewell:** saying a real and authentic 'goodbye' to people and places you care about, and not avoiding or cushioning this process.

'T' for **Think Destination:** learning about and visualizing what life will be like in the next place, and cultivating a genuine readiness to be there.

The 'RAFT' idea from *Third Culture Kids* has resulted in concrete programs at international schools to help students and adults navigate these four steps, which has resulted in the improved moving experience for countless numbers of individuals around the world.

We now step from Pollock and Van Reken's 'RAFT' to a larger idea and vessel, by way of the first portion of the nautical tale in *Chapter 7: Three-Part Parable of a Seasick Sailor*. The reader will recall that our fictitious seasick passenger started to recover when we moved him towards the stern of the vessel, sending him *aft*. Building on Pollock and Van Reken's 'RAFT' work, we can thus introduce a new acronym to describe what works well for the individual passenger:

move AFT on your RAFT for health that will LAST.

Seasickness can be likened to an attachment system that has lost its bearings. For people to feel normal again, they're going to have to reclaim a sense of mastery in their attachment systems. They're going to have to feel they know what to do to maintain and manage an attachment system that has been pummeled.

When psychologists are trying to help people make the kinds of improvements they would like to make to their lives, we often talk about three pathways to change via:

- thoughts

- feelings

- behavior

All too often, people want to change their uncomfortable feelings directly, by turning feeling 'sad' or 'depressed' directly into 'feeling better.' It is worth considering the other two pathways to change – changing how one is *thinking* or changing one's *actions* or *behavior*. This three-way concept or triangle re-sides at the foundation of what is known as cognitive-behavioral therapy.

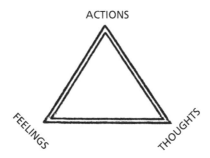

FIGURE 8.1 Three pathways to change

The orientation of this triangle is arbitrary. 'Actions' and 'thoughts' and 'feelings' are equal partners, meaning that one is not more important or more causal than the other. You could say sad feelings lead to sad thinking ("I'm depressed again, and I'm never going to feel better"), which contributes to sad behavior (i.e. not going to the gym, even though you feel great every time you do). This kind of choice of behavior only reinforces the depressive feelings and thoughts, fueling the vicious cycle.

But you could also say the cycle starts with sad behavior (not going to the gym), which keeps the endorphin, serotonin and dopamine levels in the blood and brain from rising, maintaining the sluggish feelings and the associated sluggish thoughts that we label as 'feeling depressed.' The point is that the above triangle can be rotated in any direction, putting any of the three words 'on top.' And all three versions are valid. In general, neither feelings, nor actions, nor thoughts can be said to definitively *cause* any of the events of our lives – they all feed and reinforce each other.

A successful transitions program helps people ready themselves to perform the actions that will help them feel the feelings that will lead them to thinking the thoughts that contribute to the successful navigating of transitions.

If any of the three pathways of actions, feelings, or thoughts is a useful route to change for a human being, then it stands to reason that an effective comprehensive transitions program should help people on all three levels. In other words: a successful transitions program helps people ready themselves to perform the actions that will help them feel the feelings that will lead them to thinking the thoughts that contribute to the successful navigating of transitions.

Moreover, these actions, feelings, and thoughts need to be maintained throughout all phases of the mobility cycle, from **L**eaving, to **A**rriving, to **ST**aying, in order to produce cumulative change that will **LAST.**

But we can be even more specific. If a successful transitions program helps people to maintain their attachment systems, then a successful transitions program helps people both tighten and loosen their relational bonds when the time is right. Combining this concept with the actions-feelings-thoughts triangle above, we could postulate that:

a successful comprehensive transitions program helps all members of an international school community maintain their attachment systems so they can feel the *feelings,* think the *thoughts,* and perform the *actions* that lead to the loosening and establishing of attachment bonds at all of the appropriate times in the transitions cycle.

At last we have arrived at some concrete concepts of what successful transitions programs should be accomplishing. And these concepts are measurable across time, at least at the individual level.

The 'Transitions Passport' on the following page is a document that can be used for any individual – be it student, parent, or staff member – to gauge the degree to which their attachment system is ready to act, feel, and think in ways that are conducive to transitioning well. These actions, feelings, and thoughts need to occur throughout all three phases of the mobility cycle, from leaving, to arriving, to staying. Future research will have to validate the instrument. By first grounding it in the attachment literature and the practice of cognitive-behavioral therapy, this entire book represents the rationale behind the use of an instrument like this.

Since the process of transitions spans multiple schools, this Transitions Passport is meant to be carried by one individual across time, to gauge how he or she is faring in moves from one school community to another. It maps how likely he or she is to be taking the actions, feeling the feelings, and thinking the thoughts that contribute to the healthy management of his or

TRANSITIONS PASSPORT (PART 1)		
	LEAVING	**A**RRIVING	**ST**AYING
Filled in by whom?	*BY ALL STUDENTS, REGARDLESS OF WHETHER YOU'RE NEW TO THE SCHOOL OR A VETERAN.*	*BY ALL STUDENTS, REGARDLESS OF WHETHER YOU'RE NEW TO THE SCHOOL OR A VETERAN.*	*BY PEOPLE WHO ARE STAYING. 'STAYING' = YOU ARE IN AT LEAST YOUR SECOND YEAR AT THIS SCHOOL*
Filled in when?	*IDEALLY TO BE COMPLETED TWICE: 1ST: ONE MONTH PRIOR TO END OF YEAR. MARK WITH A '▲'* *2ND: ONE WEEK PRIOR TO END OF YEAR. MARK WITH AN '●'*	*IDEALLY TO BE COMPLETED TWICE: 1ST: AT START OF YEAR MARK WITH A '▲'* *2ND: ONE MONTH AFTER START OF YEAR. MARK WITH AN '●'*	*TO BE COMPLETED ONCE, CLOSE TO THE MIDDLE OF THE SCHOOL YEAR. MARK WITH A '▲'* *MARK EACH NEW '▲' WITH THE YEAR.*
ACTIONS	*DEPARTING STUDENTS:* I AM ACTIVELY DOING THINGS TO SAY GOODBYE TO THE PEOPLE I CARE ABOUT HERE. *STAYING STUDENTS:* I AM ACTIVELY DOING THINGS TO SAY GOODBYE TO THE PEOPLE WHO ARE LEAVING: 1 2 3 4 5 6 7 NOT TRUE VERY TRUE	*ARRIVING STUDENTS:* I AM ACTIVELY DOING THINGS TO TRY TO MAKE NEW FRIENDS AND CONNECTIONS HERE. *VETERAN STUDENTS:* I AM ACTIVELY DOING THINGS TO TRY TO CONNECT WITH NEW STUDENTS. 1 2 3 4 5 6 7 NOT TRUE VERY TRUE	I AM ACTIVELY INVOLVED IN ACTIVITIES HERE. I DO THINGS WITH FRIENDS ON A REGULAR BASIS. 1 2 3 4 5 6 7 NOT TRUE VERY TRUE
FEELINGS	*DEPARTING STUDENTS:* I FEEL SAD ABOUT LEAVING THIS PLACE. *STAYING STUDENTS:* I FEEL SAD TO SEE MY FRIENDS LEAVE. 1 2 3 4 5 6 7 NOT TRUE VERY TRUE	*ARRIVING STUDENTS:* I FEEL OKAY ABOUT MOVING TO THIS NEW SCHOOL. *VETERAN STUDENTS:* I FEEL OKAY ABOUT MAKING FRIENDS WITH NEW STUDENTS THIS YEAR. 1 2 3 4 5 6 7 NOT TRUE VERY TRUE	I FEEL GOOD ABOUT MY LIFE AT THIS SCHOOL. I FEEL LIKE I'M A PART OF THIS SCHOOL, LIKE I BELONG HERE. 1 2 3 4 5 6 7 NOT TRUE VERY TRUE
THOUGHTS	*DEPARTING STUDENTS:* I AM GRADUALLY GETTING READY TO LEAVE. *STAYING STUDENTS:* I AM GRADUALLY GETTING READY TO SEE MY FRIENDS GO. 1 2 3 4 5 6 7 NOT TRUE VERY TRUE	*ARRIVING STUDENTS:* I AM READY TO START MY NEW LIFE HERE. *VETERAN STUDENTS:* I AM READY TO MAKE FRIENDS WITH SOME OF THE NEW STUDENTS. 1 2 3 4 5 6 7 NOT TRUE VERY TRUE	THIS SCHOOL AND COMMUNITY HAVE BECOME LIKE A 'HOME' TO ME. I BELONG HERE NOW. 1 2 3 4 5 6 7 NOT TRUE VERY TRUE

TABLE 8.2. Transitions passport (part 1)

her attachments, be it the relinquishing of good friendships or the gradual formation of new ones.

The first three rows cover the actions, feelings, and thinking in the **AFT** part of the vessel that I am arguing we should help people occupy on their Pollockian RAFTs. The columns move across time, from **L**eaving (since that's where the process begins), to **A**rriving, to **St**aying, all of which should add up to behaviors that help the attachment system **LAST**.

What is particularly new about a document like this is the notion that it would travel with the student, wherever the student goes – just as passports do. The issues involved with mobility across cultures traverse schools and are not confined to – or entirely measureable by – any one school. What is needed to accurately assess what is occurring with any one individual is a series of measurements that follow a person 'longitudinally,' as it's called in research circles, to capture what happens to them over time.

Of course there are massive practical considerations before such a Transitions Passport system could work. A family would have to 'turn in' their children's transitions passports upon matriculation, and they would receive them again upon departure. In the space between, the school would have to have systems for managing and using the passports, such as incorporating them into advisory or pastoral care lessons at appropriate junctures throughout the year. When the family moves, the school would have to see to it that the Transitions Passport gets returned to the family before they leave.

The purpose of this brief exploration of the Transitions Passport is not to delve into the practical hurdles that would obviously need to be overcome. The purpose here is to launch the conversation. Let's look at practical applications for the Transitions Passport like this.

USES OF PART 1 OF THE TRANSITION PASSPORT

Future research will have to explore the validity and utility of what the Transitions Passport might be measuring. But even prior to exploring the scientific validity of the Transitions Passport, it already has a variety of potential uses:

- As the basis of conversation between a new student and school personnel, after the new student fills in his or her Transitions Passport after arrival.

- As a conversation builder during advisory or small-group conversations at the end of the year, after students fill in the 'leaving' column.

- In aggregated fashion, to assess the effectiveness of a new Transitions Program. Collective scores of large groups of people could be examined to see if positive shifts are, in fact, occurring after a comprehensive transitions program gets launched.

- To see what areas need improvement in the school's program, based on scores that indicate an overall 'unreadiness' of the attachment system for large groups of people at a particular phase or juncture.

- To examine shifts in an individual's score between the first measurement (one month before the end of school, or one week after new arrivals) and the second measurement (one week prior to the end of school, or one month after new arrivals), as a possible indicator for growth or improvement in the attachment system.

- As an overall way to boost awareness and self-reflection regarding how well one is dealing with a particular phase of the cycle.

- As a way of spotting individuals who are clearly in need of intervention.

In other words, the possible uses for a Transitions Passport such as this are extensive. Future research, dialogue, and usage will determine to what degree any of these uses are feasible.

The second half of the Passport focuses upon how well the school – at least in the experience of the individual completing the Passport – is handling the challenges of mobility across cultures. This 'Part 2' is presented in the next chapter, where we look at assessing an entire school's harbor.

Chapter 9

ASSESSING THE HARBOR – A TRANSITIONS PROGRAM FOR AN INDIVIDUAL SCHOOL

"Esse est percipi." ("To be is to be perceived.")
  – George Berkeley

Given so few comprehensive programs exist for addressing the challenges of mobility across cultures, it should come as no surprise that an instrument for assessing the quality of a transitions program also does not exist – at least not to my knowledge.

If the purpose of *Chapter 8: Assessing the Sailor* was to assess the experience of the individual, the purpose of this chapter is to pan back and to broaden the scope to assessing how well the entire school is addressing the challenges involved. This chapter briefly presents two instruments that could provide the building blocks for achieving such a goal.

The first instrument looks at school programs from the perspective of the students themselves. The second instrument looks at school programs from the perspective of those most intimately involved with and knowledgeable of the programs involved, namely the members of the Transitions Team.

THE FIRST INSTRUMENT FOR ASSESSING HOW WELL A SCHOOL IS ADDRESSING MOBILITY

Part 2 of the Transitions Passport examines how each individual feels about how their current school is handling issues related to mobility across cultures. It assesses how aware the individual is of the school's efforts to provide safe passage. It also asks how much the individual deems these efforts successful. In other words, how much does the person *feel* that the school has the *intention* of providing safe passage to the next school? And *how successful* does the person think the school actually is in providing safe passage?

If these school-sponsored programs have been helpful, then theoretically they should have helped the person make healthier choices in managing his or her attachment system. Choices about how to manage one's attachment system can be made at three points in time:

- during the leave-taking phase, when attachment bonds need to be loosened

- during the arrival phase, when new attachment bonds could be getting established

- during the staying phase, when a person needs to take very good care of his or her attachment system in order to be able to continue doing anything meaningful for the legions of people leaving and arriving annually

Part 2 could be completed at the same time as students complete Part 1. But the focus of Part 2 is entirely different. Part 2 needs to be on a physically different piece of paper (or other medium) than Part 1. Unlike Part 1, which would need to travel with the student, Part 2 would remain the property of the school.

Students are generally unaware of the macro-structures and processes involved in running and managing a school. Part 2 of the Passport doesn't ask them directly about their conscious awareness of what the school is, or isn't, doing with regards to mobility across cultures. Instead, it chooses for a much looser, general, and child-friendly kind of language. Each phrase begins with "People here… ", followed by a general statement.

Students again complete the Passport from the perspective of the phase they currently occupy. Are they in the 'leaving', 'arriving', or 'staying' phase? Are they the one doing the departing, or are they the one being left behind? Students would complete the Passport at set times throughout the year, where the Passports are distributed during guidance, advisory, or pastoral care lessons, for example. Afterwards, all Passports are collected, and the school continues with its own tailored system for managing Passports internally.

TRANSITIONS PASSPORT (PART 2)		
	LEAVING	**A**RRIVING	**ST**AYING
FILLED IN BY WHOM?	BY ALL STUDENTS, REGARDLESS OF WHETHER YOU'RE NEW TO THE SCHOOL OR A VETERAN.	BY ALL STUDENTS, REGARDLESS OF WHETHER YOU'RE NEW TO THE SCHOOL OR A VETERAN.	BY PEOPLE WHO ARE _STAYING_. 'STAYING' = YOU ARE IN AT LEAST YOUR SECOND YEAR AT THIS SCHOOL.
FILLED IN WHEN?	IDEALLY TO BE COMPLETED TWICE: 1ST: ONE MONTH PRIOR TO END OF YEAR. MARK WITH A '▲' 2ND: ONE WEEK PRIOR TO END OF YEAR. MARK WITH AN '●'	IDEALLY TO BE COMPLETED TWICE: 1ST: AT START OF YEAR MARK WITH A '▲' 2ND: ONE MONTH AFTER START OF YEAR. MARK WITH AN '●'	TO BE COMPLETED ONCE, CLOSE TO THE MIDDLE OF THE SCHOOL YEAR. MARK WITH A '▲' MARK EACH NEW '▲' WITH THE YEAR.
HOW IS THIS SCHOOL DOING?	DEPARTING STUDENTS: PEOPLE HERE HAVE TRIED TO HELP ME GET READY TO LEAVE THIS SCHOOL WELL. STAYING STUDENTS: PEOPLE HERE HAVE TRIED TO HELP ME GET READY TO SAY GOODBYE WELL TO PEOPLE WHO ARE LEAVING. 1 2 3 4 5 6 7 NOT TRUE VERY TRUE	NEW STUDENTS: PEOPLE HERE HAVE TRIED TO HELP ME ARRIVE AND FIT IT WELL AT THIS SCHOOL. VETERAN STUDENTS: PEOPLE HERE HAVE TRIED TO HELP ME BE ABLE TO CONNECT WITH THE NEW STUDENTS THIS YEAR. 1 2 3 4 5 6 7 NOT TRUE VERY TRUE	IT'S HARD TO BE A 'STAYER' WHEN EVERYONE IS ALWAYS ARRIVING AND LEAVING. BUT I FEEL LIKE PEOPLE HERE REALLY UNDERSTAND THAT. 1 2 3 4 5 6 7 NOT TRUE VERY TRUE
	DEPARTING STUDENTS: THE THINGS PEOPLE HERE HAVE DONE TO TRY TO HELP ME LEAVE WELL REALLY HAVE HELPED ME. STAYING STUDENTS: THE THINGS PEOPLE HERE HAVE DONE TO HELP ME SAY GOODBYE WELL TO THE PEOPLE WHO ARE LEAVING HAVE REALLY HELPED ME. 1 2 3 4 5 6 7 NOT TRUE VERY TRUE	NEW STUDENTS: THE THINGS PEOPLE HERE HAVE DONE TO HELP ME ARRIVE WELL REALLY HAVE HELPED ME. VETERAN STUDENTS: THE THINGS PEOPLE HAVE DONE TO HELP ME CONNECT WITH THE NEW STUDENTS REALLY HAVE HELPED ME. 1 2 3 4 5 6 7 NOT TRUE VERY TRUE	PEOPLE AT THIS SCHOOL DO THINGS THAT MAKE US 'STAYERS' FEEL REALLY SEEN AND VALUED. 1 2 3 4 5 6 7 NOT TRUE VERY TRUE

TABLE. 9.1: Transitions passport (part 2)

USES OF PART 2 OF THE TRANSITIONS PASSPORT

This part of the Passport could lead to more macro, management-type kinds of conversation about transitions services at the school:

- As a conversation starter during guidance or advisory lessons, discussing what the school does well with regards to mobility across culture, and what could be improved.
- In aggregated fashion, to see how large groups of people feel the school is handling mobility across cultures.
- To see what areas need improvement in the school's program, based on scores that indicate an overall 'unreadiness' of the attachment system for large groups of people at a particular phase or juncture.
- As an overall way to boost awareness of the issues involved with a particular phase or perspective of the annual transitions cycle.
- As a way of spotting individuals who are clearly in need of intervention.
- As a way to follow the adjustment of people longitudinally over time, to evaluate which schools are more successfully helping their students manage transitions effectively, and which ones are not.
- As an instrument that could provide data demonstrating the meeting of the standards for accreditation, including the standards proposed later in this book
- As a broad research tool.

THE SECOND INSTRUMENT FOR ASSESSING HOW WELL A SCHOOL IS ADDRESSING MOBILITY

The second instrument for assessing how well a school is addressing the challenges of mobility is essentially a one-page summary of *Part II: Finding A Safe Harbor: Building Programs To Match The Challenge,* of this book.

The 'Rubric for Assessing a School's Comprehensive Transitions Program' presented in Table 9.2 splits the assessment of a school's transitions services into two fundamental domains:

- an area that has to do with structural components
- an area that has to do with support components

Structural components pertain to the layout and architecture of the comprehensive Transitions Program. As has been explored in this book, a comprehensive Transitions Program has to attend to:

- All three populations of the school, namely students, parents, staff, where staff also includes administrators. This is captured by the term **parity**, a word which also evokes the equal nature of these populations' needs, and the necessity of addressing the needs of all three populations in proportional fashion.

- Needs over time. To focus only on arrivers, without attending to the needs of leavers or stayers, verges on neglect. **Longitudinality** is a term that seeks to convey the importance *of addressing needs over time,* throughout the academic calendar.

- All of the cultures and heritages involved at the school. If people's life stories need to be seen and read in order for them to feel validated and thrive, then the program's **focus** must be inclusive of all the cultures involved. The program must seek to incorporate those cultures in creating a school where cross-cultural understanding can grow and develop. To be explicit, the program's focus must *not* only be upon the needs and perspectives of those from the dominant culture.

Support components seek to assess the level of 'buy-in' of school personnel with regards to a comprehensive transitions program. If people see and understand that something is important, it has a chance of thriving. If people question something's importance, it has less of a chance of surviving. The reason why math classes generally thrive and would never be discarded from educational systems worldwide is because general buy-in exists about the importance of math.

How important do people consider the issues described by this book, the issues involved with mobility across cultures? This question can be evaluated at several levels:

- *At the school management level:* If heads of school, directors, principals, HR managers, and curriculum directors believe comprehensive transitions programs are worth building and supporting, then we can speak of **empowerment.**

- *At the level of organizational membership:* Support of school management does not directly lead to a changed experience for a student in the classroom. People across the board, from teachers to support staff to parents to students, have to recognize the part they each play in shaping the climate of the school. How much **responsibility** do all people at a school generally take for assuming responsibility and initiating constructive action with regards to the challenges involved with mobility across cultures?

- To what degree has the ownership of the transitions program been sufficiently infused into the 'fabric' or 'DNA' of the school, so that ownership resides in and throughout the **organization**?

Using the example statements laid out within the rubric, these six components can be scored for a given school.

It is then time to pan back to the highest level of abstraction. How 'good' is a given school's transitions program? Taking an average of the scores in the six columns discussed above leads to a corresponding **'Developmental Stage'**[37] of the Transitions Program. This single number should roughly match the descriptive phrase in the 'Summary' column, providing a single digit indicator on a 1-7 scale of how well developed the school's comprehensive transitions program actually is.

The descriptors run from a score of 1 for a situation where members of the school community generally have no awareness whatsoever that mobility can pose a challenge, to a score of 7 for a school where all community members appear completely engaged with regards to issues surrounding mobility across cultures. While a 7 is probably unlikely anywhere, there are schools – particularly in domestic school systems – where 1 might be the reality.[38]

---

37 This notion of 'developmental stage' originated from ASH's first ECIS presentation on the work of its new transitions program. I am indebted to my colleagues Carol Mecklenburg, Peter Loy, and Dianne Banasco for providing the starting ideas and inspiration that led to this rubric. Barbara Schaetti provided valuable feedback during its development in 2007.

38 The admittedly tongue-in-cheek statement that "Nobody comes and nobody leaves" also dates back to our first presentation and was an attempt to use humor to cope with schools we knew must exist, but whose imagined hallways felt to us like the Dark Ages.

The Limitations Of Self-Report Measures

The shortcomings that are inherently involved with self-report measures like the two instruments above should be readily acknowledged. Self-report measures are scores given by people about their own experience. In the case of the Transitions Passport and the Rubric, the people filling in the forms may or may not be invested in the programs, both of which could bias results.

Consider one student filling out Part 2 of the Transitions Passport, who happens to be heavily involved with the Student Ambassador program. This student is very knowledgeable about what 'people here' are doing to help students at various stages and phases of the mobility cycle. Her scores on Part 2 of the Transitions Passport are likely to be quite positive, especially compared to a relatively uninvolved student in her group who is also filling out the Passport. This latter student's scores are likely to be low.

Or consider the Transitions Team member who is similarly highly invested and informed in programs provided by the school to address mobility across culture, whose perspective on what the school does may be totally different from a veteran 3rd grade teacher just down the hall. That 3rd grade teacher could be an expert on second- and third-language acquisition, but she might – for whatever reason – know nothing about the programs sponsored by the school for transitions. The first teacher might score the school at a 6 on the Rubric, whereas the second teacher might rate it at a 3.

And the same holds true, of course, for the discrepancy that would likely be found between the active parent volunteer versus the isolated stay-at-home father. Both send their children to the same school, but their perspectives on what 'people here' are doing regarding transitions might be drastically different.

My purpose in providing these instruments for assessing a school is not to help the reader arrive at the objectively 'right' answer as to 'exactly' how well a school is doing. Such a clear answer doesn't exist. Rather, the Passport and the Rubric are intended to help create a platform upon which thoughtful dialogue and reflection can begin to occur. Just as hiking boots have solid soles, it is my hope that these instruments help to create some traction on the slippery slopes of mobility.

After all, having good boots is only the beginning of any journey. Once you strap them on and begin walking, it's time to discuss some of the cliffs and ravines they might carry you to.

STAGE	STRUCTURAL COMPONENTS		
	PARITY	LONGITUDINALITY	FOCUS
DEVELOPMENTAL STAGE ↓ & CORRESPONDING GUIDING QUESTIONS →	*TO WHAT DEGREE DOES THE PROGRAM TOUCH THE NEEDS OF ALL FOUR POPULATIONS: STUDENTS, PARENTS, STAFF, & ADMINISTRATORS?*	*TO WHAT DEGREE DOES THE PROGRAM ADDRESS ALL PHASES OF THE MOBILITY CYCLE, FROM LEAVING, TO ARRIVING, AND INCLUDING STAYING?*	*TO WHAT DEGREE IS THE PROGRAM ACTIVE IN INVOLVING PEOPLE FROM OUTSIDE OF THE SCHOOL'S DOMINANT CULTURE(S)?*
1 TRANSITIONS? WHAT'S THAT?	NONE OF THE THREE POPULATIONS' NEEDS ARE ADDRESSED.	THERE IS NO WORK DONE AT ANY POINT ON THE CYCLE.	WHAT OTHER CULTURES?
2 ONE OR MORE INDIVIDUAL INITIATIVES	SOME ACTIVITY EXISTS FOR ONE POPULATION.	SINGLE PROJECT, OFTENTIMES TARGETING ARRIVAL.	THE ORGANIZATION FOCUSES ON ITS OWN NEEDS.
3 VARIOUS INITIATIVES, BUT NOT CONNECTED	SEVERAL ACTIVITIES EXIST FOR ONE OR TWO POPULATIONS.	MULTIPLE PROJECTS TARGETING ARRIVAL.	SOME ASPECTS OF MOBILITY ARE ADDRESSED, BUT IN A MONOCULTURAL WAY.
4 CONNECTION & DIALOGUE BETWEEN INDIVIDUAL INITIATIVES	WORK IS BEING DONE TO ADDRESS TWO OR THREE OF THE FOUR POPULATIONS' NEEDS.	ORIENTATION AND ARRIVAL PROGRAM WELL DEVELOPED.	RECOGNITION THAT NATIONALITY & MOTHER-TONGUE IMPACT EXPERIENCE OF MOBILITY
5 TEAM-BASED COORDINATION AND OWNERSHIP	WORK IS BEING DONE TO ADDRESS THREE OR FOUR OF THE POPULATIONS' NEEDS.	LEAVETAKING PROGRAMS FORM; UNDERSTANDING EXISTS THAT "YOU HAVE TO SAY A CLEAR GOODBYE TO SAY A CLEAR HELLO."	CULTURAL TRANSITIONS START TO BE ADDRESSED, ALONG WITH GEOGRAPHIC TRANSITIONS.
6 PROGRAM ATTENDS TO OWN TRANSITIONS-RELATED NEEDS.	ALL FOUR POPULATIONS' NEEDS ARE BEING MET ADEQUATELY AND PROPORTIONALLY.	PROGRAMS EXIST THAT FULLY ADDRESS ISSUES OF LEAVING, ARRIVING, AND STAYING.	EFFORTS DELIBERATELY TARGET DEVELOPMENT OF INTERCULTURAL SENSITIVITY COMPETENCE.
7 TRANSITIONS! AN OPPORTUNITY FULLY GRASPED BY ALL!	VARIOUS "LEGS" OF THE STOOL PROVIDE SERVICES FOR EACH OTHER (I.E. "CROSS-HATCHING").	ENTIRE "CYCLE" OF TRANSITIONS FULLY UNDERSTOOD AND ADDRESSED THROUGHOUT ORGANIZATION.	ORGANIZATION IS A "LIVING LAB" FOR DEVELOPING INTERCULTURAL COMPETENCE.

TABLE. 9.2: Rubric for assessing a school's comprehensive transitions program

SUPPORT COMPONENTS			SUMMARY
EMPOWERMENT	RESPONSIBILITY	OWNERSHIP	
TO WHAT DEGREE DOES THE SCHOOL SUPPORT PEOPLE IN TAKING LEADERSHIP IN ADDRESSING MOBILITY ACROSS CULTURES?	*TO WHAT DEGREE DO MEMBERS OF THE SCHOOL COMMUNITY FEEL IT IS THEIR RESPONSIBILITY TO SUPPORT PROGRAMS THAT ADDRESS THE CHALLENGES OF MOBILITY ACROSS CULTURES?*	*TO WHAT DEGREE ARE THE PROGRAMS THAT ADDRESS MOBILITY ACROSS CULTURES OWNED BY THE ORGANIZATION AS A WHOLE, AS OPPOSED TO BY THE INDIVIDUAL?*	*TO WHAT DEGREE DOES THE SCHOOL SEE THE CHALLENGES AND OPPORTUNITIES INHERENT IN MOBILITY ACROSS CULTURES?*
THERE'S NOTHING TO ADDRESS. IT'S NOT EVEN A PROBLEM.	THERE'S NOTHING TO EVEN TAKE RESPONSIBILITY FOR.	NOBODY OWNS THE CHALLENGE.	TRANSITIONS ARE NOT AN ISSUE. NOBODY COMES. NOBODY LEAVES.
I FEEL NO SUPPORT IN TAKING A LEADERSHIP ROLE ON TRANSITIONS.	A COLLEAGUE DOES THAT ONE ACTIVITY, BUT IT'S NOT REALLY NECESSARY.	ONE OR MORE INDIVIDUALS OWN A FEW PROJECTS.	A PERSON SOMETIMES COMES OR LEAVES. BUT WHO CARES?
PEOPLE THINK IT'S INTERESTING WHAT WE DO, BUT THEY'RE NOT VERY SUPPORTIVE.	THEY DO THOSE ACTIVITIES, BUT THEY'RE NOT REALLY NECESSARY.	MANY INDIVIDUALS OWN MANY PROJECTS; NO COLLECTIVE OWNERSHIP YET.	LOTS OF PEOPLE COME AND GO. IT'S HARD, BUT WHAT CAN YOU DO?
MODERATE SUPPORT FOR INITIATIVES, AS LONG AS THEY DON'T COST TOO MUCH TIME OR MONEY.	THERE'S A BUNCH OF PEOPLE DOING THINGS. SHOULD I GET INVOLVED?	INDIVIDUALS BEGINNING TO DISCUSS & CONNECT EFFORTS.	IS THIS SOMETHING THAT AFFECTS LOTS OF PEOPLE HERE?
SOME REAL, PRACTICAL, AND FINANCIAL SUPPORT TO TAKE A LEADERSHIP ROLE.	IT'S THE TRANSITIONS PROGRAM'S JOB. BUT SHOULD I MAYBE BE DOING SOMETHING TOO?	START OF COLLECTIVE OWNERSHIP AS BUFFER AGAINST DEPARTURE OF ANY INDIVIDUAL.	IT'S NOT EASY TO REINVENT SELF: MOBILITY ACROSS CULTURES AFFECTS EVERYONE HERE!
CONSIDERABLE SUPPORT EXISTS FOR ADDRESSING CHALLENGES OF MOBILITY ACROSS CULTURES.	IT'S REALLY IMPORTANT, AND MOST PEOPLE ARE INVOLVED IN SOME WAY.	MEMBERS & COMMITTEE CHAIRS REPLACE THEMSELVES; CLOSURE FOR DEPARTING TEAM MEMBERS.	TRANSITIONS-RELATED CHALLENGES RESIDE NEAR THE CORE OF EVERY COMMUNITY MEMBER'S EXPERIENCE.
COMPLETE SUPPORT IN TAKING A LEADERSHIP ROLE IN ADDRESSING TRANSITIONS.	IT'S EVERYONE'S RESPONSIBILITY, INCLUDING MY OWN.	THE ORGANIZATION FULLY OWNS THE CHALLENGE AND THE PROGRAMS TO ADDRESS THAT CHALLENGE.	ALL MEMBERS INVOLVED IN ORGANIZATION FULLY AWARE OF IMPORTANCE OF ADDRESSING TRANSITIONS.

SOME OF THE LIMITATIONS OF A COMPREHENSIVE TRANSITIONS PROGRAM

The last thing this book aspires to do is to assign full responsibility for the thriving of student, parent, or staff member entirely to the school or its transitions program. The school's willingness to be a transitional object and to provide a solid Transitions Program is analogous to the life buoy that is thrown out to the swimmer. To make it to the buoy and use it to get out of the water, the swimmer still needs to swim.

More importantly, there are many factors that have to do with the swimmer himself. What about his personality, and how outgoing or sociable or assertive he is? Or how shy, reserved, or closed he is? These kinds of factors have repeatedly been shown to influence how well a person will transition or not, with a clear advantage going to the sociable, assertive types of personalities [50, 51, 52, 53, 54, 55]. What about a person's motivation to make the transition? Or the degree of control he perceives regarding the choice to move or not? Research has consistently indicated that the perception of choice and the sense that one has some control over one's fate and direction positively influence outcomes, including the outcome of something like moving [24].

What about family factors, and the degree of harmony and protection a family gives its members during the stress and challenge of a move? What about past experiences of moving, both positive and negative, and how they might affect a person's expectations of how the upcoming move will turn out?

All these questions focus upon the arriving process, but they can easily be turned towards departing and staying too. For example, what effect does a shy personality have in terms of how somebody navigates the process of leaving? Or what effect would that shy personality have on somebody who stays, somebody who repeatedly has best friends leave?

A school obviously has no control over the personalities of its students, parents, or teachers, or the people with whom they forge friendships. Certainly a school can't tackle all these variables.

What, then, *is* a school's responsibility?

A Very Brief Sojourn Into Statistics

One of this book's main points is that focused investments in developing effective and comprehensive Transitions Programs will positively influence the experience of those who attend schools with a high degree of turnover.

What does that mean? In non-statistical terms, it means that many factors contribute to whether somebody thrives or struggles through a challenge like mobility across cultures. The mix of factors are slightly different for each person.

The only way to address all the factors involved would be to develop an individualized approach for each and every student, parent, and teacher to help them throughout the entire transition cycle.

Someone with unlimited reserves might have the resources for a program like that. But most schools do not. And with an eye on what's been said about the work of Winnicott and 'the good enough' school (see page 33), the better question is whether such a program would actually be good for those involved. After all, each person does need to learn skills for coping with adversity.

In non-statistical terms, the phrase above, namely "developing effective and comprehensive Transitions Programs that positively influence the experience of those who attend schools with a high degree of turnover," simply means that a good transitions program is like a multivitamin. It has ingredients everyone needs. In other words, like those factors at the bottom of Maslow's hierarchy of needs, good transitions programs cut to common denominators. Attention to these core issues benefits everyone, *regardless* of personality or past experience.

> *A good transitions program is like a multivitamin. It has ingredients everyone needs.*

So What Am I Saying?

My argument here is not to claim the school is the only, or even the most important, contributing factor to a student's working models of social relationships. But I am arguing that it would be folly, and ethically irresponsible, for educators at international schools to ignore their part in shaping a child's attachment style.

When our students throw litter out of the window and we correct them, only to be told that "everyone does it," our natural response is to say "that doesn't make it right," or perhaps even "a cleaner environment begins with your own behavior." We teach our students to take their share of responsibility in the world.

As parents and informed educators, shouldn't we be doing the same in terms of how we shape our schools?

You cannot necessarily see the effects of the aforementioned multivitamin by zooming in only on individuals or small groups of individuals. However, when you pan back and look at the progress of more and more of the whole population of a school, the positive effects of a Transitions Program should become more evident. In fact, the finding in *Visible Learning* that mobility hurts learning can – and arguably should – be taken as evidence that not receiving the multivitamin of an effective Transitions Program is detrimental to all involved.

IN CLOSING

Talk really is not enough. As Hattie has shown in his research, the quality of children's learning is at stake. Perhaps more importantly, the quality of life on this planet is at stake. We must not forget George Walker's wise words:

> *"Against our contemporary background of a renewed sense of precarious isolation, the vocabulary of international education – responsible citizenship, compassionate thinking, tolerance, diversity within a shared humanity, cultural understanding – no longer sounds like high-flown idealism but seems, on the contrary, to offer the only practical hope for the future of humankind."*
> [5, p. 209]

And the simple reality is that students at international schools are in a privileged position to truly learn, from a young age, how to be and live with people who are different. In the era of globalization, this planet is getting smaller, not bigger. It is incumbent upon us, therefore, not to just talk about what would make our schools great, but to insure that they *are* great.

It is for this reason that the closing chapter turns to accrediting bodies. They, and they alone, are in a position to say "this is best practice," and that such practices require installation prior to receiving, or extending, accreditation.

Accrediting bodies can enforce safe passage between harbors. Let's find out how.

Chapter 10

ASSESSING NETWORKS OF SCHOOLS – ENSURING SAFE PASSAGE

"Twenty years from now you will be more disappointed by the things that you didn't do than by the ones you did do. So throw off the bowlines. Sail away from safe harbor. Catch the trade winds in your sails. Explore. Dream. Discover."
– Mark Twain

"It always seems impossible until it is done."
– Nelson Mandela

The bench where I started the project of writing this book beckons from beyond the library. Returning to the same scuffed wooden planks where the book began a year earlier, I take in the scenery. Verdant woodlands abut a sparkling canal. The hiss of traffic fades in the face of this Dutch urban beauty.

A mother duck leaps out of the canal, flanked by two downy ducklings.

I am drawn to the amber of her eyes, eyes that radiate a calm, piercing vigilance. *If you are a threat to my ducklings, I will see you.* Her voice repeats a faint, guttural chirp, not loud enough to qualify as a 'quack,' but constant, like a faint pulse of radar. The chirp says *I am here, I am here, I am here.* She escorts her two ducklings across the path before me, and lets them nibble at grass blades between my feet. She watches me, assessing. *If you are a threat to my ducklings, I will see you.*

Convinced of my harmlessness, she escorts her duo closer, underneath my bench, and into the taller grasses and flowers behind me. The ducklings nibble at everything in reach, trying flowers, tasting weeds, pecking at pebbles. The mother accompanies them, positioning herself nearby, but allowing them to explore. *I am here,* she quietly clucks.

Sipping my cappuccino, I gaze into the greenery.

I am here.

The ducklings have disappeared into the grass, visible only indirectly, as the taller grasses and flowers flex, betraying the ducklings' downy locations.

I am here.

I think of cats, of hawks, of rats, of the six or so reasons there must be why this mother's original brood – which probably started at eight – is now down to two.

I am here.

I wait, noticing my mouth is hovering open above my cooling cappuccino. Flowers wave, grasses wave, a duckling jumps.

I am here.

The ducklings scurry back to their mother, like two spirits parting the grass. *I am here.* They are safe. The trio waddles back under the bench, back across the path, back to the edge of the canal, and into the water.

I realize I have just seen attachment in motion.

I have just witnessed safe passage.

OUR POINT OF DEPARTURE: SOUND REASONS AND MOTIVATIONS

You are well on your way towards helping your school build, or improve, a safe harbor, a place where people can find solace and shelter when they are faced with the vulnerabilities of arriving at, or departing for, a foreign dock. You are well on your way towards building a harbor that attends to its dockworkers as well as those arriving and leaving, in the full awareness these 'stayers' are the ones who create and maintain the harbor's safe culture. You are well on your way to appreciating that the real safety of the harbor does not exist in the wood used, or in the gauge of the bolts binding the wood together, or even in the sheer number of available dock workers. You know the harbor's real safety resides in the hearts of those who build and maintain it.

It is for this reason I have not gone into great detail regarding what actual programs need to look like. I have not recommended the actual design of specific programs, procedures, or protocols. The rationale for the lack of prescriptive detail in this text is fourfold:

1. The culture of each school is unique. Each school must shape the ideas in this book in ways that work for it.

2. Shaping the ideas themselves allows people to invest the program with their personalities and 'stamp,' thereby boosting people's sense of ownership and investment in the program.

3. This sense of ownership is essential for the program to survive the tests of time, rather than simply being an 'upwelling' of enthusiasm by a few people for a few years, only to disappear thereafter.

However important those first three reasons might be, the fourth reason is the main driving factor in the style I have adopted for this text:

4. A program born from the right reasons and motivations, namely genuine care for the well-being of other human beings, will, *when equipped with the requisite tools*, naturally give rise to and continuously shape programs that have the best chance of achieving their goals.

This book has attempted to strike a balance between providing the reader with reasons to work towards addressing mobility at his or her respective school, while also providing the reader with the tools needed to do so. But even assuming I got the balance between reasons and means correct, which I earnestly hope I did, we still haven't reached our final destination.

WHY SOUND REASONS AND MOTIVATIONS AT INDIVIDUAL SCHOOLS ARE NOT ENOUGH

At a number of earlier points in this text, I have alluded to the uncomfortable reality that no single school can successfully address all of the issues associated with mobility on its own.

In other words, even if you run with the ideas put forth in this book and create the most outstanding comprehensive Transitions Program on the planet, you still won't be done, for the simple reason that you can't address the challenge in isolation.

Why not? The answer resides in something David Pollock was implying in his oft-repeated observation that "It takes six months to pack up your heart, and six months to unpack it."[39]

Unmanaged mobility is the single largest detrimental factor in educational outcomes ever documented.

On one end, the emotional ripples associated with mobility begin long before people arrive at your school. At the other end, the value of the transitions-related work your school invests in them will only become clear after these people have left. The emotional processes generated by transitions transcend school walls and ignore academic calendars. Like swells on the open oceans, these emotional waves are impossible to block or contain. They will run their course and only come to rest when the energy they contain has dissipated.

What are schools to do? The only meaningful way forward with the issues at hand is for international schools with any degree of turnover to work together. The only complete solution to challenges of this magnitude entails combining the efforts of all the schools involved into a concerted whole. A starting point can be found in the framework and vocabulary of attachment and life stories presented in this book.

But the only way to guarantee transition needs are met is to insure that evaluations of appropriate transition programs are adopted into the standards for accreditation or quality assurance measures for all schools involved.

This chapter will propose a means to do just that. But before doing so, we need to review the answers to two core questions:

- Is it worth it?
- Why hasn't it happened yet?

IS IT WORTH IT?

This book sets forth the argument that efforts to address the challenges of mobility across cultures are worth it. Beginning with the largest study in the

---

39 *I would say that six months is relatively quick!*

history of educational research, as published by John Hattie in *Visible Learning*, we noted that unmanaged mobility is the single largest detrimental factor in educational outcomes ever documented. I argued that it doesn't have to be this way, and the means and methods of 'managed mobility' as set forth in this book provide hopeful directions for the future.

But we learned it goes deeper than just educational outcomes. We learned that a child's experiences of how caregivers respond to their cries for help eventually coalesce into a stable pattern of expectations that psychologists refer to as an attachment style. We learned that people with secure types of attachment styles have internalized the conviction they can rely on their fellow human beings for support when support is needed. And we saw that people with secure types of attachment outperform their less-securely attached counterparts on every single measure of human functioning across the life span, be it in personal health, success at work, or effectiveness as a parent.

Against that backdrop, we considered what mobility does to a person's attachment system. We considered the perennial strains that moving and being left behind place upon a person's ability to truly trust, to truly open him - or herself up to being known by another human being. We considered, in other words, how the development of more insecure forms of attachment would be a *logical reaction* to the experience of moving across cultures, at least when that experience is occurring in a way that is not well managed. "Why should I make a new friend," a young child will logically ask, "if she is just going to leave me too?"

In other words, we considered the role international schools are playing – or, perhaps more accurately, *not* playing – with regards to the development of attachment style in the young people they service. If a secure attachment style is such an asset to a human life, shouldn't schools be paying attention to the kinds of attachment styles that are crystallizing within their walls? Marks and grades are important. But won't people be carrying their attachment styles with them long after they can no longer remember what they got in math or Spanish class?

WHY HASN'T IT HAPPENED YET?

As of the publication of this book, there are still very few schools worldwide, international or otherwise, that have successfully developed and maintained comprehensive programs for addressing transitions. And this is true in spite of the regularity with which I, and many capable others, continue to present at schools and conferences worldwide on the importance of addressing mobility.

Why is this? I believe there are four main reasons.

The first reason is awareness. The splash from David Pollock and Ruth Van Reken's *Third Culture Kids,* first published in 2001, still has not reached every shore. Many people still have not considered the issues of identity and loss that are involved. Readers still regularly report the 'aha!' moment of validation, the sheer relief of recognition, when they finally encounter the ideas in *Third Culture Kids.*

But awareness alone is not enough to account for the slowness with which schools have developed comprehensive transitions programs.

The second reason is discrimination. As discussed earlier in the book, many in schools continue to believe that emotional issues do not reside near the core business of an educational institution. Certain people may themselves be uncomfortable with the issues that are at stake. Mobility-related initiatives that otherwise could have been launched get stifled on the launchpad.

But awareness and discrimination alone are not enough to account for the slowness with which schools have developed comprehensive transitions programs.

The third reason is that it's difficult. Developing comprehensive transitions programs is hard work, both practically and emotionally. It requires dedicated individuals who are willing to sustain hard work over time, and a team that can sustain momentum even in the face of its own grief, such as when key members of the team leave. Working on a Transitions Team can sometimes feel like trying to construct a home on a muddy, sliding slope.

Awareness, discrimination, and the sheer difficulty of the task are still not enough to account for the slowness with which schools have developed comprehensive transitions programs.

I believe there is a fourth reason at work, which I will refer to as 'the problem of the commons.' This fourth reason is inspired by the classic 1968 essay by biologist Garret Hardin, entitled *The Tragedy of the Commons* [56]. This fourth reason is fundamentally a problem of who should take responsibility. A deep understanding of what Hardin meant by 'the commons' will point us towards a solution for finally addressing the unacceptable reality that few schools have comprehensive transitions programs in place.

THE PROBLEM OF THE COMMONS

In 1798, Thomas Malthus published his pamphlet *An Essay on the Principal of Population.* Given that populations tend to grow exponentially, whereas food supply increases linearly, Malthus argued we could expect periodic crashes in population due to hunger, famine, disease, or conflict. This 'Malthusian' principle, as it came to be called, was a matter of straightforward logic. Hardin's essay *The Tragedy of the Commons* was an attempt to argue the need for a non-technical solution to this Malthusian principle.

Technical solutions had been tried. People could farm more efficiently to increase the productivity of the land, but one of the simple realities Hardin focused upon was the mathematical impossibility of sustaining an unlimited population on a limited planet. No amount of technical creativity to support a burgeoning human population would ever sidestep the reality that the planet and its resources were finite.

Not only was the planet finite, it was also shared. As a shared space, Hardin likened the planet and its resources to a 'commons.' The reason for 'the tragedy of the commons' is because shared spaces lead to a paradoxical type of shared behavior.

Hardin provides the example of a shared pasture. If every herdsman follows what is in his rational self-interest, it makes sense to add another head of cattle to his herd. His cattle count becomes +1, and because he alone will benefit from the sale of this head of cattle, he reaps all the benefits. From the point of view of rational self-interest, it makes sense for him to add another head of cattle, and another, and so forth.

Each additional head of cattle comes with a price of -1, mostly in the form of additional grazing on the land. But all the users of the land *share* this price that gets paid, making the actual cost to the fictitious herdsman only a fraction of the -1. The herdsman knows his line of reasoning will ultimately lead to the depletion of the shared pasture, but he reasons that "everyone else is doing it." Not adding the additional heads of cattle seems to our herdsman to carry an unacceptable cost.

Hardin points out that 'the commons' takes on many shapes. The commons includes tangible resources such as forests, rainforests, oceans and fisheries. But it also includes less tangible resources such as national parks, water quality, and pollution-free spaces. Should a factory spend the considerable expense to treat its waste products safely, when it bears the costs of such treatment entirely on its own? Or should it dump them into the ocean, when the obvious costs of doing so get shared by all users of the ocean – in other words by all of humanity? Dumping is cheaper, at least in terms of the factory's financial bottom line.

Remember this fictitious factory. It's more than metaphor. We will return to it below, because it may have more to do with something happening in our schools than we like to think.

THE SOLUTION TO THE COMMONS

When rational self-interest leads people to behave in ways that are not in the wider interests of the larger group, a different solution is necessary. In his essay, Hardin calls for 'coercion,' not because he enjoys the nasty connotations the word generally carries, but because the term is honest and straightforward. The "coercion I recommend," Hardin writes, "is mutual coercion, mutually agreed upon by the majority of the people affected" [56]. What is called for, in other words, is a higher au-

To protect ourselves from ourselves, we must allow ourselves to be coerced into doing that which is best, not necessarily for our individual selves, but for the larger whole.

thority all parties agree to abide by, an authority which guards over the commons by constraining the behavior of all, as everyone is logically trying to maximize their own interests. To protect ourselves from ourselves, we must allow ourselves to be coerced into doing that which is best, not necessarily for our individual selves, but for the larger whole.

If we stick to this book's maritime metaphor and look at the oceans, then this type of "mutual coercion, mutually agreed upon" was successfully established in the form of the United Nations Convention on the Law of the Sea (UNCLOS). Ratified by 166 parties, which include 165 states and the entire European Union, the convention defines the ownership, management, and protection of the earth's marine spaces. The International Maritime Organization is charged by the UN with enforcing the UNCLOS, including the prevention of pollution of our shared oceans by the vessels that navigate them.

And along the coasts of most developed and civilized countries, each country's own local legislation generally seeks to reduce and prevent the dumping of raw sewage and other pollutants into marine spaces and wider oceans. It might be cheaper to an individual factory to do so in the short term, but it is now widely understood and accepted that the costs in the longer term are unacceptable.

Defining 'the commons' and the appropriate means of protecting it creates lively debate on many levels. Consider contemporary discussions of the environment as a commons. Consider rising sea levels as a problem of the commons. My point here is not to enter any of these debates, but to draw a link between Hardin's article and a different kind of commons, a shared space most people have likely never considered before.

I'm going to call this shared space 'the inside of our students.'

A NEW PROBLEM OF THE COMMONS: THE INSIDE OF OUR STUDENTS

The inside of our students is also a shared common space. Inside that space are thoughts, experiences, and feelings. Inside that space is an attachment system learning how it feels when loved ones leave or cherished souls are lost. Inside that space is an attachment system learning how others are likely to respond in times of emotional need. Inside that space is an attachment system with masts and sails straining in the gale force winds of mobility.

Admittedly, what I am suggesting here requires a leap of imagination. After all, how can something that is inside somebody also be shared? How can individual attachment systems be considered a 'commons'? We share the environment and the oceans, but a student's attachment system resides *inside* the student, right?

Attachment systems play out in the shared spaces between people.

Wrong. The neurological basis of an individual's attachment system certainly resides solely inside that individual, in his or her memory networks, but this attachment system leads to certain ways of behaving and connecting with other human beings. In other words, *attachment systems play out in the shared spaces between people.*

As students grow on our watch, their attachment systems are paying close attention. They are watching us. What do we, the adults, do in the face of mobility's gale force winds? How should they, the students, behave when they see sails snapping, when the masts of their little vessels tip dangerously towards the surf?

The inside of each student is observing us, taking notes, and learning. This interior space is filling with charts that will guide these young sailors on their future journeys. Each student's invisible attachment system – invisible to the naked eye – is collecting the nautical maps the student will use to navigate the rising and ebbing tides of human relationships, without getting battered on the rocks.

What kinds of maps are we giving them? What kind of ways of behaving and connecting do these maps produce, in the shared space between people where attachment occurs?

Our students' attachment systems are an invisible, but critical, commons. Students often move from school to school, giving each school only a certain amount of influence over how that student's inner space takes shape. But that an influence does occur is unquestionable.

The leap of imagination that is required in the way I am using 'shared space' is two-fold. The attachment systems inside students dictate how they will behave and connect with others, in the shared space where attachment plays out. But these attachment systems themselves are also shared spaces, by virtue of the fact that internationally mobile students bring them from school to school.

Who is willing to take responsibility for the influence they bring to bear on this shared space?

Carrying forth Hardin's central arguments, the rational self-interest of an individual school would predict that it is not cost-effective or in the individual school's interests to take responsibility for this shared space. For reasons outlined above, it is challenging to do a good job of molding a person's attachment style towards a 'secure' shape. It requires work, predictability, availability, commitment. Many of these students only attend our schools for very a limited time. Then they move on, taking all of our hard work being predictable, available, and committed with them, right out the door.

And we have no idea if the student's next school is even going to try to continue the good work we did. Is that school going to maintain it? Or will that school community simply pollute the clean waters we worked to create and protect?

Worse still, we have no control over the way a particular student's attachment system was treated at his or her last school. Was it neglected? Was it tainted with the toxins of teasing or the heavy metals of marginalization? Educating a child well is already challenging enough. Are we now being given the daunting task of decontamination when these students wash up on our shores?

How in the world, you wonder, are you – as a single, solitary, committed individual – supposed to take responsibility for this new commons, this shared space inside our shared students?

The blunt, realistic answer is that you can't. A larger, more concerted effort is needed to safeguard this commons. And this, in my opinion, is the fourth compelling reason why comprehensive transitions programs have not taken off at many schools worldwide.

Most people have probably never considered the issue in these terms. And I would not suggest the problem of the commons leads school personnel to consciously reach the conclusion that 'there's no point' in building a comprehensive transitions program. Nonetheless, I believe the problem of the commons provides a compelling framework for understanding why comprehensive transitions programs have been so slow to get off the ground at international schools worldwide, or at any school with a high degree of turnover. "What is the point," schools might be unconsciously asking themselves, "in trying to attend to this commons when our influence is so limited, and when nobody else seems to be taking their responsibility for their effect on the commons?"

As mentioned earlier, Hardin had a solution for this question. What is needed is some form of recognized federal authority that integrates each individual school's pursuit of its own self-interests into a larger whole, into an orchestrated set of activities that protects the commons. All schools involved in any significant way with mobility must subscribe to the kinds of practices that protect the attachment systems of their members. What is called for is "mutual coercion, mutually agreed upon."

And this is where the swells described in this book begin to converge. An 80-foot problem is rolling across the seas, namely that no single school can fully address the challenges associated with mobility on its own. Hardin offered us an 80-foot solution that is also circling the oceans, namely that individuals must subscribe to a higher authority if they want to resolve problems of the commons.

Hold on. Two 80-foot swells are about to converge. When waves meet, physicists speak of 'constructive interference.' At the point of convergence, the energy of waves combines. The 80-foot problem is about to meet Hardin's 80-foot solution. And the time has come for schools to consider what can be done to harness the energy in a 160-foot surge.

COLLECTIVE INTERFERENCE, AND THE SOLUTION TO THE COMMONS

The swells described by this book converge at a simple point. *If no school can fully address mobility on its own, then all schools must subscribe to the practices that will guarantee the integrity of the commons.* Like national parks or clean water systems, the attachment systems at stake inside our students can only be safeguarded if we agree to abide by the same rules. To oversee the rules, we will need agencies bigger than individual schools, agencies with the authority to implement and oversee the guarantors of quality. And we will have to be willing to abide by the decisions of these agencies, for our own good, but more importantly for the good of the students we are educating.

In other words, we need accrediting agencies or other quality-assurance bodies in education to adopt the kinds of standards into their evaluation protocols that will protect the commons. We need the kinds of standards and end measures that shield our students' attachment systems from the howling winds of mobility and loss. We need to know our families' last harbor is sending them on their way well nourished. We want guarantees that our students' next port of call will be protecting their emotional experiences as well as we have.

Those who are doing the voyaging want the same thing. As they pull into their next harbor, they should be able to look for the signs and symbols that guarantee it is a *safe* harbor. In the same way as universal navigational signs

FIGURE 10.1: Nautical flag 'P': meaning 'ready to sail' (flag border is blue in real life)

and symbols exist, meaning the exact same things to an Indonesian captain arriving in Rotterdam as they do to a Dutch captain sailing into Jakarta, so too do we need a universal set of symbols and measurements that tell people when and where safe passage is taken seriously. People want to know what a potential port has to offer. They deserve to know how seriously a potential port takes the issues that are important to them. Just as the international nautical flag for 'P' conveys to all who see it that the ship is 'ready to sail,' so too do we need universal means of efficiently conveying the message that a school takes safe passage seriously.

FIGURE 10.2: Possible stamp to designate a school with a comprehensive transitions program

Accrediting agencies or quality-assurance bodies such as school inspectorates are the logical organizations to develop, implement, and oversee these systems. They are the organizations to which we can collectively turn to request Hardin's "mutual coercion, mutually agreed upon." This line of thinking can be extended in three practical directions:

- Accrediting agencies should devise and adopt appropriate measures into their accreditation standards to ensure that the needs associated with mobility across cultures are properly addressed.

- Any school with a significant degree of turnover can decide to hold itself accountable by being accredited, or seeking accreditation, by an agency with such standards in place.

- The parents, teachers, and even students who read this book can and arguably should insist that these kinds of standards end up in outcome measures which assess, accredit, or license their schools.

To assist in that dialogue, such a proposed list of accreditation standards is presented in *Appendix C*, starting on page 275. These standards are drafted in the same language and format as the 8th Edition (version 8.2) of the Council of International Schools' Accreditation Standards, reprinted with permission in *Appendix B*, starting on page 261.

It is my hope these proposed Standards foster a fruitful dialogue whose time has come. It is my hope the use of such end-of-the-line measures can fundamentally improve the experience of real students in real classrooms by addressing the attachment and life-story needs at the foundation of that experience.

PULLING INTO PORT

In closing, I sincerely hope this text has provided you, the reader, with the blueprints, inspiration, and some of the tools to start generating activity in your respective harbors.

Over the course of the years ahead, I hope the harbors we all contribute to will gradually become increasingly interlinked, and that it will become the collective goal of all schools with any considerable degree of turnover to ensure that everyone involved flourishes. I have dedicated my career to the reduction and prevention of suffering, and this call to arms is certainly about the reduction and prevention of suffering at international schools.

THE TALE OF THE SWALLOW

A swallow tattoo signified amongst sailors of old that its owner had covered 5000 nautical miles. Two swallows, often tattooed facing each other, signified 10000 nautical miles. In the pre-industrial age, when vessels required wind and navigation knew no GPS, sailing vast distances was dangerous. Sailors sometimes did not return.

The more swallows you had on your chest,
the more respect you deserved.

The swallow's small size doesn't deter it from migrating large distances. European swallows commute from breeding grounds throughout Europe all the way to southern Africa. North American swallows set their sights on Argentina for the winter. They cover 8000 to 9000 kilometers in each direction, eating on the fly, and returning in many cases to the same mud nests they built – or were born in – in previous years. Mating for life, swallows around the world are associated with loyalty. Family. Reliability.

Except when forced to cross large bodies of water like the Mediterranean Sea, swallows tend to follow the contours of the land. So when a swallow alighted on a ship's masts, it was a good omen. It meant the swallow could see the coast from its airborne perspective, meaning land was nearby. You had almost reached your destination. In the best of cases, the swallow meant you were almost home.

In Egyptian mythology, a swallow sat on the prow of the solar boat that would carry the sun god Ra, after setting, safely through the underworld. That same swallow would guide Ra safely into the next dawn, to rise and be ferried across another day's sky.

Since the dawn of human civilization, the swallow has signified 'Safe Passage.'

An international school – like any school – should be about the facilitation of optimal human development.

But there is a catch. We should invest in such optimal development not only for the good of the direct recipients, but also because these individuals have something very important to give back.

My vision and hope are founded on the sober conviction that the students who attend an international school are fortunate because they are in a position to acquire a profound understanding about the accessibility of other cultures. Echoing the IBO's mission statement, these students are in a position to acquire a genuine awareness that there is more than one way of being right. The goal of understanding there is more than one way of being right in the world can become a felt experience that is as self-evident to a child as his or her ability to speak several languages without thinking. He or she just knows how. Those ways of speaking, thinking, and being, were introduced during a critical phase in life, when his or her mind was like a sponge.

Recent studies in neuroplasticity suggest it's never too late for our brain to adapt and grow. But a real openness to other ways of being becomes painfully difficult for people to learn as they get older, so much so they are willing to do harm or even go to war to annihilate the other. Perhaps, then, it is wise to start with the brains and hearts still developing on our watch. The "prototypical citizen of the twenty-first century" Ward described decades ago is very much here – in the harbors of our schools, international and otherwise. The brains and hearts of these young twenty-first century citizens are only too willing and able to learn the language of curiosity for the other, the feeling of comfort in the face of multiple answers to the same question, and the conviction that we can make it work all together on this planet we call Earth.

"After all," says the hypothetical student who attended a series of visionary educational institutions, "that's what I learned at school."

AFTERWORD

"The war occurred half a lifetime ago, and yet the
remembering makes it now. And sometimes remembering
will lead to a story, which makes it forever. That's what
stories are for. Stories are for joining the past to the future.
Stories are for those late hours in the night when you can't
remember how you got from where you were to where you are.
Stories are for eternity, when memory is erased,
when there is nothing to remember except the story."
> – Tim O'Brien,
> *The Things They Carried*

Safe Passage is a book Doug Ota simply had to write. Given his professional experience as an international school counselor and psychologist specializing in adolescent behavior, and given his personal experience growing up across cultures, he couldn't not write this book. Doug had to write this book because... well... because it was in his DNA to capture and pull together the disparate components of successful – and unsuccessful – transitions he had lived and witnessed and assisted throughout his life.

The professional literature on transitions and third culture kids is relatively sparse, and this book is a huge contribution to the field of mobility and transitions. As should be all too clear to most of us by now, traditional geographic stability – where a person experiences childhood, grows into young adulthood, is educated, and then spends his or her professional life all in the same place – is becoming increasingly less common. With *Safe Passage,* Doug has written the guidebook (the navigational chart, to use his metaphorical conceit) that will direct countless parents, teachers, school administrators, and mental health professionals in how to celebrate the many ways in which moving across cultures enriches our lives and enables our growth through contact with diversity in all its forms. This book should also help us understand, and mitigate, the downsides of mobility cited through research findings such as those of John Hattie. With his book, Doug adds a compelling and comprehensive manual to the still limited body of work on transitions, providing not only conceptual underpinning for transition support but also nuts-and-bolts advice on how to institute and maintain an effective transitions program.

This speaks to me personally for a couple of reasons. First, in thirty years of working outside our home culture, my wife and I have raised two children born in Africa, schooled in Tunisia and Vienna, and university educated in the USA. Both struggled to find identity in their 'home' culture. Our daughter (she only later confided) resented that her friends moved away every two or three years. She chose to marry a young man who works in his father's accounting firm in California and she hopes never to move again in her adult life. Our son, on the other hand, could not wait to return to international life and now lives and works in Dubai. The lessons in this book help illuminate the lives and thoughts of children and adults such as ours, and the soon-to-be millions like them who will move from culture to culture in their formative years.

The second reason this book touches me is even more powerful, yet painful. The colleague of Ruth Van Reken (author of the Foreword of this book) who first drew my attention to transitions and mobility was David Pollock, her co-author of the then-definitive *Third Culture Kids: Growing Up Among Worlds*. Pollock was staying in our home and preparing to give a workshop to the parents of TCKs at the American International School of Vienna, where I was then the director, when he collapsed and was rushed to the hospital. My wife and I were at his bedside when he passed away a few days later. To this day, I grieve that I couldn't prevent one of the great educators and researchers on the topic of transitions from slipping away on my watch. When I left Vienna a few years later and moved to the American School of The Hague, I pledged my complete support to the school's Safe Harbour program (see *Chapter 6: An Exemplar Harbor*) in Pollock's name. I believe Doug Ota's book has the potential to advance our knowledge and practice on mobility to new and even more effective levels. If so, this is exactly what David Pollock would have wanted, and this book will pay Pollock the homage he deserves, honoring his memory and life's work. Pollock dedicated his life to third culture kids – so has Doug Ota.

He has picked up the baton from Pollock and Van Reken and carried it forward, and for this my children, and those many like them to follow, will be better off.

Dr. Richard L. Spradling, Ph.D.
Director/ Superintendent
American School of The Hague
The Netherlands

APPENDICES

"*Somewhere there's a place for us.*"
    – West Side Story

APPENDIX A: MESSAGES IN BOTTLES

In what follows, I offer different entry points for *Safe Passage*. Like messages washed up on a beach, bottled and corked, I hope they find the right people. I hope they get read. Their location here at the back of this text is not an indication that these messages are less important. They simply don't fit smoothly in the construction of the text's main arguments.

Everyone experiences the issue of mobility differently. These 'messages in a bottle' seek to focus attention on the specific experience of various subgroups. How do various subpopulations experience issues of mobility across cultures differently? I knew this book was most likely to be effective if people felt it was relevant. While it may be impossible to adapt a single text to all the backgrounds and personalities readers possess, several distinct types of people addressed by this book can be identified, including:

1.   Administrators
2.   Board Members
3.   Parents
4.   Students
5.   Counselors
6.   Teachers and Members of Staff
7.   Human Resource Managers
8.   Admissions Directors

Each of the following 'messages in a bottle' addresses one of these subpopulations.

The reader will naturally be inclined to read the message or messages that most pertain to his or her role or position in the school. Conversely, the reader is likely to disregard messages addressed to other populations.

I want to emphasize that all these messages deserve to be uncorked and read by everyone.

While the reader may understandably begin with the most relevant (to them) message or messages first, I strongly encourage serious readers of this text to read every message. Doing so will help you understand how issues of mobility affect those with different roles within a school. Doing so will help reinforce the reality that what we share in common in the challenges of transition far outweighs the ways in which we are different. Doing so will help Transitions Teams better understand the experiences and realities of their fellow team members, further strengthening the team approach essential for handling challenges of this magnitude.

In other words, consider the following messages to be a fleet of bottles, washing simultaneously onto your sandy beach. Kick off your shoes, cross the warm sands down to the water's edge, and grab the first bottle that catches your eye.

Then grab the rest.

And uncork them all.

MESSAGE 1

Dear Administrator,

The first message lands on your shore because lasting, systemic growth and change at a school is only possible with your support. A comprehensive Transitions Team will only drop anchor and flourish at your school if you are convinced that it should.

Period.

For the purposes of argument, I'll assume you're not convinced, so I can employ the remainder of this letter trying to convince you.

Getting Maslow's Hierarchy Right-Side-Up

Maslow's hierarchy of needs indicates that human beings can only thrive in the upper echelons of their experience when their basic needs are met. Translated to an educational setting, human beings can only grow cognitively and intellectually when their fundamental needs for physical and emotional safety and belonging are intact. Mobility erodes these foundational layers. Any educational endeavor that attempts to foster learning when this fundamental bedrock has been whisked away can be likened to the construction of a building without a foundation.

Students who have had to give up life as they know it may not yet feel they even *exist* in their new setting. Students who have had a best friend depart may be struggling with a level of grief that interferes with their ability to even *listen* to Mr. Jones in math. Worse still, these students are often misdiagnosed as having a 'motivation problem' or worse, a behavioral one.

These students have one or both parents who might similarly be struggling with undiagnosed grief or adjustment problems. These same parents may be stuck at home depressed, with all the associated consequences for their sons and daughters, or sitting outside your office with a complaint about Mr. Jones – an example of misdirected anger my professional field calls 'displacement.' Other students might have a teacher who really does have a problem. This teacher may, for example, go 'home' to an apartment that's still empty because her shipment's been lost. She's still sleeping on a blow-up mattress and eating take-out food in the second month of the school year, but she hasn't told a soul. How well do you think she's teaching?

This rundown of problems I've cited may remind you of the kinds of things that cross your desk, too, where people seem to collect problems and dump them on your doorstep, expecting solutions. Let me assure you this book is not an inventory of problems for you to solve. This book represents several decades of thinking and practice in identifying several of the root causes to many of the problems school personnel – and the students and parents for whom they do their work – encounter.

The thinking and programs outlined in this book will help you and your school identify and address several common themes all members of the school community grapple with, whether they know it or not. Addressing these common themes will not provide you with a silver bullet that eradicates your school's issues and magically clears your desk. But the addressing of these transitions-related themes will help your school convert the underlying dynamic of transitions from something which fuels problems towards something that fosters school community.

Compounding the issue is that *most human beings find it challenging to ask directly for their basic needs lower on the hierarchy, particularly when they're feeling vulnerable.* Unusual is the parent who shows up saying, "I'm feeling vulnerable and alone. Can you help me?" Such transparency is not generally socially sanctioned. Worse still, the stress of mobility can activate our 'fight or flight' response, making people who do not currently feel a sense of emotional safety or belonging feel and sound edgy or even aggressive.

We all need to belong. But society conditions us not to ask for what we need openly and honestly. What is a school to do?

Giving People What they Need – Before they Know they Need It.

By having systems and processes in place to address people's needs without their having to ask for it, an international school with a comprehensive transitions program can effectively sidestep social etiquette – by administering effective preventative psychological first aid free of stigmatization. As all portions of the school community participate in various programs, 'grappling with transitions' becomes a unifying factor rather than a pathologizing agent. *Everyone* is involved because *everyone* is affected.

When people come and go from our midst, it does something to us. The more we care about these people who come and go, the *more* it does to us. Short of those with profound forms of autism, every member of the international school community, be it student or parent or staff member or administrator, must, in his or her own way, navigate the ramifications of having to repeatedly both build and loosen affectional bonds.

This pertains to you too. Positions of responsibility do nothing to shield a human from the wear and tear on the psyche amidst the rapid-fire building and loosening of affectional bonds typical at international schools. The professional distance principals and heads of school are often expected to maintain from their staff may place those in management positions more at risk than other staff members, as their hurt is more likely to go unseen, unnamed, and therefore unaddressed.

This is a real and fundamental human challenge an international school ignores at its own peril. Certainly we don't want students drawing the conclusion that, since leaving hurts, they won't allow themselves to build deep human relationships. But this is exactly what many students will logically tend to do – and what their teachers and parents and administrators may all be inadvertently modeling – if the dynamic of transitions is not openly dealt with.

Embraced as an opportunity, the challenge of transitions – as with any challenge in life – can be harnessed to yield growth. Building a program which simultaneously reduces mobility's fallout, while exploiting its positive potential, is the focus of this book. And along the lines of the old adage 'a stitch in time saves nine,' building such a program will ultimately save you and your personnel time. Energy becomes focused where it belongs, namely on core human needs that get rattled by transitions. These are the strains feeding, and in many cases driving, some of the issues appearing in your office, your counselors' offices, and your teachers' classrooms.

I hope you will continue to read on.

Yours Truly,

Doug Ota

MESSAGE 2

Dear Board Members,[40]

You are the stewards and guardians of the school. It is generally accepted a school board has three explicit purposes:

1. Hiring and evaluating the Head of school.
2. Overseeing legal and financial probity.
3. Overseeing implementation of the school's Strategic Plan.

While often not explicitly stated in the literature on governance, a fourth function of a board is implicit:

4. Providing stewardship of the school's values.

My letter to you addresses the first and last of these board – related tasks. I begin with stewardship of the school's values, because a school's values ultimately provide, or should provide, the foundation upon which every decision is based.

Stewardship Of The School's Values

What kind of a school are you? Who are the students and families you serve? What are the things you believe are important to accomplish as you serve this population? Where does the school stand on big -picture issues such as culture, internationalism, language, and inclusion? The answers to these questions reside at the core of a school's identity. The answers therefore appropriately find their way into the school's vision and mission statements. While heads of schools have their own personalities, strengths, and priorities, heads of schools come and go. The mission and vision of a school move more slowly and deliberately because they belong to the community from which the school sprang.

The board is tasked with safeguarding the nature and pursuit of these value statements. The school's mission rests upon the bedrock of these values, and one moves from there to formulate a strategic plan grounded in the mission, policies based on the strategic plan, and a means of monitoring the

----

40 I am deeply indebted to Dr. Graham Ranger, Director of Accreditation at the Council of International Schools, for helping me to sharpen many of the ideas presented in this message.

implementation for the policies. The school's management carries out the implementation and provides the board with the regular updates it needs to make the necessary decisions of governing the school.

While there are as many different values as there are schools, and while the variety of possible mission statements for schools is therefore infinite, we can identify a number of factors held dear by many international schools' core values worldwide. In one way, shape, or form, most international schools would agree it is important to:

- raise global citizens
- welcome an international mix of students into their school
- foster an international, outward looking orientation in their students as opposed to a parochial, inward looking focus
- help all students achieve and maximize their potential
- build a positive alliance between home and school

If schools wish to cultivate global citizens with an international mindset, one of the best ways to do so is to bring students from different walks of life together in the same place. *But this requirement will obviously entail students moving or being moved away from.* Such mobility unleashes the forces described and addressed in this text, forces which require attention if a child is to achieve his or her potential.

And as for the building of positive home/ school alliances, the kind of attention needed to address the issues of mobility across cultures is the very attention which helps foster alliances between the home and the school. Mobility across cultures creates opportunities for the building of home/ school alliances that less mobile communities can only dream of. As explained repeatedly throughout this text, given any significant degree of annual turnover, mobility across cultures is a challenge faced by all members of an international community, be it a student, parent, teacher, administrator, or board member. And there is nothing that builds alliances better than an externalized common opponent. The famous Arabic phrase attributed to Bedouin tribes runs:

> "Me against my brothers
> Me and my brothers against my cousins
> Me and my brother and my cousins against the world"

Challenges or threats from without give those within a shared sense of purpose and identity. Mobility is one such challenge. Rallying together is necessary to address a challenge of this scope at a school; doing so has the added benefit of creating and supporting a shared sense of purpose and identity. This fact should have our attention, because the educational literature is unequivocal on the positive effect a sense of community has on educational outcomes [57].

Hiring And Evaluating The Head Of School

Board decisions shape schools. They therefore shape, in a fundamental fashion, the children who spend any portion of their developmental years within these schools. That massive responsibility is not generally matched by any awareness on the part of the students of the importance of the board. (Rare is the child who wonders, "what is the board going to do about X?" When I hear a child speak like that, he or she is invariably related to a board member.)

Nowhere are the positive opportunities for shaping the organization felt more keenly than in the hiring and evaluation of the head of school. This individual translates board policy into actions and programs that can be implemented. Excellent leadership skills are necessary – though not sufficient – for the building and sustaining of excellent schools.

More challenging still, excellence as a leader in a monocultural, monolingual school does not translate directly into excellence as a leader in a multicultural, multilingual school. In his groundbreaking book *Frames of Mind: The Theory of Multiple Intelligences,* Professor Howard Gardner, of Harvard's School of Education, formulated a definition of intelligence to underpin his 'theory of multiple intelligences.'

Intelligence, as he defined it, had to encompass "those intellectual strengths that prove of some importance within a cultural context" [58, p. 65]. Any 'roles and skills valued by human culture' had to 'make the cut' of what qualified as intelligence. Conversely, because some cultures may value a skill differently than others does not mean the skill is more or less important on some objective hierarchy. Valuations of various intelligences vary across cultures.

Returning to the board's task of hiring and evaluating a chief executive, a head of school with an outstanding track record in largely monocultural, monolingual settings will not necessarily be able to transfer this excellence to a multicultural, multilingual setting. To complete the analogy with Gardner's definition of intelligence, the roles and skills of the head of school will be valued and perceived differently in different cultural contexts. The forthrightness and directness valued in the head of an elite preparatory school in North America or Western Europe might be viewed as brusque and rude in a head of school in Mumbai. Inversely, the prolonged, overt interest in the well-being of extended family members shown by a successful head of school in Mumbai might sound strangely indirect and inefficient coming from a head of school in London [59].

This is but one example of the importance of cross –– cultural literacy, and filling this book with additional examples (as many capable authors before me have) will do nothing to address or create the essential ingredient required by a head of school in a multicultural, multilingual setting: *experience in recognizing one's own cultural frame of reference.* The only way to become adept at recognizing the existence of one's own cultural frame of reference, and the biases and prejudices which naturally issue from those baseline assumptions, is to have that frame of reference jolted by being surrounded by others who organize their experience differently. This experience has been variously described by terms ranging from 'culture shock' to 'alienation.'

Any term will do; the head of an international school with any degree of mobility across cultures needs to be intimately familiar with the experience in order to understand and reflect upon the experience of his or her clientele. Such experience and sensitivity cannot be taught. To make an analogy with the cryptic sayings of Zen masters, it is *that* which cannot be pointed to directly, *that* which can only be described in terms of what something is *not.*

School leaders with these kinds of abilities recognize the importance of not only evaluating the progress of the school in more traditional terms (i.e. educational outcomes, enrollment, finances), but also evaluating how the institution is performing interculturally. What are the experiences of all the members of the school community, not only those from the more dominant or outspoken cultural groups? The head of school is also reflective of how to go about achieving this level of evaluation. For example, where face-to-face interviews, surveys, or focus groups may be an appropriate and familiar means in one cultural context, they may be alien or inappropriate in another. The culturally competent head of school is comfortable with the reality that different cultures value different outcomes and means, and he or she is agile in adjusting management's goals to the idiosyncrasies of the cultural moment at hand.

This book seeks to help readers build comprehensive Transitions Teams in their schools. By virtue of their culturally representative natures, effective comprehensive Transitions Teams potentially provide heads of school with powerful vehicles for helping to effectively gather input on how the school is performing interculturally. The Council of International Schools (www.cois.org) is also developing tools to assist leaders in international schools in evaluating and boosting their degree of intercultural competence and sensitivity.

In Closing

I would like to close by encouraging you, in your capacity as a member of the board, to open all the preceding and following bottles and read each of the enclosed messages. Each message is relevant to your role by virtue of the scope of your mandate. Students at international schools need and deserve the programs detailed in this book. You'll have to hear what I've said in the other messages, and hopefully in this entire book, to fully understand why. At that point, I hope it will be clear why you want to support the establishment of a comprehensive transitions program at your school.

Yours Truly,

Doug Ota

MESSAGE 3

Dear Parents,

Help!

Parents are to a Transitions Team what wind is to a ship's sails. Without you, the ship won't move, and we're stuck. I'm glad this bottle found you!

International relocations are almost always driven by one parent's job, meaning there is usually a 'trailing spouse' who, more often than not these days, gives up a career in order to allow his or her spouse to pursue a promotion. In the ideal scenario, the promise of adventure abroad and a life-expanding experience for the entire family compensates for the sacrifice. In less fortunate scenarios, the trailing spouse experiences little choice in the matter: the decision gets made for them by the head office. They have to go.

These days, the fact more and more trailing spouses are male does little to change a reality that had begun to dawn over the course of the latter half of the twentieth century – that the trailing spouse is often highly educated. He or she is often equipped with a skill set that gets placed on hold due to difficulties of finding a job in the host country, acquiring the requisite work visas, combining work with family in a foreign setting – or all of the above.

Do you recognize parts of yourself in the above description? If so, I would say you are likely part of a diverse, skilled, and motivated crew, but a crew that doesn't yet know each other and is in search of a vessel.

Now let me add some tiny ripples.

Have you ever longed for a place you used to call 'home'? Have you ever felt the person you used to be – perhaps one with a job and a profession and a career you felt was a big part of 'who you were' – just got erased? Have you ever looked over your shoulder at a former time and wondered, "Was that really me? Did I really used to do all that?" Have you ever felt that nobody in your new place knows who you *really* were?

Now let me add some small waves.

Have you ever felt there were few or no people around you who really understood your culture, and how the people where you come from really think, what they really value? Have you ever felt the things that are essential to *who* you are as a person don't exist in the minds of most people around you, that the values and traditions and things you miss are even *invisible* in the society where you find yourself?

Now let me add some larger swells.

Have you ever wondered if you were doing the right thing by your children, taking them 'on the road' like this and exposing them to such a life at an international school? Have you ever feared they were missing a 'normal life' like the kids where you come from – making them destined to feel like global nomads for the rest of their lives, without a clear sense of home? Have you ever wondered if you were damaging them by not staying rooted, by introducing them to a life where they get torn away from friends, and friends get torn away from them, with all the grief that returns on an annual basis?

Now let me add some massive breakers.

Have you ever felt everybody else seemed to be doing just fine? Have you ever wondered if you were the only parent or family struggling with the move? Or have you ever felt you couldn't turn to your friends and family back home for support, because they might think, "everything abroad must be such an awesome experience"? Or, if you shared any of the difficult aspects of this mobile lifestyle, would friends and family reproach you, saying (or thinking to themselves) you had 'chosen it yourself', 'nobody forced you' or – worse still – that they had 'warned you'?

And now let me launch a tidal wave.

As if things weren't already hard enough, have you ever had a time when your spouse was constantly gone because of the demands of his or her new job, and one or more of your children was furious with you, screaming "you've ruined my life!" and "it's all your fault!" and that they "just want to go home!" Your spouse is away on an important business trip, but you desperately hit your phone's speed dial anyway to try to get some emotional support.

But you get your partner's voicemail.

If you made it through that list of ripples, waves, swells, breakers, and even the tidal wave without feeling the cold sea at least licking your toes, then your soul is cut from a hardier wood than mine. (And I'm not inclined to believe you!) An internationally mobile lifestyle *does* expose us to the riches of distant cultures and continents, which are an abstraction to most families. To reach those distant experiences without being buffeted by some gales and storms is, statistically speaking, highly unlikely. And, quite frankly, the waves and gales are an essential part of the experience. We learn and grow from the challenges we face, not the successes we accomplish. The peak experiences of an international lifestyle can only be reached via the troughs that precede each wave.

Your Role As A Parent

So what does your role as a parent in your international school have to do with the successful establishment and maintenance of an effective Transitions Team? Everything.

You are the key stakeholders in determining the course the school charged with educating your children chooses. There are various dimensions to the school's chosen course, such as the cognitive, physical, artistic, social, and emotional areas of development. While it is true that schools generally (and successfully) hire and employ staff who can address the cognitive, physical, artistic, social, and emotional needs of their students, the type of needs created when large portions of the school population constantly relocate are poorly addressed in most teacher training programs and staff development curricula.

Many inspired individuals at schools around the world accurately perceive the very real needs such a dynamic creates, but these people cannot adequately address the challenges involved for one simple reason – *a systemic challenge requires a systemic solution.* These talented individuals might give birth to inspired programs at the schools where they work and parent, but they inadvertently take their programs with them when they leave, simply because they own the program. Ownership of the program was never successfully passed to, or adopted by, the institution.

As the key stakeholders in your school, you have the ability to form a critical mass around this issue. You can be a force administrators simultaneously dread and dream of: you can insist on improvements (the kind of uncompromising forcefulness some administrators dread), while at the same time providing the volunteer person power to collaborate on effecting those improvements (the solution-focused approach administrators dream of). "If you bring me a problem," I once read on one administrator's bulletin board, "bring me a solution too."

This book is a rallying point for you and the fellow volunteers you will hopefully both find and inspire to join you. Your own transitions-related needs are every bit as important as your children's. If you're happy and well-adjusted in your wider parent community, you're serving as a role model and stabilizing factor for your son or daughter to imitate. (Unfortunately, the opposite is also true: if mobility has made you miserable – or if you have let it make you miserable – then your kids are more likely to do or feel the same.)

The Role Of 'Parents' At Your Current School

An important caveat worth mentioning here is that the spirit of this message is informed by certain assumptions about the place and role of 'the parent' in a school community. These assumptions are admittedly USAmerican, due to my upbringing and that I have spent much of my career in international schools, colored by USAmerican educational values. The 'volunteer mentality' in most USAmerican schools means it is considered normal for parents to be physically present in the school building, as well as involved in projects and activities sponsored by the school. This is not the case in every culture, where it may not be the norm, and perhaps even unacceptable, for parents to regularly enter and seek to be deeply involved in the life of the school.

If you are a parent involved in a school where active parental involvement is not the norm, let me say the following. Cultures can change. The statement "that's just how we do things around here" cannot serve as the gold standard for acceptable or unacceptable behaviors. The best guideline I have ever found for informing difficult decisions I've had to make as an educator – in fact the *only* guideline I fall back on when interests begin to conflict and pressures come to bear from multiple directions – is "What is in the best interests of this child?"

Or, translated to the school as a whole, the statement could run, "What is in the best interests of all the children?"

Certainly children deserve a school that is attending well to their cognitive, physical, artistic, social, and emotional needs. *But children attending an international school, with a high degree of mobility across cultures, face an additional set of developmental needs that children in most national schools around the world never need to contemplate.* The massive questions they silently ask themselves reveal the underlying need for guidance that we, the adults, must provide them. They ask themselves things such as:

- How do I say goodbye to my very best friend?

- What do I do if I'm a bit angry at my parents for making me move here?

- What should I do at recess if I don't have any friends yet?

- What should I do at lunchtime if I don't have a group of people to sit with?

- Everybody's nice to me here, but I just want to go home. What do I do?

- What do I do if kids say and do things that I was taught are wrong?

- How should I behave if lots of kids don't like the country I'm from?

- What if I'm convinced that making friends just leads to getting hurt?

Children do not spontaneously discover the answers to complex real-life questions any more than they learn algebra by sleeping on a math book. Learning how to navigate complex emotional issues requires adult guidance, preferably from all the adults in the proverbial 'village' it takes to 'raise a child' well. Only when all the adults involved in the educational enterprise are trying to row the boat in the same direction can complex issues such as transitions, grief, and culture begin to be adequately addressed by an international school. Only when all the parents join forces with all of the students and teachers can transitions across cultures be comprehensively tackled.

Pull Together, Get Started, And Enjoy The Ride

So align yourselves. Create an inspired group of parents consisting of a representative cross section of the parents and families that attend your school. Create a book group and begin to foster conversation on how to launch a Transitions Team. Last but not least, enjoy yourselves. I know from the many parents I've worked with over the years that being a parent volunteer on a team like this can be one of the most gratifying aspects of your experience as a parent in an international school setting. The fact you are rallying around a common goal with people from all walks of life elevates international experience to what it is at its best: an opportunity to see through our cultural differences to the shared humanity that links us at our cores. Bon voyage!

Yours Truly,

Doug Ota

MESSAGE 4

Dear Student,

Hi there. My name's Mr. Ota, and I'm really glad you're reading this. I need your help. More importantly, your fellow students need your help.

I'm not too worried about whether you picked out this book yourself or whether an adult suggested you read it. The fact is, I've got a chance to talk to you directly right now. I might understand some things about your life a lot of people don't. I wrote this book to help more people understand those things, and to help your school do something about them. Let me explain.

Ever Feel Like You Got Erased?

What a lot of people don't understand is that by being a student at an international school where lots of people come and go, your life is different from most students' lives. Sure, everybody talks about the positive things, such as seeing the world and getting to know people from lots of different countries. That's all true, and all exciting. But there's another more difficult side to this, too.

Moving, and having good friends move away from you, can feel like the hardest thing in your life. It can feel like somebody has erased you. Have you ever felt that who you are just went 'poof,' like you disappeared into thin air? You move to your new school, and nobody knows what you're interested in, nobody knows what you're good at, nobody even understands your jokes! The first day is hard enough, when you're just trying to figure out where to go and where to sit at lunch. It's only after a few months that reality settles in. *That person you used to be… That life you used to have… Where did it all go?*

You might sometimes wonder if you're even the same person!

Or what about when a good friend tells you he or she is going to be leaving? Has that ever happened to you? If it has, it might have felt like a bomb went off in your life.

Or what if you're from a country or culture that's not part of the main culture of your school? Let's say you're from the Middle East, or you're from Japan, and there's hardly anyone else familiar with your home and culture at the school? Students behave differently. Teachers expect different kinds of things from you. It's all so different and confusing, like somebody changed all the unwritten rules! All the other students seem to 'get it', but you feel like you're trying to find the 'Unwritten Rules Handbook.' You feel like you landed on Mars.

What Your School Is Doing About It – Or Not

Unfortunately, lots of schools don't yet deal with these kinds of challenges very well. The purpose of this book is to try to change that. And the reason I'm writing this letter *to you* is because you really can play an important part in making that happen. In fact, *you play a crucial role!* Let me explain.

Back in the last century, a sociologist named Ted Ward at Michigan State University said students like you are the "prototypical citizens of the 21st century." What he meant is that students like you are on the cutting edge of a kind of life which eventually all people will know, as technology makes our world smaller and smaller and brings us more and more in touch with people from other walks of life. You may be from Pennsylvania and sit at lunch with somebody from Pakistan or Peru, and you know exactly where Paraguay is on the map – when most people from outside South America probably don't. Technology and transportation may one day have most people around the world interacting daily with people from other places and mindsets. The human race is not there yet, but we're not so very far removed.

Especially you guys. International schools provide a training ground for interacting and building friendships with kids from other walks of life. Most kids just go to school with kids from their own neighborhoods. You go to school with students who may have come from every corner of the earth. Now this sounds special, and it is special, but there's a catch. With these special circumstances come exceptional challenges. And you know what I'm talking about. Going to an international school where lots of students come and go involves a lot of grief.

You might think grief is something that only happens when somebody dies. But grief also happens anytime you lose something important to you. That can be a person, but it can also be a place, or even a dream.

What You Can Do

Your school has a responsibility to help you with that grief. Sure, there are lots of positive things about your school and the opportunities in an internationally mobile lifestyle. But your feelings – and those of your fellow students – also need attention before you can grab those opportunities.

This is why I want you to get involved in your school's Transitions Program. The people reading this book may be thinking about how to build or improve a program that helps not only students, but also parents and teachers, with the challenges associated with moving across cultures. Let me be a cheerleader for you and offer any support I can by writing me at info@dougota.nl.

They Can't Do It Without You!

The adults cannot build this program well without you. So get on the Transitions Team, and stay on the Transitions Team! Make sure you're not alone, because you need several motivated and visionary students to make a program like this take off. Make sure there are students in different age groups, so you and the group of students don't all graduate at the same time. By helping a Transitions Team get started well, you have a special chance to help students who will come to or leave your school in the future, students you may never even know! That's a pretty cool thing to be able to do, don't you think?

So how can you help specifically? By really believing me when I tell you that *you can help the adults understand and remember what it's like to be a student at your school.* What is it like to have friends move away? What happens when friends keep moving away, or when you have to move every few years? What does that do to your sense of where you belong? Where *do* you feel like you belong, or where *does* 'home' feel like it is. *Tell the adults.* Just because they are older and more experienced at this thing called 'life' does not mean your experience is less important to making a Transitions Team at your school successful. You are no less than any other member at the table! Don't be afraid to make a difference! Good luck!

Yours Truly,

Doug Ota

MESSAGE 5

Dear Counselors,

We're colleagues, and for me, that makes this a special, personal message. For nearly fifteen years I occupied the position of High School counselor at the American School of The Hague (ASH), and it was from that role I helped co-found the school's Transitions Program, a program I chaired for a decade and eventually helped rebrand as the Safe Harbour program.

Preaching To The Choir

The position of counselor – which may have a different title in school systems not based in North America, such as 'mentor' or 'head of year' or even 'dean' – is one that logically combines with a leadership role for a transitions program. Counselors are natural helpers, generally highly invested in the welfare of students specifically, and human growth more generally. As such, we gravitate towards the establishment of programs such as transitions programs because we recognize they are geared towards assisting people in a proactive, preventative fashion. (And we know it's always better to prevent a problem than to solve it later.) The 'face validity' of such programs is so high and readily apparent that we 'counselor types' quickly perceive the obvious value of what the programs are trying to achieve, making us ready to launch into whatever work is required to make such a program successful because 'we get it.'

Being Wary Of Burnout

The obvious benefits of such motivation are simultaneously our Achilles' heel. Like all helping professionals, counselors run an elevated risk for burnout. As we attempt to address the needs we perceive, we risk shifting our own towards a lower priority. This is dangerous enough on an individual basis, where there are dozens, and sometimes hundreds, of individual student needs we're attending to. But it is a recipe for disaster when confronting a systemic challenge such as mobility across cultures at an average international school – a challenge that can simultaneously involve many thousands of people.

Why? *Because mobility at an average international school affects every single individual affiliated with the school.* Every single student, parent, teacher, and staff member is involved in and affected by real human beings moving in and out of the school community. The only way to address a challenge of this magnitude is to create and sustain a team equipped to address the scale of the challenge. Counselors can and should play key roles on such a team, and counselors can logically be the chairperson of such a team. But counselors must focus more on being process managers than actual agents of implementation if they want to be able to sustain their work on transitions over time.

I learned this the hard way. In addition to the normal responsibilities that came with my task as High School counselor, I became passionately involved with launching the Transitions Program at ASH. But in those days, there was no counselor available to coach me in the difference between process management and program implementation. I was passionate about the development and management of the program, but I was also one of the only people – or, stated differently, I allowed myself in my ignorance to *become* one of the only people – to implement the programs we devised. Such ambition is fine in the 'honeymoon phase', when the adrenaline of a new project is coursing through your veins, and you know your work is helping people and making a difference. But there are two reasons why such an approach is not sustainable:

- Budding programs need to be maintained and managed, leaving little time or energy for developing the next generation of additional programs in subsequent years – at least if you're also implementing the early programs yourself. Without additional personnel, the energy of an early Transitions Team, if spearheaded primarily by the counselors, hits a glass ceiling that can leave everyone surprised and discouraged in years two, three, and beyond.

- Just as programs are needing ongoing management and improvement to be sustained and to truly get into the 'fabric' of the school culture, certain people who were key to the early Team – including counselors – may leave. In other words, the issue the Transitions Program is seeking to address can strike the very Team doing the addressing.

Forewarned Is Forearmed

I send this message in a bottle not wanting to discourage you, but rather to give you the tools to avoid navigating yourself into the dire straits in which I found myself in the late 1990s. At that time I was the chair of a Team doing great work, but I was tired from all of my own hands-on activities, and several key people – including counselors and parent members of the founding Team – announced they were leaving. We had created little provision for recruitment, and the school leadership was not yet fully on board in terms of backing our efforts. This recipe for disaster culminated in me feeling depleted and resentful, and it very nearly led to the program – which was being heralded in ECIS (European Council of International Schools) circles as the best and most innovative of its kind – collapsing.

So my counsel to counselors is as follows: play *a,* or even *the,* key leadership role in the development of a comprehensive transitions program at your school, but make sure your process is healthy. A healthy process is your goal, not the actual programs. If the process is healthy, the programs follow suit. What I mean by a 'healthy process' is the topic of this book, explored particularly in *Chapter 4: Building the Harbor* and *Chapter 5: Sustaining the Team* of *Part II.*

To wrap up, let me say thank you for opening this bottle, and let me wish you my heartfelt best wishes for an inspiring ride through the seas and straights that lie ahead, which I hope you will choose to explore. Parent crew members are ready and waiting, so rally them together with a few visionary students and members of the school leadership, and you have the basis for a crew that can take on the gales mobility will blow your way.

Yours Truly,

Doug Ota

MESSAGE 6

Dear Teachers and Members of Staff,

All Legs are Equal

You represent one of the four key 'legs of the stool' of any school community. I've already written to the members of the other three 'legs' – the administrators and students and parents – but an international school, or any school for that matter, depends upon *your* energy in order to function, *your* professionalism in order to excel, and *your* dedication to keep growing.

Your needs are equally as important as those of the other three 'legs.' A school that seeks to address the transitions-related needs of its students, parents, and administrators without attending to the transitions-related needs of its staff is like a furniture maker who cuts costs by eliminating legs.

Practicing What We Preach

The reason why is simple. As adults, we can only help others with issues we have resolved for ourselves.[41] If we haven't resolved an issue for ourselves, how can we help anybody else with it?

Nowhere is this truth more clear than around the topic of grief. For students to process the amounts of grief generated at an international school with a substantial degree of turnover, the professionals working with these students have to be comfortable in dealing with grief themselves.

For me to personalize what I'm saying, I have to ask you to put yourself into the right subcategory of 'teacher and staff' first. This 'subcategory' depends less on what you do at school, and more on how long you do it.

Two Kinds Of Staff Members

Do you identify with the expats and those who regularly move to a new teaching or working location? Or do you identify with those who feel deeper ties to the local culture, either because of the duration of your tenure, a relationship with somebody from the local culture, or your own heritage?

---

41   *This is a given for psychologists and others in the helping professions, who must ideally have had counseling for themselves to resolve their own issues, before trying to help others with theirs. It is also true for parents, which is why those of them who say "I'm going to do X so much differently than my own parents" find themselves often dismayed, and discouraged, when 'X' comes to pass in their own families.*

The direction of this identification is more important than your actual role at school for two reasons.

The first is cultural. For teachers or members of staff who identify with the local culture, 'going to work' can be equivalent to crossing a cultural divide – particularly during the first months and years of one's employment at a new international school. You might live in Santiago, Chile, or The Hague in the Netherlands, but by making your commute to Nido de Aguilas International School or the American School of The Hague every day, you cross an invisible membrane and enter a numinal space that is *other*. Your sense of place becomes disoriented when you enter that international bubble, but it also becomes disoriented when you leave. Try describing your workplace to people from the local culture. You can't. It's an international, third culture space, and the only way to understand the experience is to live it.

The perspective of this 'local' employee is alien to many veteran international educators – and vice versa. Two members of staff, even members of the same grade-team or department, could be occupying vastly different personal spaces invisible to the naked eye. One is rooted in the local culture and sees the veteran international educators as 'rolling stones' that pass through briefly. The other is rooted in the 'global nomad' culture, a culture 'between borders', and he or she views the long-term placement of the long-term local as an overdose of stability lacking in adventure, one that misses the point of a career in international education.

Two Ways Of Responding To Grief

Moving tires us, because moving makes us grieve, and grief is unpleasant, difficult, emotionally exhausting work. Our natural human inclination in the face of unpleasant, difficult tasks is to avoid them. (Be honest, do you really look forward to submitting your taxes every year?) Even if we don't tend to be the avoidant type, the sheer volume of goodbyes that life in an international school can throw at you can fatigue what I referred to in *Chapter 1: Attachment,* as your 'attachment system.' So many people can come and go over the years it becomes challenging to keep up with the emotions involved. Have you ever had a dear friend leave, and then another one the next year, and then several more the next, making you wish for a break, making you desperately hope that any remaining good friends don't also announce they're leaving?

This is where the two types of staff members sketched above, the 'locals' and the 'internationals', intersect with two ways of dealing with grief. Given enough time in international education, everyone begins to experience what might be termed 'grief fatigue,' which can be dealt with by attempting to:

- 'stay on top' of it by continuously processing the grief

- avoid it altogether, because it is painful

Four Types Of People

Given the preceding discussion identifies two main categories for staff (the 'local' and those on an 'international assignment'), and given there are two extremes in how to deal with grief ('avoid it' or 'process it'), we could argue there are four types of staff members, as depicted by the following axes:

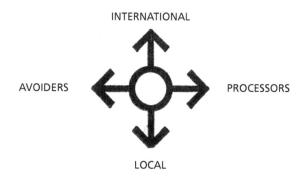

Staff members who *process* their grief, be it as a local or as somebody on international assignment, remain psychologically healthy, sad to see dear colleagues leave, but able nonetheless to make and maintain new friendships and connections over time. Because they process their feelings, they're more likely to be able to make connections with others, regardless of an 'international' or 'local' orientation.

The two manifestations of *avoidance* of grief can look different, depending on whether it's from the perspective of the 'international' or 'local' staff member. Those who would identify themselves more as international, with a tendency to move to a new school every three or so years, can often develop what relocation experts have dubbed a 'quick attach and quick release' system. They are quick to make new connections in a new setting, but the new connections might stop at a certain level of intimacy, almost as a safeguard against growing connections that would hurt to sever. When it is time to move on, these individuals are adept at doing the 'quick release', whereby they let go of friendships quickly. This 'quick release' is facilitated by the fact the connections weren't allowed to run deeply in the first place. Fundamentally, the 'quick release' is a means of coping with grief.

Those members of staff who would identify themselves as more 'local' tend to remain at the school for longer, sometimes for a large portion of their careers, and this fosters in them the perspective of 'the stayer.' 'Stayers' see so many colleagues come and go that their attachment systems *(Chapter 1: Attachment)* begin to fatigue, making such individuals lean towards identifications and associations with like-minded others, i.e. with 'those who won't go.' This is another way of avoiding grief because it steers clear of making deep connections with those with whom it will likely be difficult to stay connected.

These two avoidant adaptations to grief are logical and predictable. Both make sense from the perspective of protecting the person involved. So what's the problem?

Why Staff Can – And Must – Do Better

If 'avoidance' is our answer to how to deal with the massive amount of grief inherent in a career in international education, then we cannot expect to effectively help our students or their parents in developing the skills needed to *process* this most human of challenges. If teachers and staff members are 'role models' and 'parental figures' for students (and often, by extension, for the students' parents too), and if it is true that kids tend to mimic adults in both good ways and bad, then we can reasonably expect our students to learn and practice a strategy of avoidance for coping with grief if that is what they observe in us, the professionals. In other words:

By not actively managing our own grief as staff members, we risk stunting an important dimension of our own emotional lives and modeling that stunted development for the students looking up to us.

I hear your doubts. Skeptics often ask me how kids can possibly notice such deeply-seated convictions or attitudes, particularly if they are never openly discussed. My rejoinder is to ask you to consider where your own convictions, values, beliefs, and prohibitions came from. Did things always have to be openly said in your family of origin for certain values or convictions to be transmitted? Does a student's mother or father need to state something verbally for kids to get the message? Or is a certain tone of voice, a certain look, enough to make abundantly clear whether something is smiled at or frowned upon?

I have heard adult clients claim "the kids don't know we're having problems" because "we always make sure we talk about these things after they're in bed." *Kids always know.* Children are wired to be highly attuned to their caregivers' opinions and preferences because their very survival, evolutionarily speaking, depended upon it. Put yourself in the child's shoes. As a child, you are completely dependent on the adults. So wouldn't it make very good sense to develop antenna that would help you decipher the adults' deepest wishes. If some of those deeper, unspoken wishes include injunctions against speaking about difficult topics – and grief is one such topic – the child will get the message.

Staff Unity

Not paying explicit attention to the dynamics of how we and our fellow colleagues manage the challenges of grief can also allow staff to inadvertently create factions and subfactions, effectively dividing the team. Based on the discussion above, it would be very possible – and this is all too often the case – that staff members who identify with the 'local' staff member description would associate with 'fellow locals,' whereas staff identifying with 'international' and on the move would associate with other 'internationals.' There is nothing wrong with a preference for a certain type of person. But when that preference hardens into an inability to understand the perspective or experience of somebody with a different background, we have the beginning of a problem – or more extremely, the beginning of marginalization or discrimination.

For example, when staff members who were hired locally are not given the same degree of orientation and understanding as those hired internationally, certain assumptions can creep into the system which imply – without being implicitly stated – that the needs of the local hires are somehow less complicated or less pressing than those of the staff members hired internationally. And this distinction is the first step towards these members of staff also feeling, or sensing they are perceived as, less important.

Although they might have a decade of experience, already understand the language, and even own a home, the locally-hired teacher new to international education is faced with the massive challenge of understanding the curriculum, grading, parent body, values, and future aspirations of the international school students he or she is now teaching. Is this challenge any less daunting than that of the newly relocated but experienced international teacher who, while still needing a home and a working phone connection, at least already understands the curriculum, grading, parent body, values, and future orientation of his or her students?

What Staff Should be Discussing – At Least Once In A While

The danger is not in having a preference for 'fellow teachers' with your type of background, but rather in *not understanding where that preference comes from and what it has to do with grief.* These issues do not need discussion every day at the faculty lunch table, but issues and questions like these deserve examination every few years for every staff team of every international school with any significant degree of turnover:

- What is it like for you to work in a place where people you care about have to leave, or where you might have to leave? How do you cope with that?

- If you tend to move around every few years, what do you think it's like to work here for somebody who's been here for a long time? How do they cope with mobility in a place like this? How do they perceive somebody like you? Talk to one of them and find out!

- If you've worked here for a long time, or if you plan to, what do you think it's like for staff members who move around every few years? How do they cope with mobility? How do they perceive somebody like you who tends to stay put longer? Talk to one of them and find out!

Questions like these can be broached in small groups as part of a staff workshop on mobility, for example.

The point here is that understanding dissolves boundaries, or at least prevents them from hardening and calcifying. And insuring boundaries do not form and harden amongst one's staff would seem to be a worthwhile goal, particularly in light of the fact that kids are watching. Students imitate adults. If we want to create the conditions for our students to believe in and pursue their shared humanity as part of Walker's higher calling for international education (see page LV), then it stands to reason we need to take care of our own emotional health amidst the challenges of mobility – making sure we don't harden to our own experiences, and those of our colleagues, with grief.

By becoming involved in programs designed to help you and your fellow colleagues better cope with the challenges of mobility across cultures in international education, you are positioning yourself to model for your students a way of being in life that leads to the long-term maintenance of emotional health and the ability to tighten and loosen relational bonds. I would argue that the true international educator does more than just an outstanding job in the classroom. The true international educator models how to cope with the human challenges of living at the confluence points of grief and culture, the junctures of connections and losses, so his or her students can also learn how to deal with what we could aptly refer to as the 'hidden curriculum' of the global age.

Yours Truly,

Doug Ota

MESSAGE 7

Dear HR Managers,

Every HR Manager I have ever known is efficient, pragmatic, and pressed for time. Many have felt like their departments are overworked and understaffed. Staff members may turn to you for issues varying from visas to job descriptions, and school leadership expects you to have all the 't's' in contracts crossed and the 'i's' in incomes dotted.

So let me say at the outset of this epistle that a likely byproduct of this entire book is your job becomes more efficient and enjoyable, and therefore more effective.

Let me try now to back that up.

Staff Well-Being

One of the important aspects of your job probably has to do with maintaining staff well-being, and one of the focal points you are probably expected to help coordinate in order to bolster this well-being probably centers on staff orientation. The logic is solid: if new staff get well orientated and incorporated into their new organization, they stand a better chance of flourishing, teaching well, and staying for a healthy tenure. Hiring and firing are extremely time consuming and expensive processes for organizations, making it clear why a robust hiring and orientation process pays massive dividends. Additional re-hiring will not be quickly necessary because the new staff member stays; expensive firing processes will not be necessary because the right person adjusts well to his or her new role – and most important of all, given that we are talking about schools, the teacher who feels well teaches well, meaning students learn well. With staff who settle and function well, the school is in a position to pursue the achievement of its mission.

While the Superintendent, Director, Headmaster or Headmistress of a school plays the key gatekeeper role in the hiring process, you as an HR manager enter the picture soon after, and the process of gradually helping a new hiree become comfortable in his or her new professional community gets underway. The formal 'Orientation Program for New Staff' probably falls to you to organize or oversee in some degree or another. But the informal process of orienting a new staff member spans a far greater amount of time, beginning the moment a staff member is hired and only ending when the staff member no longer describes him or herself as 'new.' This process spans at least one year, and may more appropriately be considered in terms of two years.

Throughout that span of time, new hires may perceive an invisible life buoy mounted on the outside of your door.

For HR managers who take the staff welfare portions of their jobs seriously, that is a lot of pressure. It can feel as if the new hiree's flourishing or floundering is riding on the effectiveness of your office. Though I've never been an HR manager, a few decades of experience as a psychologist has taught me that this sense of pressure – so typical for those in any kind of a helping or supportive profession – forms a significant contributor to job-related stress and burnout. The purpose of this letter to you is to point out how you can:

- make your efforts to address that stress more effective

- distribute that stress more evenly, so it's not solely on your shoulders, but on the shoulders of many – where it belongs

Human beings crave connection. Everything in our being and biology propels us to make and maintain connections with others. Just as Isaac Newton stated in his third law of motion "for every force there is an equal and opposite force," so too is connection a two-way street, meaning that for every human connection in one direction, there must be an equal and opposite connection in the other direction. In other words, relationships are mutual. Friendship is liking somebody's company *and* knowing that person enjoys yours.

The ramifications of this idea are quite vast, and can be summarized in what is referred to in this book as the Second Law of Transitions:

For a person to connect to somebody else, that other person must be willing and able to make the connection.

In other words, all our efforts to build exemplary orientation programs, if focused only on those who are moving or new, are only hitting one half of this Second Law of Transitions, i.e. the moving half. What about the receiving half? What energies are we spending on those who have stayed *to be willing and able to make connections* with the new half? Too often, we're doing too little.

Yet what are the ramifications of the Second Law of Transitions when juxtaposed next to the First Law of Transitions:

"You have to say a clear 'goodbye' in order to say a clear 'hello.'"

For the receiving half of staff to be able and willing to connect with the new half, which would seem like a prerequisite for the successful orientation and integration of the new half, this receiving half of staff needs to say a clear goodbye to all the staff members they have lost in the previous transition(s). Why? Because the ramifications of the inverse of the First Law of Transitions, when phrased negatively, are unmistakable in their implications:

Staff members who have not said a clear 'goodbye' to departing staff will be unable and unwilling to say a clear 'hello' to arriving staff.

This raises the next logical question, namely: What is your school doing to insure that staff say clear and effective farewells to one another? As HR manager, this should be your point of investment.

Any entry-point to staff assistance that skips this step is akin to trying to address symptoms without first attending to sources.[42] An entry point to staff assistance that starts with the process of goodbye has the greatest chance of getting a full return on its investment. This is why I have repeatedly said – and will continue to do so through this text – that the academic calendar may begin in August or September, but the emotional calendar begins six months earlier, in February or March.[43] It is at the cusp between winter and spring that the first seeds of a successful goodbye need to be planted, so those who leave and those who are being left behind can reap the benefits of well-said farewells. Failing to plant these seeds and to truly grieve the loss of dear colleagues and friends leads to the stunting of our emotional apparatus, and therefore to a compromised ability to connect when new people arrive. New staff will never be able to consciously see these processes. But I can guarantee they feel it.

First Things First

The trick for staff, and perhaps for HR managers in particular, is to refocus the lion's share of energies back where it belongs, upon a thorough goodbye process that *honors* the loss of key connections, thereby clearing the way for the *building* of new ones.

One thing that makes the American School of The Hague's (ASH) treatment of staff stand out is the degree of attention it spends on this Second Law

---

42 *The Dutch have many remarkable sayings that 'hit the nail on the head' in particular circumstances. One that comes to mind in this situation is 'it's like mopping the floor without turning off the faucet.' (Dat is dweilen met de kraan open.)*

43 *For readers in the Southern Hemisphere, where the academic calendar begins after January 1st, I would shift my statement accordingly, such that the emotional calendar begins around July.*

of Transitions, namely the fostering of the kinds of conditions that assist staff members in saying farewell to one another. Early announcement of departures; division-specific traditions for holding farewell ceremonies for departees; signing the permanent signature boards framed centrally in the school; recognition speeches by colleagues, principals, and directors – all of these events are telltales signs of an institution that takes 'goodbye' seriously. An even more poignant example is ASH's annual longevity ceremony, when the school leadership pays tribute to those staff who have stayed for longer periods of time, holding a ceremony to honor those who have served the school at key points in their careers (10 years, 15 years, 20 years, 25 years, and longer). In a well-attended ceremony packed with fellow colleagues, the school's Director prepares brief but poignant speeches about all honorees, with input gleaned from colleagues via school-wide email exchanges, so his words of appreciation are interspersed with those of colleagues. As gifts and plaques are presented, both honoree and audience are validated.

Most 'longevity award' recipients continue their tenure at ASH. Why, then, is this ceremony an example of addressing the Second Law of Transitions? Because it assuages some of the grief associated with longevity. These staff members have been faithful educators and assistants, but they have also provided the spine that has borne much of the institutional load dealt by departure. The longevity ceremonies massage and soothe the grief muscles that receive such intensive use amongst long-term staff. When so many leave, fewer remain to carry the institution's memory. Periodic recognition of this fact sustains the people involved and the willpower required to live within the bounds of the Second Law of Transitions.

To sum up, it is all good and well to welcome new staff thoroughly, but the effectiveness of that welcoming process is in direct proportion to the effectiveness of the farewells said months earlier – or not. It is all good and well to welcome new staff thoroughly, but if veteran staff do not feel recognized and valued for the continuity and organizational memory they provide in the face of turnover, then the 'receiving end' of the new connections formed at the beginning of each cycle will not be properly primed, and the orientation process will not flow as well as it could.

The Paradigm Shift You're After

Dr. Richard Spradling, Director of the American School of The Hague for many years, collaborated with the HR department and the Transitions Team to create and maintain the programs and processes described above. But more importantly for the purposes of this letter, they did not attempt to carry these transitions-related programs for staff on their own. *They helped create an organization that would own these processes.* An effective transitions program is perhaps the key agent in that shift to organizational ownership of staff-related transitions issues, and this is where we arrive at the second focus of this letter – how you can distribute the pressure of addressing staff needs more evenly, so it's not solely on the shoulders of the HR department.

The paradigm shift that needs to occur is as follows. At least as it relates to the challenges of mobility across cultures, staff are best positioned to address the emotional welfare of staff, not the HR department. Like the best of managers, the HR department can be involved in managing and helping to oversee the *process* of how the staff's transitions-related needs can be met – it does not need to be an *actor* in executing these processes. HR departments that do take the primary or sole lead in program administration for new staff risk overburdening their own staff and depriving the wider staff of a key opportunity to establish new connections.

And a staff for whom the First Law of Transitions has been respected is primed and ready to establish those new connections. Staff who have appropriately and adequately grieved for those who have left have 'worked through' the emotional processes that must precede the building of new collaborations and friendships, and are therefore ready and seeking these new collaborations and friendships. This is where an HR department has a veritable army of willing personnel to tap into – and where an HR Manager's job starts to become more effective, and potentially a whole lot easier.

Mobilizing The Personnel To Pull This Off

By helping to create programs that will help staff work through their own emotional needs in relation to transitions – whether staff are aware of these needs or not – an HR department creates the conditions for mobilizing a large force of willing colleagues and unleashing a win-win process that benefits both the 'arriving half' and the 'receiving half.' Embedding these staff-related programs in a community-wide transitions program stabilizes the programs within a wider team, aligning the needs of staff with the needs of both students and parents alike, as all are working to cope with a challenging dynamic, namely the tightening and loosening of relationships in the face of mobility across cultures.

And as I've said with regards to happier students who learn better, happier and well-adjusted staff members teach better – both those who are new as well as those who have seen cherished colleagues leave. The literature is unequivocal about the costs to society of unhappiness, maladjustment, and depression. Depression is now the single most expensive disorder on the planet. The connection between an unhappy employee and an employee who misses work for appointments or illness – while sometimes difficult to 'prove'– is unquestionable, and ultimately very expensive to the organization. An HR Department that contributes to maintaining the emotional gears of the staff is making significant contributions towards helping the school operate smoothly and achieve its mission.

I hope I have started to make good on the promise made in the second paragraph of this message. If so, my next promise is that this book provides you with the map for how to achieve what sounds so good in theory.

Yours Truly,

Doug Ota

MESSAGE 8

Dear Admissions Directors,

Yours is probably the first smiling face families will remember when they think of their first contact with your school. You provide people with a safe and caring place to dock. As a Director of Admissions at an international school, you are probably charged with some or all of the following:

1. Maintaining and attracting relationships with the kinds of organizations that have families who already send, or may consider sending, their children to your school.

2. Overseeing the processes needed to distinguish between the students for whom your school is appropriate versus inappropriate, and making sure the former student is admitted, while admission is denied to the latter.

3. Contributing to a process whereby both the student and the family make a smooth transition into your school's community.

Implicit in an Admission Director's job – as is true for all members of the school's leadership team – is a fourth mandate:

4. To keep enrollment up – a school needs students to be a school, and a school needs enough students if it wants to be a school that survives.

When there are more schooling options available to a relocating family, it is the welcoming warmth of an Admission Director's personality that often convinces parents to enroll their children in your school.

Creating or improving a comprehensive transitions program at your school will contribute to helping you achieve all four of the above objectives. I'll begin my letter with the most obvious objectives, and move to those that may not be readily apparent. I will start with the third task, namely to help students and their families make a smooth transition to your school.

Thousands Of Mouths To Feed

First impressions are important, and it is essential an Admissions Director and Admissions staff are naturals at putting people at ease and helping them feel welcome. The way things start in the Admissions Office sets the initial trajectory of the welcoming process. As this welcoming process goes on for months and often the entire first year, it is essential welcoming services from the Admissions Office are well articulated with ongoing welcoming services sponsored by other groups long after acceptance and enrollment.

A school community with one thousand students is very easily a community with two to four thousand family members currently involved in the school – more if you count alumni students and parents – and there is no realistic way for the Admissions Office itself to appropriately match the right student with the right student, or the right parent with the right parent. They can make a start, but larger processes are needed, involving far more people to manage this kind of volume. Admissions Officers do not have the time to accompany every lonely student to the appropriate lunch table, or to play tennis with every trailing spouse. (I know many who care enough about people to want to try, but that's a different chapter.)

From a transitions perspective then, the effective Admissions Director sees him or herself as a process manager: he or she helps the student and the parents participate in processes that assist them in finding long-term friendships, lunch mates, and tennis partners.

This is why a comprehensive Transitions Team can be your best friend. If you aren't one of the most active proponents of starting or improving your Team, then the purpose of this letter is an attempt to persuade you to change that. In the fictitious school of a thousand students cited above, hundreds of students and hundreds of parents need to be involved in ushering the new students and parents into the community – in a way that leads to their meeting the right students and the right parents, the ones with whom friendships can grow, the ones who will help them arrive sooner rather than later at a feeling of not being new anymore.

Doing The Right Thing

Do not get me wrong – it's very possible to run a school without doing it this way, by letting students and parents find their own way. Research shows that the most outgoing and assertive will do fine; "the others," one could argue as a hardliner, "will simply have to find a way to survive, because that's how it works in the real world."

One of the ethical questions underpinning this entire text is whether we can, in good conscience, run our international schools based on 'survival of the fittest' norms. Students or parents with a more introverted or anxious character or personality profile are automatically at more risk for the stresses of mobility across cultures, but organizations do not (as a rule) investigate the personality profiles of an employee's dependents before reassigning that employee to a new post. Nobody gets to pick their personality at birth, but students and parents who are more shy, less social, and less assertive also deserve support.[44]

Boosting Enrollment

Reasons 1 and 4 in the start of this message pertain directly to enrollment. As word gets out about how well your school handles the challenge of mobility (initially because of your front door efforts, but now augmented a hundred-fold by the efforts of your new Transitions Team and the PR on the excellent job it is doing!), then your school's front door immediately becomes more attractive. Positive PR and word-of-mouth is the best advertising around, something that begins to distinguish your school from the competition. People begin to make decisions about where to relocate – to choose, for example, the posting near your school as opposed to the posting near a school without a well-known transitions program – because of your school's approach to dealing with this challenge. Seasoned expats who have perhaps had challenging experiences with mobility are even more likely to be on the lookout for schools like your own. And the reality, at least as I write these paragraphs, is there are shockingly few schools dealing with mobility's challenges well.

As your front door PR improves, so too will your school's ability to maintain enrollment, because you will have fewer students dropping out due to poor adjustment. This is admittedly likely to be only a few students per year, but the cost to your school can be significant – to say nothing of the cost to that young person's confidence and life trajectory. Smooth transitions, like most preventative work, saves significant time, money, and effort over the long haul. It might seem expensive to take your car for its annual check up, but it's far more expensive over time not to.

So far, we have explored why a comprehensive transitions program can assist in attracting families, smoothing the relocation process, and keeping enrollment up. Can a Transitions Team really help with '2' too, namely your need to admit those students for whom your school is appropriate, while denying admission to the students your school can't serve?

----

44   *Noteworthy in this respect is Susan Cain's talk on introversion [see 60]*

Boosting Enrollment A Bit Further

Yes, to a degree. An effective Transitions Team will not, of course, increase the intelligence or drive of a student who is not academically strong enough or sufficiently motivated to succeed at your school. But there are many other gradients on which to evaluate students. One of these gradients is psychological or character-based. Some students may have struggled at their last school, and one of the reasons they may have struggled was because of psychological factors making them more vulnerable. Perhaps they did not feel they fit in culturally. Perhaps they were bullied. Perhaps they got off to a bad start and never found their way back onto a more successful trajectory, be it academic or social. Most strikingly, perhaps their last school was infused with the self-same 'survival of the fittest' mentality mentioned above, and they were not one of the fittest.

We are not talking about a massive number of students who would suddenly fit the criteria for your school by virtue of your school developing a comprehensive transitions program. But we are talking about a particular bandwidth, and the parents of prospective students like these are likely to hear of your school during their search, as your school develops its reputation for caring and for taking transitions seriously. *The process of developing and participating in a comprehensive transitions program run by an effective Transitions Team will help you in your task of recognizing 'appropriate students' by broadening the definition of this type of student.* Your school's catchment net will broaden slightly. And this, of course, will also produce a slight but non-negligible positive impact on enrollment.

Why An Admissions Office Should Be Involved In Departures Too

Let me close this message by encouraging you to open the bottle I sent to the HR Manager, and by emphasizing an idea in that message. The main requirement for being effective at the front door entails being effective at the back door. This is what I've referred to as the First Law of Transitions:

"You have to say a clear 'goodbye' in order to say a clear 'hello.'"

In your great efforts to make an effective 'hello' process, you must keep in mind that the new people are being met by veterans of goodbyes, and that these veterans will only be fully open to effective 'hello's' if their own goodbyes have been thoroughly worked through. As a Director of Admissions, you most likely have little direct influence in this domain. People expect you, after all, to be helping students arrive at school, and not to be focusing on what they're doing when people are leaving. Many an eyebrow might go up if your office, the 'Office of Admissions,' suddenly began wanting to sponsor activities at school targeting leaving and departure!

Yet, as I wrote in my letter to the HR Manager, these processes are absolutely fundamental to readying the school 'soil' for the new arrivals. Without 'stayers' who are emotionally ready and willing to connect, the 'arrivers' have nobody to connect with – or at least to fully connect with, in the full human sense. This Second Law of Transitions demands:

"For every connection there is an equal and opposite connection."

Yet how are you, as a Director of Admissions, supposed to exert an influence on a process that would seem to have no relation to your office?

The answer, as you will have guessed, is to be found in the comprehensive transitions program, and in either helping to form, to join, or to improve the Transitions Team needed to manage such a program for your school. Such goodbye programs for students exceed the reach of your office when we consider the goals of your office in job description terms. But a more holistic and total view of the community's well-being targeted by an effective Transitions Team puts these goals appropriately on your radar.

This book will show you how to proceed. I hope you will read on.

Yours Truly,

Doug Ota

APPENDIX B: CIS ACCREDITATION STANDARDS, VERSION 8.2

COUNCIL OF INTERNATIONAL SCHOOLS (CIS)
SCHOOL IMPROVEMENT THROUGH ACCREDITATION

Guide to School Evaluation and Accreditation - 8th Edition (Version 8.2)
STANDARDS AND INDICATORS

SECTION A SCHOOL GUIDING STATEMENTS

Note: The term "governing body" includes any school ownership structure.

STANDARD A1
The school shall be guided by clear and broadly accepted Guiding Statements of vision, mission, and educational objectives (or the equivalent using the school's chosen nomenclature and format) for students.
A1a
INDICATORS RELATED TO STANDARD A1
The school's Guiding Statements establish clear expectations for student learning and guidelines for the well-being of the whole school community.
A1b
Monitoring procedures exist which show that the school's Guiding Statements enjoy a high degree of support from the governing body, school leadership, staff, parents and students with this support being demonstrated by the actions of all these school sectors.
A1c
There is evidence which shows that the school's Guiding Statements drive decision-making, planning, action and review at multiple levels of school life.
A1d
There are periodic, data-driven reviews of the school's Guiding Statements which involve the broad school community and which ensure that the statements remain vibrant and relevant.
A1e
A formal process and defined indicators are used to assess the school's success in achieving its aims as laid out in its Guiding Statements.

STANDARD A2
The school's Guiding Statements shall clearly demonstrate a commitment to internationalism/interculturalism in education, and this shall be reflected throughout the life of the institution.
A2a
INDICATORS RELATED TO STANDARD A2
The school has created an engaging and contextually appropriate definition of internationalism/
interculturalism in education.
A2b
The school puts into action its definition of internationalism/interculturalism in education, both inside and outside the classroom, as evidenced by impact on students.
A2c
The school expresses its commitment to internationalism/interculturalism in education through as many avenues as possible.

STANDARD A3
The school's Vision for Students (or similar) shall demonstrate a clear commitment to fostering desirable traits related to internationalism/interculturalism, and this shall impact upon all students.
INDICATORS RELATED TO STANDARD A3
The school is committed to, and is actively promoting in its students, internationalism/interculturalism in education through ....
A3a
.... discussion of substantive matters of principle from multiple perspectives.
A3b
.... the understanding of the histories, cultures, beliefs, values and perspectives of a range of individuals and peoples.
A3c
.... the understanding of current issues of global significance relating to geopolitics, the environment, health, trade, sustainable development and human rights.
A3d
.... development of fluency in the language(s) of instruction, in another language, and - with as much support as the school can offer - in student mother tongues.

A3e
.... the development of their disposition to serve the community - local and global - through engagement in meaningful and reflective service.
A3f
.... the acquisition and refinement of the skills of leading and following, collaborating, adapting to the ideas of others, constructive problem-solving, and conflict-resolution through experiencing leadership in authentic contexts.

STANDARD A4
The school's admissions policies and practices shall ensure there is alignment between its Guiding Statements, its programmes, and the students admitted to and remaining at the school.
A4a
INDICATORS RELATED TO STANDARD A4
The school's promotional materials and activities project a realistic picture of the school and its mission, objectives and programmes, hence enabling parents to appraise the school's suitability for their children.
A4b
The school's admissions policies and practices require that adequate information be obtained, and that appropriate evaluations be carried out, to ensure that there is alignment between a student's needs/abilities and the programmes offered.

SECTION B TEACHING AND LEARNING

STANDARD B1
The curriculum, in its content, design, implementation, assessment and review, shall reflect the school's mission, learning objectives, and policies and shall foster global citizenship and student achievement.
B1a
INDICATORS RELATED TO STANDARD B1
The school's curriculum design, teaching practices, and student learning experiences are aligned with its mission and objectives.
B1b
The school's curriculum and programmes are supported by a comprehensive set of teaching and learning policies.
B1c
The formal curriculum offers an appropriate range of disciplines, including those that foster the development of global citizenship.
B1d
There is evidence of alignment between the written curriculum, the taught curriculum and student learning.
B1e
The school has a clearly articulated vision of quality learning and defined practices that support student achievement.

STANDARD B2
Students shall have access to a curriculum that provides challenge but also supports varied developmental, academic, social, physical and emotional needs and fosters the development of skills and abilities that prepare students for lifelong learning.
B2a
INDICATORS RELATED TO STANDARD B2
The effectiveness of the school's curriculum design and the varied implementation methods used, is evidenced by students being full participants in the learning process.
B2b
The curriculum design, teaching strategies, and support resources provided ensure that all students can profit from school offerings and that all students are challenged by the content of their courses.
B2c
The curriculum emphasizes the processes of gathering, organizing, presenting, and applying ideas and information as well as the mastery of content knowledge.
B2d
The curriculum provides students with opportunities to learn, develop, and apply skills in critical thinking, evaluating, interpreting, synthesizing, and problem solving.
B2e
The curriculum provides opportunities for students to develop and demonstrate awareness of their own learning styles.
B2f
The curriculum includes opportunities for students to acquire skills in accessing and evaluating information from print and media resources and in using the tools of technology.

STANDARD B3
Teaching and learning shall be guided by comprehensive curriculum documentation that reflects horizontal and vertical articulation as a means of providing students with meaningful connections among and between disciplines and continuity within disciplines.
B3a
INDICATORS RELATED TO STANDARD B3
Written curriculum materials specify expected learning outcomes in terms of what students should know, understand, and be able to do.
B3b
Written curriculum materials indicate content and sequence for each course/grade.
B3c
Written curriculum materials include references to the methodologies, teaching materials and resources that are used.
B3d
Written curriculum materials include references to the assessments that are used to measure student progress.
B3e
Written curriculum materials include references to links within and across disciplines.
B3f
The written curriculum describes multi-disciplinary experiences and/or activities, where appropriate, to foster authentic learning.
B3g
There is clear designation of responsibility for overseeing effective school-wide curriculum planning, design, articulation, implementation, and review.
B3h
Teachers meet with colleagues, as necessary, to strengthen vertical curriculum articulation and to ensure a logical sequence that minimizes overlap or gaps in content.
B3i
Teachers meet with colleagues, as necessary, to strengthen horizontal curriculum articulation that enhances meaning and connections for students.

STANDARD B4
Students shall benefit from a curriculum and related activities that shall be enhanced by the cultural diversity of both the host country and the school community, hence contributing to the development of global citizenship in students.
B4a
INDICATORS RELATED TO STANDARD B4
Information about the local culture and physical environment is imbedded into the curriculum and related activities to enhance student learning and contribute to the development of global citizens.
B4b
The school can cite specific examples indicating that the diversity of the school community is used to enrich the curriculum, enhance student learning and contribute to the development of global citizens.

STANDARD B5
The school shall provide ongoing professional development that improves the design, implementation, and assessment of the curriculum, reflects the needs of the faculty, and benefits student learning.
B5a
INDICATORS RELATED TO STANDARD B5
The school provides relevant professional development to assist teachers in designing curriculum and developing assessments that provide evidence of student learning.
B5b
The school provides professional development in content areas relevant to teachers' assignments.
B5c
The school provides professional development to assist teachers in improving pedagogy, for example through reference to best practices and the use of technology, in order to enhance teaching / learning and strengthen student engagement.
B5d
The faculty has an avenue for input into the planning of professional development activities.
B5e
Planning for professional development includes attention to needs that are identified through analysis of student achievement, review of school goals, and the faculty appraisal process.

STANDARD B6
Teaching practices shall reflect an understanding of the different ways in which students learn, and this is evidenced by student engagement and performance.

B6a
INDICATORS RELATED TO STANDARD B6
Teaching methods and student learning activities are varied according to the nature of the subject matter.
B6b
Teachers create stimulating learning environments that are evidenced by students who are engaged and active participants in their learning.
B6c
Teachers use varied methods, materials and technology to address individual student needs, abilities and learning styles.
B6d
Teaching methods provide appropriately for students for whom English (or other language of instruction) is not the first language.

STANDARD B7
The school shall provide appropriate support and resources to implement the curriculum and allow access and full participation by all students.
B7a
INDICATORS RELATED TO STANDARD B7
Class sizes are defined according to the subject and/or grade, student needs, and the number and qualifications of staff members present.
B7b
The school provides suitable texts, an age-appropriate library/media collection, and other print materials to support learning objectives.
B7c
Technology and media resources are up-to-date, accessible to all, and available in sufficient supply to support learning objectives.
B7d
Specialized equipment is available, up-to-date, and well maintained to support learning objectives in those areas that require it (e.g. science labs, AV/ICT, PE and Arts materials, etc.).
B7e
Assignment of teachers reflects expertise and qualifications in the appropriate subject/content area(s).
B7f
Support staff members are assigned to assist teachers in those areas where it is appropriate.
B7g
Library/media personnel are available and suitably qualified to collaborate with faculty, engage in curriculum development, and support students in acquiring and applying research skills to achieve curriculum goals.
B7h
IT personnel are available and suitably qualified to collaborate with faculty, engage in curriculum development, and support students and faculty in acquiring and applying IT skills.

STANDARD B8
The school shall have formal procedures and defined criteria to effectively and regularly assess the impact of teaching strategies and the level of student performance.
B8a
INDICATORS RELATED TO STANDARD B8
Teachers develop and implement assessments that can be used to ascertain student achievement of the desired outcomes.
B8b
Expected learner outcomes and grading standards and criteria are clearly stated and available in advance to students and parents.
B8c
Students demonstrate their learning through a variety of assessment models such as formal testing, self assessment, peer review, projects, etc.
B8d
The school has processes for comparing and analyzing its students' achievements with those of similar students elsewhere.
B8e
Teachers can cite examples of the use of the results of student assessment in a formative way to effectively modify teaching and to improve learning.

STANDARD B9
Curriculum review and revisions shall be completed at periodic intervals, and changes shall reflect the school's mission, current educational practice, and the results of student assessment, with the goal of enhancing student participation and performance.
B9a
INDICATORS RELATED TO STANDARD B9
Teachers, school administrators and relevant members of the support staff collaborate to develop,

review and revise the curriculum on a regular basis.
B9b
The school encourages pilot curriculum innovations and exploration of new teaching strategies, monitored by appropriate assessment techniques.
B9c
There is evidence that current educational practice is considered in revising curriculum and instruction.
B9d
Curriculum revisions reflect the school's mission and objectives, and are informed by the results of student achievement.
B9e
Curriculum revisions and changes are made in the context of an overarching curriculum plan.

STANDARD B10
The school shall have formal processes for recording, analyzing, and reporting evidence of both school-wide achievement and individual student performance to parents and other appropriate members of the school community as a means of measuring success in meeting stated goals.
B10a
INDICATORS RELATED TO STANDARD B10
The school has thorough and effective systems for tracking, analyzing and reporting on school-wide and individual student performance, and for measuring success in meeting stated goals.
B10b
The school provides timely, meaningful and clearly understood information that helps parents remain advised of their child's achievements and enables them to support on-going progress.
B10c
The overall results of external tests/examination, if used, are shared with appropriate members of the school community and are analyzed to support on-going student achievement.
B10d
Data gathered from graduates or past students is considered when determining the effectiveness of the school's programme.

SECTION C: GOVERNANCE AND LEADERSHIP

Note: The term "governing body" includes any school ownership structure.

STANDARD C1
The governing body shall be so constituted, with regard to membership and organization, as to provide the school with sound direction, continuity of leadership, and effective support in the current and long term life of the school.
C1a
INDICATORS RELATED TO STANDARD C1
The governing body shapes and upholds the mission, articulates a compelling vision, and ensures that its decisions support and further the mission.
C1b
The governing body promotes strong ethical values and compliance through appropriate and effective oversight.
C1c
The governing body effectively measures the school's success in putting its mission and objectives into practice, and it promotes corrective action if results show this is needed.
C1d
The governing body invigorates itself through planned membership, thoughtful recruitment, and inclusiveness.
C1e
The governing body provides appropriate orientation and on-going training for its members in the understanding and performance of their duties and in understanding policies and their implications.
C1f
The governing body is so constituted that it can fulfill essential governance duties and provide continuity for the school in the event of sudden change in ownership, governance, and/or administration.

STANDARD C2
There shall be a co-operative and effective working relationship between the governing body and the head of school so as to establish and sustain high morale, quality relationships, and a positive climate for teaching, learning, and student well-being throughout the school.
C2a
INDICATORS RELATED TO STANDARD C2
There is a clear and effective understanding by the governing body and the head of school of their respective functions, and these understandings are set out in written form.

C2b
There is a partnership between the governing body and head of school which recognises that the effectiveness of the parties is interdependent.
C2c
The governing body and the head of school enjoy a positive, open, and mutually supportive relationship.

STANDARD C3
The head of school, while accountable to a higher authority, shall be the responsible leader to ensure that teaching, learning, and student well-being are supported and that the school's mission is achieved.
C3a
INDICATORS RELATED TO STANDARD C3
The governing body has developed a clear, written job description for the head of school.
C3b
The head of school provides leadership for the total school programme.
C3c
The head of school sets educational priorities and outlines funding implications for submission to the governing body.
C3d
The head of school has final responsibility for the recruitment, selection, assignment, orientation, deployment and appraisal of all the administrators, teachers and support staff.
C3e
The governing body ensures that all issues pertaining to the day-to-day operations of the school are addressed through the head of school.
C3f
The head of school effectively delegates responsibility through a leadership structure that is designed to fulfill the school's mission and objectives.

STANDARD C4
The governing body shall have clearly formulated written policies and practices which are applied to bring consistency and clarity to school operations.
C4a
INDICATORS RELATED TO STANDARD C4
The governing body has a comprehensive, up-to-date, and effective policy manual for both school and governance operations.
C4b
The governing body allots sufficient time to the most important concerns and issues, and continuously engages in strategic thinking about the school's direction.
C4c
In decision-making, governing body members always put the interests of the whole school above all else, avoiding favouritism towards any individual or group.
C4d
An ethos of transparency is promoted by the governing body to ensure that appropriate members of the school's constituency have access to accurate information about decisions and matters which impact them.
C4e
Governing body policies and practices include a regular and systematic appraisal of its governance organization and effectiveness.
C4f
Governing body policies and practices include a clearly defined appraisal process for the head of school, to be conducted regularly with his/her full knowledge and to include written outcomes and provisions for discussion and appeal.

STANDARD C5
The school shall have educational and financial plans for the near and long term that ensure school viability, are supportive of the mission and are explained to the school community.
C5a
INDICATORS RELATED TO STANDARD C5
There is evidence that the short and longer-term finances of the school are sufficient to ensure it can fulfill its educational and other obligations for the foreseeable future.
C5b
The school has educational and financial plans for the short, medium and long term which are tied to the school's mission.
C5c
Financial considerations and required expertise are incorporated into the governing body's vision and plans for the school.
C5d
The school's educational and financial plans are appropriately communicated to the school community.

SECTION D: FACULTY AND SUPPORT STAFF

STANDARD D1
The school shall have faculty and support staff that are sufficient in numbers and with the qualifications, competencies and sound moral character necessary to carry out the school's programmes, services, and activities, to support fulfillment of the mission and objectives, and to ensure student protection and well-being.
D1a
INDICATORS RELATED TO STANDARD D1
Recruitment and screening processes are in place to ensure that employees in all categories are appropriately qualified and of sound moral character.
D1b
The teacher-student ratio reflects the size of classrooms, instructional practices, programme requirements and the school's mission in order to foster personalized and meaningful learning experiences for students.
D1c
The head of school or his/her designees recruit and assign professional staff to teaching duties and other responsibilities according to their professional competence.
D1d
The head of school or his/her designees assign work loads that allow faculty and staff to be maximally effective in carrying out their teaching duties and/or other responsibilities.
D1e
There are procedures in place for reviewing regularly the alignment between personnel competencies and programme needs to ensure that the school can implement programmes and services in support of fulfilling the mission and objectives.

STANDARD D2
Faculty and support staff shall embrace the school's Guiding Statements and act professionally and ethically in carrying out their duties and responsibilities, inspiring excellence and students' best efforts.
D2a
INDICATORS RELATED TO STANDARD D2
Teachers utilize methods and practices which are consistent with the school's Guiding Statements and which inspire, encourage and challenge students to reach their full potential.
D2b
Faculty and staff members respect and comply with all applicable statutes, government laws and regulations and with school expectations for appropriate employee behaviour.
D2c
Teachers remain current with content and pedagogy in their areas of academic responsibility, and they maintain a high level of preparation to foster students' engagement in their learning.
D2d
Members of the faculty foster respectful interactions among and with students and with their peers, both in classrooms and about the school.

STANDARD D3
All personnel shall be employed under a written contract or employment agreement which states the principal terms of agreement between the employee and the school, and which provides for salaries and other benefits that are appropriate to the position and to the school's location.
D3a
INDICATORS RELATED TO STANDARD D3
The school provides each employee with a written contract or employment agreement in which are stated the basic facts such as salary, benefits, assignments, length of term of initial service, date during which re- employment will be decided, and conditions of termination or resignation.
D3b
The school makes clear the factors which are taken into account in determining each employee's remuneration.
D3c
Compensation is paid to employees promptly and in accordance with a predetermined schedule made known in advance of employment.
D3d
There are appropriate guarantees for the employee of job security for the term of employment, including procedures for appeals.
D3e
Compensation packages are at a level that enables the school to recruit and retain qualified and appropriately experienced staff.

STANDARD D4
Written personnel policies and guidelines shall establish expectations for the performance of faculty and support staff which shall be consistently and effectively applied.

D4a
School policies include:

INDICATORS RELATED TO STANDARD D4
i.   a statement on non-discrimination ;
ii.   recruitment and hiring guidelines that include provisions such as background checks which
      ensure the protection of students;
iii. procedures on recruitment, appointment, compensation and benefits, promotion and
      retirement;
iv.   clearly stated expectations for faculty and staff behaviour;
v.   a commitment to ethical treatment and respectful interactions between faculty, support staff
      and their supervisors.
D4b
Personnel policies and practices are described in a handbook or manual that is up-to-date and
given to all employees prior to signing a contract or employment agreement.
D4c
Policies and practices foster efficient and effective performance and enhanced morale
among all employees.

STANDARD D5
There shall be a clearly defined and implemented appraisal system for faculty and support staff
based on pre-determined, explicit criteria and supported by a programme of professional develop-
ment and/or training which is linked to appraisal outcomes and other school priorities for student
learning.
D5a
INDICATORS RELATED TO STANDARD D5
The school utilizes an effective performance appraisal system for all categories of faculty and
support staff.
D5b
Faculty and support staff appraisal reflects clearly stated criteria, is conducted with the full knowl-
edge of the staff member, and is reported in writing in a document accessible only to defined
individuals.
D5c
Employees have the opportunity to discuss and appeal against any aspect of the appraisal.
D5d
Appraisal processes involve the individuals in goal setting and provide opportunity for reflection
and self- assessment.
D5e
The school provides a programme of professional development and/or training that links to needs
or agreed upon goals identified in the appraisal process and reflects other priorities identified by
the school.

SECTION E: ACCESS TO TEACHING AND LEARNING

STANDARD E1
There shall be effective procedures for identifying the learning needs of students, both at ad-
mission and while enrolled, to ensure that students in the school can benefit from the school's
programmes.
E1a
INDICATORS RELATED TO STANDARD E1
As part of the admissions process, the school secures relevant diagnostic information about an
individual student's abilities/learning differences/talents and learning styles to assist in determining
whether the student's educational needs can be met by the school and its programmes.
E1b
The learning needs of students enrolled in the school are adequately supported by clearly defined
and effective referral systems and screening programmes.
E1c
On-going assessment procedures monitor the extent to which any given student is benefiting
from school programmes, and effective procedures are used to inform school and parent decisions
about continued
enrolment.

STANDARD E2
Children with learning differences or specific needs who are admitted into the school shall be
given support to access and enhance participation in the learning environment through
appropriate and effective programmes that are delivered by suitably qualified personnel.
E2a
INDICATORS RELATED TO STANDARD E2
The number, qualifications and levels of experience of learning support personnel are appropriate
to the number and the needs of identified students.

E2b
The school uses student data as part of the regular evaluation of the effectiveness of the learning support programme.
E2c
Personnel providing services to learning support students are clearly identified, and their roles are defined and understood by the school community.
E2d
The school makes effective use of community resources to enhance access to the curriculum for students with special learning needs.
E2e
Learning support services function as an integrated part of the school's programme with learning support staff members working in collaboration with classroom teachers, students and parents to optimize student learning.

STANDARD E3
Effective language support programmes shall assist learners to access the school's formal curriculum and other activities.
E3a
INDICATORS RELATED TO STANDARD E3
Students who need specialized language support to access the curriculum are provided with appropriate, clearly defined programmes delivered by qualified teachers.
E3b
All staff members have received appropriate training and use pedagogical approaches which support the needs of language learners.
E3c
The school provides sufficient personnel and other resources to support student language needs.
E3d
The school encourages parents to continue development of the student's home language(s).

STANDARD E4
The school shall ensure that students have access to advice and counsel on academic, personal, career and tertiary education matters to effectively support their current and future development and achievement.
E4a
INDICATORS RELATED TO STANDARD E4
Personnel providing academic, personal, career and tertiary education advice and counsel are sufficient in number and have the appropriate experience, qualifications, character and skills to provide quality services to the school community.
E4b
Counselling and advisory programmes are supported by clearly documented policies and procedures to ensure that community members understand the scope of programmes as well as the manner in which to access services.
E4c
The school provides orientation for students new to the school and/or to international education as well as transition support for those students exiting the school for home or other school systems.
E4d
Counselling and advisory programme records are available to those who need to use them, are adequately maintained, and are stored and backed up in a secure manner for an appropriate length of time.
E4e
The school regularly evaluates the effectiveness of its counselling/advisory programmes, taking into consideration student profile and achievement data.

STANDARD E5
The school shall provide appropriate health care and promote the practices of healthy living to serve student well-being and enhance access to learning opportunities.
E5a
INDICATORS RELATED TO STANDARD E5
The school provides adequate health care services to support students on the school premises and at school sponsored activities off-site.
E5b
The school's programmes, services and environment encourage the adoption of healthy life style choices.
E5c
The school facilitates for its community an awareness and understanding of local health services, local health requirements and potential health concerns.
E5d
The school assists its community in understanding and responding to potential health hazards in the local and wider community.

SECTION F SCHOOL CULTURE AND PARTNERSHIPS FOR LEARNING

STANDARD F1
A school climate characterized by fairness, trust, and mutual respect shall support student learning and well-being.
F1a
INDICATORS RELATED TO STANDARD F1
A culture of shared responsibility for the social and emotional well-being and protection of students is promoted by the school leadership and teachers through programmes to address awareness, prevention and responsiveness to issues such as child abuse, sexual harassment, substance abuse, hazing and bullying, and discrimination in any form.
F1b
The school has policies, procedures, and practices that promote and address the physical, emotional, and social well-being of students and staff.
F1c
School community members demonstrate an understanding of and appreciation for diversity, thereby supporting a climate of mutual respect.
F1d
Fairness in dealing with student concerns is enhanced by clearly written statements of expected behaviour, the consequences of non-compliance, and a mechanism for appeal.
F1e
The school celebrates students' efforts and achievements in meaningful and culturally sensitive ways.
F1f
Student, staff and parent information is treated with an appropriate degree of confidentiality.

STANDARD F2
Effective communication processes shall foster a productive home-school partnership and a positive learning community.
F2a
INDICATORS RELATED TO STANDARD F2
Effective, formal processes are in place to facilitate a flow of information and a meaningful interchange of opinions among all sectors of the school community.
F2b
A "whole-school" climate and a positive learning community are fostered by effective horizontal and vertical communication among the various sections of the school.
F2c
The school engages students and parents in creating a collaborative culture based on a shared vision, shared responsibility and a sense of belonging.
F2d
Opportunities are provided for parents to learn about the school's educational aims, programmes, and pedagogical approaches so that they can support student learning.
F2e
The school creates student learning opportunities by effectively using the skills of its own community members and by building partnerships with external agencies such as local businesses and professional organizations.

STANDARD F3
The school shall offer effective programmes and activities which complement the formal curriculum in supporting the school's Guiding Statements.
F3a
INDICATORS RELATED TO STANDARD F3
The development and delivery of the school's complementary programmes demonstrate sensitivity to the needs and beliefs of different cultures, foster engagement with the local culture and promote global citizenship.
F3b
The school actively supports the development of student leadership and encourages students to undertake service learning.
F3c
The school actively promotes and models global environmental awareness and responsibility across its community.
F3d
The school regularly evaluates its complementary programmes to ensure they remain aligned with its Guiding Statements, meet student needs and interests, and foster global citizenship.
STANDARD F4 (FOR BOARDING SCHOOLS)
Boarding services effectively support the school's Guiding Statements, and serve the well-being of all boarding students and staff.
F4a
INDICATORS RELATED TO STANDARD F4
A clear boarding educational philosophy is in place which creates a twenty- four hour, seven day a

week learning environment.
F4b
Sound, clear and effectively implemented operating procedures and systems are in place which support boarding life and provide guidelines for addressing fire, accidents, natural disasters, civil unrest, medical and any other emergencies.
F4c
The boarding programme is supported by written policies and effective record keeping which enhance the well-being of students.
F4d
Boarding staff have appropriate training and orientation for the role they play and have been effectively screened prior to appointment to ensure that they have the necessary skills and sound character to provide a supportive, safe, caring and nurturing environment.
F4e
Boarding staff members are adequately deployed to provide boarding students with a safe environment and open, positive and nurturing teacher/student relationships.
F4f
The boarding facilities effectively reflect the school's Guiding Statements and support the well-being of students and staff in the following areas:
i.   The number and needs of the boarding students. ii. The number and needs of the boarding staff.
iii.   The range of formal and informal activities.
iv.   The delivery of important services (laundry, meals, medical support, transport, technology etc)
v.   The integration of day and boarding students
F4g
The boarding facilities meet local authority safety standards and any reasonable stipulations which may be required by the accrediting agency/agencies.
F4h
The culture within the boarding programme demonstrates sensitivity to and respect for the diversity of the student body as well as a sense of home and family.
F4i
Effective channels of communication are in place between the school, boarding staff and the home to ensure that parents, teachers and residential staff work in partnership to support boarding students.
F4j
Schools with students that are privately boarded, and/or for whom the school has legal responsibility, support their well-being through clear written expectations for the students and their guardians and by active monitoring.

SECTION G OPERATIONAL SYSTEMS

Note: The term "governing body" includes any school ownership structure.

STANDARD G1
The management of school finances shall be consistent with best financial practices in international schools, in accordance with the legal requirements of the host country, and shall support the effective delivery of the school's programmes.
G1a
INDICATORS RELATED TO STANDARD G1
The head of school and the governing body regularly receive understandable financial reports which facilitate careful and regular reviews of the school's short and longer term financial health and which ensure appropriate allocation of funding.
G1b
After appropriate input and debate, the governing body establishes annual school budgets - including appropriate fee levels – which ensure funding for programmes necessary to put the school's Guiding Statements into practice in an effective way.
G1c
Parents enrolling students are informed in advance of the precise nature and scope of their financial obligations, and changes in fees are communicated to parents early enough to allow them to make arrangements to move their children to other schools if necessary.
G1d
The school regularly considers - and where feasible applies in an effective manner - culturally appropriate and effective means of raising additional funds to support delivery of its programmes.
G1e
Accounting processes are orderly, understood by all parties involved, and carried out in accordance with sound and ethical business practices.
G1f
The insurance programme is comprehensive, and provides for effective risk and liability coverage for the school and for students, employees, visitors and members of the governing body.

G1g
Total servicing of long-term debt, including both interest and principal payments, is fairly apportioned to both present and future fee payers.
G1h
An annual, external audit of the school's finances is performed by an independent accounting firm, results are discussed at appropriate levels within the school, and any necessary action is taken.

STANDARD G2
Grounds, buildings, technical installations, basic furnishings, and equipment shall effectively support delivery of the programmes required to put the school's Guiding Statements into practice.
G2a
INDICATORS RELATED TO STANDARD G2
The school's facilities/equipment provide for effective delivery of educational programmes and a positive context for learning while promoting student, staff and visitor well-being. This includes satisfactory provision of indoor and outdoor spaces, air quality, heating and cooling, shade, shelter, lighting and acoustical comfort.
G2b
Teaching, storage and work spaces are suitable in size and layout for the age, number and needs of students and for the effective delivery of programmes.
G2c
Governing body policies and school practices effectively address the adequacy, maintenance and improvement of school facilities/equipment.
G2d
If the school admits handicapped students or personnel, all reasonable provision is made for them.
G2e
Information and Communication Technology provisions (hardware, software, networks, training and maintenance) effectively support the management and operational functions of the school.

STANDARD G3
The school shall ensure that its grounds, buildings, technical installations, basic furnishings, equipment and systems provide for the health and safety of students, personnel and visitors.
G3a
INDICATORS RELATED TO STANDARD G3
School facilities meet the health and safety codes of local authorities and any reasonable stipulations which may be required by the accrediting agency/agencies.
G3b
Certificates of inspection and regulations required by law are available on file and/or posted in prominent places as appropriate.
G3c
An internal health and safety committee (or its equivalent) actively monitors conditions at the school and is effective in ensuring any deficiencies or anomalies are rapidly resolved.
G3d
Maintenance services are effective in ensuring that school premises and equipment remain in a safe and healthy condition.
G3e
Effective measures, including regular rehearsals, are in place to address fire or other emergency situations requiring evacuation.
G3f
Effective measures, including regular rehearsals, are in place to address emergencies requiring "safe haven/lock down".
G3g
The school takes all reasonable steps to operate its facilities and related services using environmentally responsible practices, hence acting as a positive model for students and the wider community.

STANDARD G4
The school shall provide or arrange for auxiliary services as required to support its declared objectives and programmes, and shall ensure that such services meet acceptable standards of safety, efficiency and comfort.
G4a
INDICATORS RELATED TO STANDARD G4
Facilities for preparing, serving and consuming food and beverages meet appropriate standards of safety, comfort, hygiene and good dietary practice.
G4b
Appropriate and regularly reviewed arrangements exist to cover threats to the security of people and premises as well as to support – to the extent possible – programme continuity under exceptional circumstances.

G4c
Vehicles used in student transportation are mechanically sound, clean, well-maintained, properly licensed and appropriately insured.

G4d
School premises are kept in an acceptably clean state at all times of the school day.

G4e
School trips are well planned and executed, ensuring a positive learning environment and supporting the school's academic or activities programme. Appropriate consideration is shown for the comfort, welfare, security and safety of students and accompanying adults.

G4f
Support staff members and employees provided by contracted suppliers who are involved in the delivery of any auxiliary service are employed in suitable numbers.

G4g
Support staff members and employees provided by contracted suppliers are properly qualified and experienced, in appropriate health, well trained, and adequately assigned and supervised.

G4h
Support staff members and employees provided by contracted suppliers make a positive and well appreciated contribution to school life.

APPENDIX C: PROPOSED ADDITIONS TO CIS ACCREDITATION STANDARDS

Proposed Section H:

Mobility Across Cultures (for schools with a transient population)

Standard H1:
The school recognizes the reality of the challenges associated with mobility across cultures.
Indicators Related to Standard H1
H1a
There is evidence that the school understands that issues related to mobility across cultures must be systemically addressed in order for the school's Guiding Statements to be achieved.
H1b
The school understands that appropriately addressing the challenges of mobility across cultures is a prerequisite for optimal student performance. Practices both inside and outside the classroom reflect a widespread appreciation of this reality.
H1c
The school recognizes that international mobility is the driving force behind two fundamental challenges faced by all members of the school community, namely a) the challenge of managing geographic transitions and b) the challenge of developing intercultural competence.
H1d
The school proactively and systemically addresses both of the challenges described in H1c.

Standard H2:
The school recognizes that the challenges associated with mobility across cultures affect all members of the international school community.
H2a
The school's Guiding Statements clearly demonstrate a commitment to assisting students, staff, and parents with the challenges associated with mobility across cultures, and this shall be reflected throughout the life of the institution.
H2b
There is evidence that the school understands that the challenges of any one population can only be optimally addressed by addressing the needs of all populations proportionally.
H2c
The school understands that stayers are also affected by issues of mobility across cultures, and that they require assistance developing a specific set of skills to deal with these challenges over time.

Standard H3
The school recognizes that the challenges associated with mobility across cultures affect members of the community throughout the calendar year.
H3a
The school's programs for addressing the challenges of mobility across cultures positively impact upon all students, parents, staff, and administrators throughout the year, at appropriate junctures throughout the annual mobility cycle.
H3b
The school provides avenues for all students to actively engage with transitions-related themes throughout the school year, thereby affording them opportunities to develop the skills needed to establish and loosen affectional bonds and to process relevant feelings at appropriate times.
H3c
The school demonstrates a clear commitment to equipping all students with the skills needed to develop intercultural competence, affording them opportunities to learn about their host country culture, to examine their own (often multicultural) cultural identities, and to both develop and apply an intentional intercultural communication practice.
H3d
The school supports appropriate avenues for teachers and other school personnel to explore, understand, and further develop their own approach to managing a lifestyle involving high turnover and high intercultural interactions, as each staff member's own approach to dealing with these two challenges influences how he or she assists students and parents with their own approach to similar challenges.
H3e
There is evidence that the school takes seriously the task of providing parents with support across the school year to manage a lifestyle involving high turnover and high intercultural interactions. This support impacts upon not only families who are arriving or leaving, but also those who are staying; and upon not only families of less-represented national backgrounds, but also those of dominant representation.

Standard H4:
A coherent and articulated curriculum exists that address the challenges of mobility across cultures for all populations throughout the school calendar.
H4a
There is evidence that appropriate school personnel are familiar with the Global Perspective Domain of the International Model for School Counseling Programs as an important means for guiding the school in helping students manage geographic transitions and develop intercultural competence.
H4b
The curriculum design, teaching strategies, and support resources provided ensure that students' feelings and perspectives related to mobility across cultures are sufficiently addressed across the year so they can all profit from the school's curriculum and offerings.
H4c
The school shall provide periodic professional development that assists staff in understanding issues associated with mobility as well as further developing their own intercultural competence.
H4d
There is evidence that staff recognize and embrace that they must be comfortable with issues associated with mobility and intercultural competence in order to be able to help students develop in these areas.
H4e
Teaching practices shall reflect an understanding of the ways in which mobility and culture can impact the way students learn and develop.
H4f
Students shall have access to a curriculum that helps them develop the skills to cope with the challenge of repeatedly making and breaking affectional bonds and of repeatedly encountering culture shock and cultural uncertainty, challenges inherent in the life of any school with a highly transient population.
H4g
The school supports the parent community in developing and implementing curricula addressing mobility across cultures, in ways that support the parent community and that are appropriate to the culture of the school.

Standard H5:
The school shall have formal procedures and defined criteria to effectively and regularly assess the impact of the services it has in place to address the challenge of mobility across cultures.
H5a
The school shall have formal processes for recording, analyzing, and reporting on the degree of success in addressing emotional challenges related to transitions, both at the school-wide level, at the individual student level, at the staff level, at the administrator level, and at the parent level.
H5b
The school shall have formal processes for recording, analyzing, and reporting on the degree of success in developing intercultural competence, at the school-wide level and at the individual student level, at the staff level, at the administrator level, and at the parent level.
H5c
Data gathered from departed students or graduates is central to determining the effectiveness of the school's programs for addressing the emotional challenges related to transitions and the effectiveness of intercultural competency development.

NOTES

1. Baumeister, R., et al., 2011.
2. Pollock, D. & Van Reken, R., 1999.
3. International Baccalaureate Organization, 2008.
4. Myers, S.L., 2013.
5. Walker, G., 2002.
6. Tiger, L., 1979.
7. Harlow, H., et al., 1965.
8. Harlow, H., et al., 1959.
9. Bowlby, J., 1979.
10. Bowlby, J., 1998a.
11. Bowlby, J., 1998b.
12. Bowlby, J., 1998c.
13. Ainsworth, M., et al., 1978.
14. Cassidy & Shaver, 1999.
15. Winnicott, D.W., 1953.
16. Johnson, S., 2008.
17. House, J.S., et al., 1988.
18. Friedman, H.S., et al., 2011.
19. Mikulincer, M., et al., 2007.
20. Friedman, R., et al., 2001.
21. Eisenberger, N.I., et al., 2006.
22. Gailliot, M.T., et al., 2007.
23. Beckes, L., et al., 2011.
24. Ota, D., 2000.
25. Gross, E.B., et al., 2013.
26. Schnall, S., et al., 2008.
27. Johnson, S.M., et al., 2013.
28. Coan, J.A., et al., 2006.
29. Conner, O.L., et al., 2012.
30. Winnicott, D., 1954.
31. Ernst Bohlmeijer, E., et al., 2007.
32. Heider, F., et al., 1944.
33. Kahneman, D., 2011.
34. Topolinski, S., 2009.

35. McAdams, D., 2008.
36. White, M., et al., 1990.
37. Warner, J., 2005.
38. Hofstede, G., 2001.
39. Hofstede, G., 2014.
40. Bennett, M.J., 1998.
41. Schwartz, B., 2004.
42. Seligman, M.E.P., 2002.
43. Schore, A.N., 2000.
44. Schore, A.N., 2009.
45. Blatt, S.J., 2008.
46. Pollock, D., 1999.
47. International Baccalaureate Organization, 2008.
48. Eliade, M., 1959.
49. Fredrickson, B.L., et al., 2005.
50. Eurelings-Bontekoe, E.H.M., et al., 1994.
51. Eurelings-Bontekoe, E.H.M., et al., 1995a.
52. Eurelings-Bontekoe, E.H.M., et al., 1995b.
53. Eurelings-Bontekoe, E.H.M., et al., 1996.
54. van Tilburg, M.A., et al., 1999.
55. Verschuur, M.J., et al., 2004.
56. Hardin, G., 1968.
57. Hargreaves, A., et al., 2009.
58. Gardner, H., 2011.
59. Walker, A., et al., 2002.
60. Cain, S., 2012.

BIBLIOGRAPHY

Allan, M. (2002). Cultural Borderlands: A Case Study of Cultural Dissonance in an International School. *Journal of Research in International Education,* 1(1), 63-90. doi: 10.1177/1475240902001001269

Anderzén, I., Arnetz, B. B., Söderström, T., & Söderman, E. (1997). Stress and sensitization in children: A controlled prospective psychophysiological study of children exposed to international relocation. *Journal of Psychosomatic Research,* 43(3), 259-269.

Bauer, J. J., McAdams, D. P., & Sakaeda, A. R. (2005). Interpreting the Good Life: Growth Memories in the Lives of Mature, Happy People. *Journal of Personality and Social Psychology,* 88(1), 203-217.

Baumeister, R., & Tierney, J. (2011). *Willpower: Rediscovering the Greatest Human Strength.* London: Penguin.

Beckes, L., & Coan, J. (2011). Social Baseline Theory: The Role of Social Proximity in Emotion and Economy of Action. *Social and Personality Psychology Compass,* 5/12, 976–988.

Belsey, T. (2001). Foucauldian Influences in Narrative Therapy: an Approach for Schools. *Journal of Educational Enquiry,* 2(2), 72-93.

Bennett, J. (1987). Towards ethnorelativism: A developmental model of intercultural sensitivity. In R. Paige (Ed.), *Cross cultural orientation: new conceptualizations and applications.* London: University Press of America.

Bennett, J. A. (1993). Cultural Marginality: Identity Issues in Intercultural Training. In M. Paige (Ed.), *Education for the intercultural experience.* Yarmouth, ME: Intercultural Press.

Bennett, J. M. (1986). Modes of Cross-Cultural Training – Conceptualizing Cross-Cultural Training as Education. *International Journal of Intercultural Relations,* 10(2), 117 - 134.

Bennett, M. J. (1998). Basic Concepts of *Intercultural Communication.* Yarmouth, Maine: Intercultural Press.

Berntsen, D., & Rubin, D. C. (2002). Emotionally charged autobiographical memories across the life span: The recall of happy, sad, traumatic and involuntary memories. *Psychology and Aging,* 17(4), 636-652.

Blatt, S. J. (2008). *Polarities of experience relatedness and self-definition in personality development, psychopathology, and the therapeutic process.* Washington, DC: American Psychological Association.

Block, J. (1982). Assimilation, Accommodation, and the Dynamics of Personality Development. *Child Development,* 53(2), 281-295.

Bowlby, J. (1979). *The making and breaking of affectional bonds.* London: Brunner-Routledge.

Bowlby, J. (1998a). *Attachment and Loss, Volume 1: Attachment.* New York: Pimico.

Bowlby, J. (1998b). *Attachment and Loss: Volume 2, Separation.* New York: Pimico.

Bowlby, J. (1998c). *Attachment and Loss: Volume 3, Loss.* New York: Pimico.

Brinegar, M. G., Salvi, L. M., Stiles, W. B., & Greenberg, L. S. (2006). Building a Meaning Bridge: Therapeutic Progress From Problem Formulation to Understanding. *Journal of Counseling Psychology,* 53(2), 165-180.

Bruner, J. (1990). *Acts of Meaning.* Cambridge, MA: Harvard.

Burrows, K. (2002). *'Sink or Swim', An investigation into the effects of induction procedures on teachers working overseas, with particular reference to the British Schools of America.* (MA), Oxford Brookes University, Oxford.

Cain, S. (2012). *The Power of Introverts.* Retrieved from http://www.ted.com/talks/susan_cain_the_power_of_introverts.

Carter, E. A. (1981). The stress of relocation on the student and his family. *International Schools Journal* (2), 31-37.

Cassidy, J., & Shaver, P. (Eds.). (1999). *Handbook of Attachment: Theory, Research, and Clinical Applications.* New York: Guilford.

Coan, J. A., Schaefer, H. S., & Davidson, R. J. (2006). Lending a hand: social regulation of the neural response to threat. *Psychol Sci,* 17(12), 1032-1039. doi: 10.1111/j.1467-9280.2006.01832.x

Conner, O. L., Siegle, G. J., McFarland, A. M., Silk, J. S., Ladouceur, C. D., Dahl, R. E., Ryan, N. D. (2012). Mom-it helps when you're right here! Attenuation of neural stress markers in anxious youths whose caregivers are present during fMRI. *PLoS One,* 7(12), e50680. doi: 10.1371/journal.pone.0050680

Coyne, J. C., & Racioppo, M. W. (2000). Never the twain shall meet? Closing the gap between coping research and clinical intervention research. *American Psychologist,* 55(6), 655-664.

Crean, H. F. (2004). Social support, conflict, major life stressors, and adaptive coping strategies in Latino middle school students: An integrative model. *Journal of Adolescent Research, 19*(6), 657-676.

Cross, W. (1995). The psychology of Nigrescence: revising the Cross Model. In J. Ponterotto, J. Casa, L. Suzuki & C. Alexander (Eds.), *Handbook of multicultural counseling.* Newbury Park: Sage.

Davis, R. P. (2001). *Wherever I lay my hat that's my home: an investigation into international student mobility and school based programmes designed to support international student transition.* (MA), University of Bath, Bath.

Delin, A. (1987). *Identity characteristics of seventh through twelfth grade third culture dependents at Cairo American College, Egypt.* (PhD), Michigan State University.

Deveney, B. (2007). How well-prepared do international school teachers believe themselves to be for teaching in culturally diverse classrooms? *Journal of Research in International Education, 6*(3), 309-332.

DeWit, D. J. (1998). Frequent childhood geographic relocation: Its impact on drug use initiation and the development of alcohol and other drug-related problems among adolescents and young adults. *Addictive Behaviors, 23*(5), 623-634.

Diamond, D. (2004). Attachment Disorganization: The Reunion of Attachment Theory and Psychoanalysis. *Psychoanalytic Psychology, 21*(2), 276-299.

Dixon, P. G. S. (2004). *On the move: A study of the views of primary age students attending an international school, concerning the impact of transition.* (MA), University of Bath, Bath, UK.

Eisenberger, N. I., Jarcho, J. M., Lieberman, M. D., & Naliboff, B. D. (2006). An experimental study of shared sensitivity to physical pain and social rejection. *Pain, 126*(1-3), 132-138. doi: 10.1016/j.pain.2006.06.024

Eliade, M. (1959). *The sacred and the profane; the nature of religion* (1st American ed.). New York: Harcourt.

Eriksen, M. (1997). *International middle school students' viewpoints from abroad: exploring the outcomes of international education, with perspectives on cross-cultural exposure, experience, and identity, and assessing the need for guidance.* (MA), Oxford Brookes University, Oxford.

Erikson, E. (1980). *Identity and the Life Cycle*. London: Norton.

Ernst Bohlmeijer, E., Mies, L., & Westerhof, G. (2007). *De betekenis van levensverhalen: theoretische beschouwingen en toepassingen in onderzoek en praktijk*. Houten, Netherlands: Bohn Stafleu van Loghum.

Eurelings-Bontekoe, E. H., Diekstra, R. F., & Verschuur, M. (1995). Psychological distress, social support and social support seeking: a prospective study among primary mental health care patients. *Soc Sci Med*, 40(8), 1083-1089.

Eurelings-Bontekoe, E. H. M., Tolsma, E., Vingerhoets, A. J. J. M., & Verschuur, M. J. (1996). Construction of a homesickness questionnaire using a female population with two types of self reported homesickness; preliminary results. *Personality and Individual Differences*, 20, 415-421.

Eurelings-Bontekoe, E. H. M., Verschuur, M. J., Koudstaal, A., van der Sar, S., & Duijsens, I. J. (1995). Construction of a homesickness questionnaire: preliminary results. *Personality and Individual Differences*, 19, 319-325.

Eurelings-Bontekoe, E. H. M., Vingerhoets, A. J. J. M., & Fontijn, T. (1994). Personality and Behavioral Antecedents of Homesickness. *Personality and Individual Differences*, 16, 229-235.

Evans, L., & Oehler-Stinnett, J. (2006). Children and natural disasters – A primer for school psychologists. *School Psychology International*, 27(1), 33-55.

Ezra, R. (2003). Culture, Language and Personality in the Context of the Internationally Mobile Child. *Journal of Research in International Education*, 2, 123-149.

Fail, H. (2002). *An examination of the life histories of a group of former international school students*. Dissertation. University of Bath.

Fail, H., Thompson, J., & Walker, G. (2004). Belonging, identity and third culture kids: life histories of former international school students. *Journal of Research in International Education*, 3(3), 319-338. doi: 10.1177/1475240904047358

Festinger, L. (1957). *A theory of cognitive dissonance*. Stanford, CA: Stanford University Press.

Folkman, S., & Moskowitz, J. T. (2000). Positive affect and the other side of coping. *American Psychologist*, 55(6), 647-654.

Fredrickson, B. L., & Losada, M. F. (2005). Positive affect and the complex dynamics of human flourishing. *American Psychologist*, 60(7), 678-686. doi: 10.1037/0003-066X.60.7.678

Friedman, H. S., & Martin, L. R. (2011). *The longevity project: surprising discoveries for health and long life from the landmark eight-decade study.* New York: Hudson Street Press.

Friedman, R., & Forster, J. (2001). The effects of promotion and prevention cues on creativity. *Journal of Personality and Social Psychology,* 81, 1001-1013.

Gardner, H. (2011). *Frames of mind: the theory of multiple intelligences.* New York: Basic Books.

Geertz, C. (1995). *After the fact.* Cambridge, MA: Harvard.

Gellar, C. (1993). How international are we? *International Schools Journal,* 26, 5-7.

Gellar, C. (2002). International education: a commitment to universal values. In M. Hayden, J. Thompson & G. Walker (Eds.), *International education in practice: dimensions for national and international schools.* London: RoutledgeFalmer.

Gergen, K. J. (1973). Social psychology as history. *Journal of Personality and Social Psychology,* 26(2), 309-320.

Goenjian, A. K., Molina, L., Steinberg, A. M., Fairbanks, L. A., Alvarez, M. L., Goenjian, H. A., & Pynoos, R. S. (2001). Posttraumatic stress and depressive reactions among Nicaraguan adolescents after hurricane mitch. *American Journal of Psychiatry,* 158(5), 788-794.

Grabner, M. (1992). *A phenomenological analysis of children's descriptions of coping with relocation.* (Master of Psychology), Saybrook Institute for Humanistic Psychology, San Francisco, CA.

Gross, E. B., & Proffitt, D. (2013). The economy of social resources and its influence on spatial perceptions. *Front Hum Neurosci,* 7, 772. doi: 10.3389/fnhum.2013.00772

Gullahorn, J., & Gullahorn, J. (1963). An extension of the U-curve hypothesis. *Journal of Social Issues,* 19, 33-47.

Halstead, J., & Taylor, M. (Eds.). (1996). *Values in education and education in values.* London: Falmer Press.

Hardin, G. (1968). The tragedy of the commons. The population problem has no technical solution; it requires a fundamental extension in morality. *Science,* 162(3859), 1243-1248.

Hardman, J. (2001). Improving Recruitment and Retention of Quality Overseas Teachers. In S. Blandford & M. Shaw (Eds.), *Managing International Schools* (pp. 123-135). London: RoutledgeFalmer.

Hargreaves, A., & Shirley, D. (2009). *The fourth way: the inspiring future for educational change.* Thousand Oaks, Calif.: Corwin Press.

Harlow, H., Dodsworth, R., & Harlow, M. (1965). Total social isolation in monkeys. *PNAS,* 54(1), 90-97.

Harlow, H., & Zimmerman, R. (1959). Affectional response in the infant monkey. *Science,* 33(3373), 421-432.

Hayden, M., & Thompson, J. (1995). International schools and international education: a relationship reviewed. *Oxford Review of Education,* 21(3), 327-345.

Hayden, M., & Thompson, J. (Eds.). (1998). *International Education: Principles and Practice.* London: Kogan Page.

Hayden, M., Thompson, J., & Walker, G. (Eds.). (2002). *International education in practice: dimensions for national and international schools.* London: RoutledgeFalmer.

Haynie, D. L., & South, S. J. (2005). Residential mobility and adolescent violence. *Social Forces,* 84(1), 361-374.

Heider, F., & Simmel, M. (1944). An Experimental Study of Apparent Behavior. *The American Journal of Psychology,* 57(2), 243-259.

Heinlein, L. M., & Shinn, M. (2000). School mobility and student achievement in an urban setting. *Psychology in the Schools,* 37(4), 349-357.

Hesse, E. (1999). The Adult Attachment Interview: Historical and Current Perspectives. In J. Cassidy & P. Shaver (Eds.), *Handbook of Attachment: Theory, Research, and Clinical Applications.* New York: Guilford.

Heyward, M. (2002). From International to Intercultural. Redefining the International School for a Globalized World. *Journal of Research in International Education,* 1, 9-32.

Hill, S., & Hayden, M. (2008). Children on the move: using Pollock's transition model for better understanding of internationally mobile primary-aged pupils. *International Schools Journal,* 27(2), 37-43.

Hobfoll, S. E., Schwarzer, R., & Chon, K. K. (1988). Disentangling the stress labyrinth: Interpreting the meaning of the term stress as it is studied in health context. *Anxiety, Stress & Coping: An International Journal,* 11(3), 181-212.

Hofstede, G. (2001). *Culture's Consequences: Comparing Values, Behaviors, Institutions and Organizations Across Nations.* Thousand Oaks CA: Sage Publications.

Hofstede, G. (Producer). (2014, March 20, 2014). Culture GPS. [Mobile App] Retrieved from http://geert-hofstede.com/mobile-apps.html

Hoshmand, L. T. (2005). Narratology, Cultural Psychology, and Counseling Research. *Journal of Counseling Psychology, 52*(2), 178-186.

House, J. S., Landis, K. R., & Umberson, D. (1988). Social relationships and health. *Science, 241*(4865), 540-545.

Hughes, C. A. (2007). *Resiliency-Building Practices to Strengthen Culturally Diverse Families in School Settings. Pre-conference Session.* Paper presented at the 8th Families in Global Transitions International Conference, Houston.

Ibarra, H., & Lineback, K. (2005). *What's your story? Harvard Business Review*(January), 65-71.

International Baccalaureate Organization. (2008). Mission Statement. Retrieved October 1, 2008, from www.ibo.org

ISC-Research. (2006). Market Overview. Retrieved December 6, 2006, from ISC Research Limited http://www.iscresearch.com

Johnson, S. M., Burgess Moser, M., Beckes, L., Smith, A., Dalgleish, T., Halchuk, R., . . . Coan, J. A. (2013). Soothing the threatened brain: leveraging contact comfort with emotionally focused therapy. *PLoS One, 8*(11), e79314. doi: 10.1371/journal.pone.0079314

Johnson, S. (2008). *Hold Me Tight.* New York: Little, Brown and Company.

Joslin, P. (2002). Teacher Relocation. Reflections in the Context of International Schools. *Journal of Research in International Education, 1*(1), 33-62.

Josselson, R. (1996). Imagining the Real: Empathy, Narrative, and the Dialogic Self. In R. Josselson & A. Lieblich (Eds.), *Interpreting experience: The Narrative Study of Lives.* Thousand Oaks, Calif.; London: Sage.

Josselson, R., & Lieblich, A. (Eds.). (1996). *Interpreting experience: The Narrative Study of Lives.* Thousand Oaks, Calif.; London: Sage.

Kahneman, D. (2011). *Thinking, Fast and Slow.* London: Penguin.

Klass, D., Silverman, P. R., & Nickman, S. (Eds.). (1996). *Continuing bonds: new understandings of grief.* Washington, DC: Taylor & Francis.

Kogut, B., & Singh, H. (1988). The effect of national culture on the choice of entry mode. *Journal of International Business Studies, 19*(3), 411–432.

Langford, M. (1997). *Internationally mobile pupils in transition: The role of the international school*. (Master in Education), University of Bath, Bath, UK.

Langford, M. (1998). Global Nomads, Third Culture Kids, and International Schools. In M. Hayden & J. Thompson (Eds.), *International Education: Principles and Practice* (pp. 28-43). London: Kogan Page.

Langford, M., Pearce, R., Rader, D., & Sears, C. (2002). *The Essential Guide for Teachers in International Schools*. Great Glemham, Suffolk: John Catt.

Lazarus, R. S. (2000). Toward better research on stress and coping. *American Psychologist, 55*(6), 665-673.

Leach, R. (1969). *International schools and their role in the field of international education*. Oxford: Pergamon Press.

Lewis, J. (1993). *The Induction of Teachers Entering an International School for the First Time*. (MA), University of Bath, Bath, UK.

Lukey, R. (2000). *An Initial Study on Improving Pastoral Care in an International School*. (MA), Oxford Brookes University, Oxford.

Lysgaard, S. (1955). Adjustment in a foreign society: Norwegian Fulbright grantees visiting the United States. *International Social Science Bulletin, VII*(1), 45-51.

Lyubomirsky, S., Sousa, L., & Dickerhoof, R. (2006). The Costs and Benefits of Writing, Talking, and Thinking About Life's Triumphs and Defeats. *Journal of Personality and Social Psychology, 90*(4), 692-708.

Maslow, A. H. (1943). A Theory of Human Motivation. *Psychological Review, 50*, 370-396.

McAdams, D. (2008). Personal Narratives and the Life Story. In O. John, R. Robins & L. Pervin (Eds.), *Handbook of Personality, Third Edition: Theory and Research* (Vol. 242-262). New York: Guilford.

McAdams, D. P. (2001). The psychology of life stories. *Review of General Psychology, 5*(2), 100-122.

McAdams, D. P., de St. Aubin, E., & Logan, R. L. (1993). Generativity among young, midlife, and older adults. *Psychology and Aging, 8*(2), 221-230.

McAdams, D. P., & Pals, J. L. (2006). A New Big Five: Fundamental Principles for an Integrative Science of Personality. *American Psychologist, 61*(3), 204-217.

McCaig, N. (1996). Understanding Global Nomads. In C. Smith (Ed.), *Strangers at Home: Essays on the Effects of Living Overseas and Coming "Home" to a Strange Land*. Bayside, NY: Aletheia.

McClain, B. (2008). *Developing Methodical Transition and Pre-Departure Programs within an International School Setting. Pre-Conference Workshop.* Paper presented at the 9th Families in Global Transitions International Conference, Houston.

McIntosh, P. (1988). White Privilege and Male Privilege: A Personal Account of Coming To See Correspondences through Work in Women's Studies. Working Paper No. 189 (pp. 25). USA; Massachusetts: Wellesley Coll., MA. Center for Research on Women. (BBB16630).

McKillop-Ostrom, A. (1999). *Addressing Transition in International Schools: Learning from the Experiences of Internationally Mobile Children.* (MA), University of Bath, Bath, UK.

McKillop-Ostrom, A. (2000). Student Mobility and the International Curriculum. In M. Hayden & J. Thompson (Eds.), *International Schools and International Education: Improving Teaching, Management & Quality* (pp. 73-84). London: Kogan Page.

Mclachlan, D. A. (2007). Global nomads in an international school. Families in transition. *Journal of Research in International Education,* 6(2), 233-249.

McLean, K. C. (2005). Late Adolescent Identity Development: Narrative Meaning Making and Memory Telling. *Developmental Psychology,* 41(4), 683-691.

Mehana, M., & Reynolds, A. J. (2004). School mobility and achievement: a meta-analysis. *Children and Youth Services Review,* 26(1), 93-119.

Meyer, B. (2002). *An investigation into student, parent and teacher attitudes toward what comprises a good induction programme in an International School.* (MA), Oxford Brookes University.

Morse, S., & Gergen, K. J. (1970). Social comparison, self-consistency, and the concept of self. *Journal of Personality and Social Psychology,* 16(1), 148-156.

Murray, C. A. (2003). *Pastoral Care, Pastoral Management and International Schools: The Experience of One International Middle School.* Oxford Brookes University, Oxford.

Myers, S. L. (2013, May 21, 2013). Persecution over beliefs is on the rise worldwide. *International Herald Tribune.*

Myers, S. M. (1999). Childhood migration and social integration in adulthood. *Journal of Marriage and the Family,* 61(3), 774-789.

Najarian, L. M., Goenjian, A. K., Pelcovitz, D., Mandel, F., & Najarian, B. (1996). Relocation after a disaster: Posttraumatic stress disorder in Armenia after the earthquake. *Journal of the American Academy of Child and Adolescent Psychiatry, 35*(3), 374-383.

Neimeyer, R. (Ed.). (2001). *Meaning reconstruction and the experience of loss.* Washington, DC: American Psychological Association.

Norford, B. C., & Medway, F. J. (2002). Adolescents mobility histories and present social adjustment. *Psychology in the Schools, 39*(1), 51-62.

Ostrom, A. M. (1999). *Addressing transition in international schools: Learning from the experiences of internationally mobile children.* (Master of Education), University of Bath, Bath, UK.

Ota. (2000). *Ambiguous Grief: The role of sense of place and attachment style in the adjustment of mobile adolescents.* (MA), Leiden University, Leiden, Netherlands.

Ota. (2006). Binoculars of Grief and Gain. *The Guardian Online.* http://www.guardianabroad.co.uk/education/article/159

Ota, D., Gibbs, L., Abrams, C., & Nelsen, S. (2007, Nov. 24, 2007). *The Journey from "Why Bother?" to "How To": The American School of the Hague's Experience of and Vision for Developing Comprehensive School-Based Transitions Programs.* Paper presented at the ECIS Conference, Madrid.

Ota, D., Hamilton, M. L., Robinson, M., Slatter, E., Kittell, A., Austin, M., . . . Schaetti, B. (2007). *Transition Programs in International Schools: Systemic Approaches that Work. Pre-conference Session.* Paper presented at the 8th Families in Global Transitions International Conference.

Ota, D., Mecklenburg, C., Hamilton, M.-L., & Roddell, J. (2001, November). *Attacking Transitions in International Schools: the Transitions Program at ASH.* Paper presented at the European Council of International Schools Annual Conference, Den Haag.

Parker, A. (1992). Coping with coping assessment: A critical review. *European Journal of Personality, 6*(5), 321-344.

Parkes, C. (2001). A historical overview of the scientific study of bereavement. In M. Stroebe, W. Stroebe, H. Schut & R. Hansson (Eds.), *Handbook of Bereavement Research* (pp. 25-46). Washington, DC: American Psychological Association.

Pearce, R. (1998). Developing cultural identity in an international school environment. In M. Hayden & J. Thompson (Eds.), *International Education: Principles and Practice* (pp. 44-64). London: Kogan Page.

Pearce, R. (2005). *Developing a Model of Identity as a means of monitoring newly-relocated students in international schools.* (PhD Dissertation), University of Bath.

Pearce, R. (2007). Culture and Identity: Exploring Individuals within Groups. In M. Hayden & J. Thompson (Eds.), *The SAGE Handbook of Research in International Education* (pp. 128-139). London: Sage.

Perry, W. (1970). *Forms of intellectual and ethical development in the college years: A scheme.* New York: Holt.

Piaget, J. (1954). *The construction of reality in the child.* New York: Basic Books.

Piaget, J. (1977). *The development of thought: equilibrium of cognitive structures.* New York: Viking.

Pickering, S. M., & Walker, L. B. (1995). Japanese American Internment: A Historical Narrative. *Social Studies and the Young Learner,* 8(2), s1.

Polkinghorne, D. E. (1988). *Narrative knowing and the human sciences.* Albany, NY: SUNY Press.

Pollock, D. (1999, November, 1999). *Transitions in International Schools. Paper presented at the Annual ECIS Conference,* Nice, France.

Pollock, D. (2001). *Third Culture Kids. Paper presented at the American School of the Hague Transitions Program Team Workshop with David Pollock,* Wassenaar, Netherlands.

Pollock, D., & Van Reken, R. (1999). *Third Culture Kids: The Experience of Growing Up Among Worlds.* Yarmouth, ME: Intercultural Press.

Pönisch, A. (1987). *Special needs and the international baccalaureate: a study of the need for and development of alternative courses to the International Baccalaureate.* (MSc), University of Oxford.

Powell, W. (2001). Orchids in the bathroom: reflections on relocation stress. *International Schools Journal,* 21(1), 19-34.

Rader, D., & Harris Sittig, L. (2003). *New Kid in School: Using Literature to Help Children in Transition.* New York: Teachers College Press.

Reeves, C. (2006). Developing a comprehensive support programme for families in transition: a working model in practice. *International Schools Journal,* 26(1), 30-36.

Rogers, C. (1989). The characteristics of a helping relationship (1958). In H. Kirschenbaum & V. Land Henderson (Eds.), *The Carl Rogers Reader.* New York: Houghton Mifflin Company.

Rossi, J. (2005). *Teacher Induction in International Schools: A literature review.* (MA), Oxford Brookes University, Oxford.

Rubinstein, P. L., & Parmelee, P. A. (1992). Attachment to place and the representation of the life course by the elderly. In I. Altman & S. Low (Eds.), *Place Attachment*. New York: Plenum Press.

Rumberger, R. W., & Larson, K. A. (1998). Student mobility and the increased risk of high school dropout. *American Journal of Education, 107*(1), 1-35.

Sanderson, J. (1981). *International schooling: the 'mobile' pupil and his educational needs*. (MSc), University of Oxford, Oxford.

Sarbin, T. R. (1986a). The Narrative as a Root Metaphor for Psychology. In T. R. Sarbin (Ed.), *Narrative Psychology* (pp. 3-21). London: Praeger.

Sarbin, T. R. (Ed.). (1986b). *Narrative psychology: the storied nature of human conduct*. London: Praeger.

Schaetti, B. (2000). Global Nomad Identity: Hypothesizing a Developmental Model. (Ph.D), Union Institute, Ohio.

Schaetti, B. (2004). *International School Transition Resource Teams*. Paper presented at the 6th Families in Global Transition Conference, Houston.

Schaetti, B. (2004). Transition resource teams: a good answer to an important question. In E. Murphy (Ed.), *The International Schools Journal Compendium. Volume 2: Culture and the International School: Living, learning and communicating across cultures*. (pp. 215-221). Saxmundham: Peridot Press.

Schnall, S., Harber, K. D., Stefanucci, J. K., & Proffitt, D. R. (2008). Social Support and the Perception of Geographical Slant. *J Exp Soc Psychol, 44*(5), 1246-1255. doi: 10.1016/j.jesp.2008.04.011

Schore, A. N. (2000). Attachment and the regulation of the right brain. *Attach Hum Dev, 2*(1), 23-47. doi: 10.1080/146167300361309

Schore, A. N. (2009). Relational trauma and the developing right brain: an interface of psychoanalytic self psychology and neuroscience. *Ann N Y Acad Sci, 1159*, 189-203. doi: 10.1111/j.1749-6632.2009.04474.x

Schwartz, B. (2004). *The paradox of choice: why more is less* (1st ed.). New York: Ecco.

Seligman, M. E. P. (2002). *Authentic happiness: using the new positive psychology to realize your potential for lasting fulfillment*. New York: Free Press.

Singer, J. A., & Bluck, S. (2001). New perspectives on autobiographical memory: The integration of narrative processing and autobiographical reasoning. *Review of General Psychology, 5*(2), 91-99.

Slatter, E. R. (2004). *Systematic Mapping of Transition Needs and Services in the International School Multicultural Environment of Seoul Foreign School.* (MA), Antioch University.

Somerfield, M. R., & McCrae, R. R. (2000). Stress and coping research: Methodological challenges, theoretical advances, and clinical applications. *American Psychologist, 55*(6), 620-625.

South, S. J., & Haynie, D. L. (2004). Friendship networks of mobile adolescents. *Social Forces, 83*(1), 315-350.

South, S. J., Haynie, D. L., & Bose, S. (2005). Residential mobility and the onset of adolescent sexual activity. *Journal of Marriage and the Family, 67*(2), 499-514.

Stirzaker, R. (2004). Staff Induction. Issues Surrounding Induction into International Schools. *Journal of Research in International Education, 3*(1), 31-49.

Stroebe, M., Hansson, R., Stroebe, W., & Schut, H. (Eds.). (2001). *Handbook of Bereavement Research.* Washington, D.C.: American Psychological Association.

Stroebe, M., & Schut, H. (1999). The dual process model of coping with bereavement: rationale and description. *Death Studies,* 23, 197-224.

Tennen, H., Affleck, G., Armeli, S., & Carney, M. A. (2000). A daily process approach to coping: Linking theory, research, and practice. *American Psychologist, 55*(6), 626-636.

Terwilliger, R. (1972). International schools – cultural crossroads. *The educational forum, 36*(3), 359-363.

Thompson, J. (1998). Towards a model for international education. In M. Hayden & J. Thompson (Eds.), *International education: principles and practice.* London: Kogan Page.

Thurber, C. A., & Sigman, M. D. (1998). Preliminary models of risk and protective factors for childhood homesickness: Review and empirical synthesis. *Child Development, 69*(4), 903-934.

Tiger, L. (1979). *Optimism: the biology of hope.* New York: Kodansha International.

Topolinski, S. (2009). The face of fluency: Semantic coherence automatically elicits a specific pattern of facial muscle reactions. *Cognition and Emotion, 23*(2), 260-271.

Useem, R., & Cotrell, A. (1996). Adult Third Culture Kids. In C. Smith (Ed.), *Strangers at Home: Essays on the Effects of Living Overseas and Coming "Home" to a Strange Land.* Bayside, NY: Aletheia.

Useem, R., & Downie, R. (1976). Third Culture Kids. *Today's Education,* Sept/Oct, 103-105.

van der Kolk, B. A., Hopper, J. W., & Osterman, J. E. (2001). Exploring the Nature of Traumatic Memory: Combining Clinical Knowledge with Laboratory Methods. *Journal of Aggression, Maltreatment, & Trauma, 4,* 9-31.

van Tilburg, M. A., Eurelings-Bontekoe, E. H., Vingerhoets, A. J., & Van Heck, G. L. (1999). An exploratory investigation into types of adult homesickness. *Psychother Psychosom, 68*(6), 313-318. doi: 12349

Verschuur, M. J., Eurelings-Bontekoe, E. H., & Spinhoven, P. (2004). Associations among homesickness, anger, anxiety, and depression. *Psychol Rep, 94*(3 Pt 2), 1155-1170.

Vygotsky, L. S. (1978). Mind and society: *The development of higher psychological processes.* Cambridge, MA: Harvard University Press.

Walker, A., & Dimmock, C. A. J. (2002). *School leadership and administration: adopting a cultural perspective.* New York: RoutledgeFalmer.

Walker, G. (1998). Home sweet home: a study, through fictional literature, of disoriented children and the significance of home. In M. Hayden & J. Thompson (Eds.), *International Education: Principles and Practice* (pp. 11-27). London: Kogan Page.

Walker, G. (2002). The language of international education. In M. Hayden, J. Thompson & G. Walker (Eds.), *International education in practice: dimensions for national and international schools.* London: RoutledgeFalmer.

Walker, G. (2004a). Joseph Conrad: International Narrator. *Journal of Research in International Education, 3*(2), 225-236. doi: 10.1177/1475240904044389

Walker, G. (2004b). *To educate the nations.* Great Glemham: John Catt Educational.

Warner, J. (2005). *Perfect Madness: Motherhood in the Age of Anxiety.* New York: Riverhead.

Weber, E. G., & Weber, D. K. (2005). Geographic relocation frequency, resilience, and military adolescent behavior. *Military Medicine, 170*(7), 638-642.

White, M. (1988). The externalizing of the problem and the re-authoring of lives and relationships. *Dulwich Centre Newsletter* (Summer), 5-28.

White, M., & Epston, D. (1990). *Narrative means to therapeutic ends.*
    New York: Norton.
Winnicott, D. (1954). Mind and Its Relation to the Psyche-Soma.
    British Journal of Medical Psychology, 27(4), 201-209.
Winnicott, D. W. (1953). Transitional Objects and Transitional
    Phenomena – A Study of the First Not-Me Possession.
    International Journal of Psychoanalysis, 34, 89-97.
Yoshikawa, M. (1988). Cross-cultural adaptation and perceptual
    development. In Y. Kim & W. Gudykunst (Eds.), *Cross-cultural
    adaptation: current approaches.* In: *International and Intercultural
    Communication Annual* (Vol. 11). Newbury Park, CA: Sage.

EFFECTIVE COMPREHENSIVE TRANSITIONS PROGRAMS AT INTERNATIONAL SCHOOLS

A Safe Harbour
American School of The Hague
Wassenaar, Netherlands
www.ash.nl/shoverview

Transitions Program Team
International School of Düsseldorf
Düsseldorf, Germany
www.isdedu.de

Transitions Program
Jakarta International School
Jakarta, Indonesia
http://www.jisedu.or.id/join/families/transitions/index.aspx

ABOUT THE AUTHOR

Doug Ota grew up in La Jolla, California, near Mission San Juan Capistrano where the swallows arrive annually from Argentina. His father descends from Japanese roots, while his mother traces her ancestry to England. Their separation when Ota was three showed him and his brother how to grow up between worlds. Ota's loss of his step-father and his brother grounded Ota in grief. He has made a career out of wondering where he – and other people – belong.

He migrated east to study Religion at Princeton University, then further east to study Clinical Child Psychology at the University of Leiden in The Netherlands, going on to become a registered child psychologist with the Dutch Psychological Association. For many years, he was a High School counselor at the American School of The Hague. He now works in private practice.

Half of Ota's professional activities are devoted to counseling with children and adolescents, individuals, couples, and families (www.dougota.nl). The other half is devoted to consulting with international schools and organizations on how to build programs to address the challenges and opportunities of mobility – programs that guarantee safe passage (www.safepassage.nl).

He lives in The Hague, in the Netherlands, with his wife and three children. For fun, he runs marathons.

ABOUT THE DESIGNER

Tom Hubbard was born in San Francisco and received his BFA from Indiana University. His work spans a variety of mediums and blurs the lines between photography, ceramics, and graphic design. Equally comfortable with a camera or found objects, kiln or encaustic wax, Hubbard's unique creations bridge past and present, linking the personal to the historical. Convinced that the solution often comes from the problem, Hubbard allows each body of work to evolve naturally, without preconceived ideas or forms. The project leads his creative process.

With projects ranging from limited edition books to gallery installations and works of public art, Hubbard moves confidently between both fine art and design studios. His work has been exhibited widely in both the US and the Netherlands and is included in several private and corporate collections.

Drawing upon his own experiences in transitioning across cultures, and inspired by international travel and the migratory practices of the passerine swallow, Hubbard's design for *Safe Passage* references antique maps and border crossings, while presenting Ota's message through a framework of clean, organized typography and stamp-like illustrations.

After nearly five years in Europe, where he met and worked with Ota on the ASH Safe Harbour program, Hubbard currently lives in Northeast Ohio with his wife and their two children.

ADDITIONAL SUMMERTIME TITLES

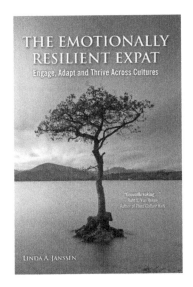

Tina L. Quick

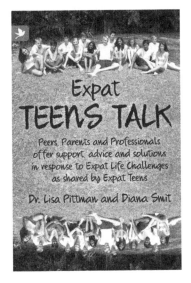

Summertime Publishing
by your side from inspiration to publication

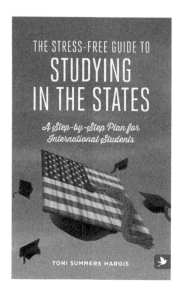

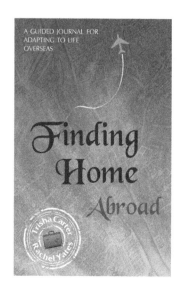

Lightning Source UK Ltd.
Milton Keynes UK
UKOW07f0809101114

241346UK00003B/17/P

9 781909 193406